I0213596

The Orderly Books of
Major General Edward Braddock
and
Selected Correspondence
of
George Washington

Also from
Normal Warfare Publications

Wilderness Wars

Historical Miniature Wargaming Rules
for
Wilderness Warfare in the Eighteenth Century

Normal Warfare Publications
P. O. Box 35
Normal, Illinois 61761

www.normalwarfare.com

Coming Soon from Normal Warfare Publications

Second Book in the *Wilderness Wars in North America* Series:

Fort McIntosh: Its Times and Men
"Fort Pitt" and Its Times
"Logstown," on the Ohio
Three Historical Sketches

by
Daniel Agnew, L.L.D.

&

Third Book in the *Wilderness Wars in North America* Series:

Jean-Daniel Dumas: Hero of the Monongahela

by
Francis-J. Audet

The Orderly Books of
Major General Edward Braddock

and
Selected Correspondence
of
George Washington
Related to the Ohio Expedition of 1755

Edited by

James A. Harris

First Book in the *Wilderness Wars in North America* Series

NORMAL WARFARE PUBLICATIONS

The Orderly Books of
Major General Edward Braddock
and
Selected Correspondence
of
George Washington
Related to the Ohio Expedition of 1755

Edited by
James A. Harris

PRODUCTION & MAP DESIGN
Philip S. Bock

GRAPHICS & COVER DESIGN
David A. Bock

ISBN 0-9748690-1-5

Normal Warfare Publications
P. O. Box 35
Normal, Illinois 61761

www.normalwarfare.com

Select portions of text © 2005 James A. Harris

All rights reserved. No part of this publication may be reproduced,
stored in a retrieval system, or transmitted in any form, or by any means,
electronic, mechanical, photocopying, recording, or otherwise,
without the prior written permission of the authors.

This book is dedicated to my wife Linda..

Table of Contents

Illustrations & Maps

ILLUSTRATIONS & MAPS

Introduction

On July 9, 1755 A small army of British redcoats and colonial troops under the command of Major General Edward Braddock, crossed the Monongahela River at the mouth of Turtle Creek in what is now Braddock, Pennsylvania. The small army, with flags waving and drums beating made an impressive sight. They were only seven miles away from their objective, Fort Duquesne at the Forks of the Ohio. Shortly thereafter the advance guard, including two companies of grenadiers, under the command of Lieutenant Colonel Thomas Gage of the 44th Regiment of Foot, marched into the forest, seemingly confident that they would meet with little resistance. However, at about 11:00 a.m., they collided with a small column of French and Indians under the command of Captain Daniel-Hyacinthe-Marie Liénard de Beaujeu.[1] What followed was one of the worst defeats in British military history.

The dispute between the French and the English over possession of the Ohio River Valley had been brewing for several years. During the War of Austrian Sucession (1741–1748) or King George's War in North America, while the French were concentrating on fighting the British in Acadia and on the frontiers of New York and New England, British traders had made inroads deep into the Ohio Country, supplying cheap goods to the Indians and fomenting hostility against the French. In 1747, a large portion of the Miami, led by Memeskia,[2] left the area around the French Fort des Miamis,[3] and settled at the village of Pickawillany[4] on the Great Miami River in Ohio. There they allowed the British to establish a trading house.

Memeskia and his band became openly hostile to the French and soon urged other tribes, particularly the closely related Wea and Piankashaw, to join them. As Memeskia's influence continued to grow, it threatened the entire French system of alliances with the western Indians. It was decided action had to be taken, and on July 21, 1752, a band of Ottawa and Ojibwa, led by Charles Michel Mouet de Langlade,[5] surprised the lightly defended Miami village and killed Memeskia.

Ange Duquesne de Menneville, Marquis Duquense (c. 1700–1778). Governor of New France, 1752–1755. Public Archives of Canada.

Meanwhile, the newly-appointed governor of New France, Ange Duquesne de Menneville, the Marquis Duquesne, arrived in Canada bringing orders from the Court at Versailles for a new strategy to prevent British incursions on the Ohio.[6] The French would occupy and fortify the upper reaches of the Ohio River, thus preventing British traders from penetrating the western territory. Captain Paul Marin de la Malgue[7] was given command of the expedition of approximately 1500 men that left Montreal in April, 1753. During the course of the summer of 1753, the French constructed Forts Presqu'Isle and Rivière aux Boeufs.[8] Marin died at Fort Rivière aux Boeufs on October 29.

Alarmed at the French advance into what he considered the territory of Virginia, Lieutenant Governor Robert Dinwiddie commissioned George Washington, a young militia officer, to deliver a summons to the French commander to withdraw. Washington, then only 22 years of age, made

Captain Daniel-Hyacinthe-Marie Liénard de Beaujeu (1711–1755). Commander of French forces at the Battle of Monongahela. He was killed in the opening minutes of the battle. From a 19th Century print.

the trip to Fort Rivière aux Boeufs, where he arrived on December 11, 1753.[9] Jacques Legardeur de Saint-Pierre, acting as commander, greeted Washington cordially but politely informed him that he would not withdraw.[10]

Washington delivered the French reply to Dinwiddie, who immediately began preparations to send an armed force to the Ohio to occupy the forks. Washington received a commission as lieutenant colonel of the newly formed Virginia Regiment. A promotion to colonel soon followed.[11]

Washington led his small force of about 300 men, supported by 100 men of the South Carolina Independent Company under Captain John Mackay,[12] into the Ohio Country. Then, on the night of May 27, 1754, Washington ambushed a small French scouting party led by Ensign Joseph Coulon de Villiers de Jumonville, at what is now called Jummonville Glen.[13] During the encounter, Jumonville was killed.

Beaujeu's Last Act. From a 19th Century print.

In retaliation for the attack, the French sent Jumonville's brother, Louis Coulon de Villiers[14] with a force of about 600 French and Canadians and 100 Indians, to drive Washington from the Ohio. He met Washington's small army on July 3 at the Great Meadows where they had hastily built a make shift stockade they named Fort Necessity.

Heavy rains fell as the French laid siege to the small stockade. After about nine hours of firing, ammunition was running low and the powder was wet. Coulon de Villiers called for a parley in which he offered a capitulation allowing the Americans to withdraw to Virginia in exchange for a promise not to return to the Ohio Country for one year. Washington, whose small force was in a desperate position agreed to the terms. Defeated, exhausted, and starving, Washington led his small force back to Fort Cumberland, conceding temporary possession of the Ohio Country to the French.

It was now clear that it would take more than a few hastily-raised recruits to drive the French from the Ohio. Decisions were made in London that would lead to an escalation of hostilities. In September, it was decided to send two regiments of Foot to North America.[15] Major-General Edward Braddock was chosen to command.

Born in 1694, Braddock was commissioned an ensign in the Coldstream Guards on October 10, 1710, and remained with the regiment for the next forty-three years. He slowly climbed in rank during long years of garrison duty in London—lieutenant in 1734, captain in 1736, major in 1743, and lieutenant colonel in 1745. He commanded two battalions of the Guards during the Jacobite Rebellion of 1745 but saw no action. He then served in Flanders, 1746–1747, but again saw no action. On February 17, 1753 Braddock was named colonel of the 14th Regiment of Foot and was commissioned major general on March 29, 1754. He was serving as governor of Gibraltar when he received word to return to London. There he received his commission as commander-in-chief of the British Army in North America on November 10.[16]

Major General Braddock landed at Hampton, Virginia on February 20, 1755.[17] He had been given detailed instructions drafted by William Augustus, Duke of Cumberland for the conduct of the military campaign against the French in North America. The plan of operations called for a four-pronged advance consisting of an attack on the French position in Acadia, another against Crown Point on Lake Champlain, and one against Fort Niagara. Braddock himself would command the main attack against Fort Duquesne on the Ohio River.[18]

It was not long after his arrival that Braddock called on the services of young George Washington. Shortly after the defeat at Great Meadows, Governor Dinwiddie had reorganized the Virginia forces, breaking up the Regiment into independent companies. Washington was faced with the choice of accepting a reduction in rank to captain or resigning his commission. Washington chose to resign.[19] However, Washington knew the country and the Indians and would be of great use on the campaign. The young Virginian readily accepted the opportunity to serve as an aide-de-camp without rank and made plans to join the general.[20]

Although Braddock had originally ordered the troops to be distributed in several camps throughout Virginia and Maryland, by the time the transports carrying the troops arrived in March it had been decided to concentrate the entire army in Alexandria, Virginia.[21] This army consisted of two regiments from the Irish Establishment, the 44th and 48th, which had been augmented to 500 men through drafts from the other regiments in Ireland. Once in North America Braddock recruited additional men to increase the strength of the regiments to 750 men each. In addition, he would command provincial troops and independent companies.

In preparation for the upcoming campaign, recruits were drafted and drilled, and attempts were made to purchase wagons and horses. Supplies were to be brought in from Pennsylvania to a storehouse at the mouth of the Conococheague River in Maryland. From there they were to be transported west to Fort Cumberland. The army finally marched west in early April in two divisions. Colonel Peter Halkett's Division marched through Virginia, while Braddock, with Colonel Thomas Dunbar's Division crossed the Potomac into Maryland and marched to Fort Frederick.

Hampered by a lack of wagons and horses, he was forced to leave the artillery at Alexandria under the command of Lieutenant Colonel Thomas Gage with orders to bring them forward as soon as transportation could be procured.[22] Braddock and his staff arrived at Fort Frederick, Maryland on April 22.[23] There he was met by 49-year-old Benjamin Franklin who assured him he could procure 150 wagons and ease his most pressing transportation problems.[24] However, at Fort Frederick Braddock discovered that there were no roads through western Maryland and he was forced to send Dunbar's Division back across the Potomac at the mouth of the Conococheague. It was about this time that Washington arrived at Fort Frederick to join the general's staff.[25]

The General next went to Winchester, Virginia, where he hoped to hold council with the Cherokee, Catawba, and other southern tribes. Lieutenant Governor Robert Dinwiddie of Virginia had assured him of their assistance, but after waiting in vain for four days for the Indians to appear, he departed for Fort Cumberland, Maryland in frustration on May 7.[26]

Braddock arrived at Fort Cumberland on May 10[27] where he found noted Indian trader George Croghan[28] waiting for him with approximately 100 Indians from Ohio and Pennsylvania led by Scarroyady. The party included approximately 40 warriors while the remainder were women and children.[29] Relations between Braddock and the Indians deteriorated quickly. On May 11, he issued orders prohibiting Native American women from entering the camp and later that day he issued supplementary orders prohibiting the distribution of liquor to the warriors.[30]

Braddock held council with the Indians on May 12, but it did not go well when they learned the gifts he was to distribute had not yet arrived.[31] A second council was held on May 18, in which he ordered them to send their women home. All but eight warriors left the next day. Many of the Ohio Indians, who had been wavering between the British and French, had been so alienated by Braddock's haughty demeanor that they immediately gave there support to the French.[32]

Meanwhile, the month of May, 1755 was spent in preparation for the upcoming march to the Ohio Country. By the end of the month, the army was ready to proceed. On May 29 an advance guard of 600 men under Lieutenant Colonel John St. Clair and Major Russell Chapman were sent ahead to the Little Meadows, near present day Grantsville, Maryland, to secure an advance post.[33]

The entire day was spent transporting their baggage over Wills Mountain, just west of Fort Cumberland.[34] It was clear an easier passage had to be found. On June 2 Lieutenant Charles Spendelowe reported finding a route around the north side of the mountain through a narrow valley.[35] The next day engineer Harry Gordon and 120 men began clearing the new route, commonly known as "Spendelowe's Road."[36]

Spendelowe's Road was completed on June 7 and Halkett's Division marched from Fort Cumberland that same day.[37] It was not until June 12 that the entire army arrived at Spendelowe's Camp, five miles from Fort Cumberland. Later that day a council of war was held in which it was determined to send back two six-pound artillery pieces along with powder and stores freeing up 20 wagons. The Virginia company of Captain Peter Hogg, which was being sent to Pennsylvania, was given charge of escorting the artillery back to Fort Cumberland.[38]

Halkett's Division left Spendelowe's Camp on June 13. Over the next few days the small army of approximately 2100 men snaked its way through the wilderness of western Maryland.[39] Braddock, with Halkett's Division joined St. Clair at Little Meadows on June 16. Dunbar's Division arrived on June 17.

On that day Braddock held a council of war. Acting on a suggestion said to have come from George Washington, it was decided to create a "flying column." Braddock would travel forward as quickly as possible to Fort Duquesne with the veteran regulars and most of the artillery, but would bring only essential provisions. Dunbar would command the second division, following up with the wagons and most of the baggage. That day Braddock issued orders specifying the troops to be included in the flying column as well as the officers who would serve.[40] Braddock's flying column marched from Little Meadows on June 19.

Meanwhile, George Washington had fallen ill and was left behind with Dunbar's Division. On June 14 he was seized with a violent fever and pains that did not subside until June 23.

On July 3 Washington accompanied a detachment of 100 men commanded by Captain Adam Stephen who were escorting 100 packhorses of flour being sent forward to replenish Braddock's supplies.[41] They arrived at Braddock's Camp on Great Sewickley Creek in Pennsylvania on July 5.[42] Braddock's column continued its slow march forward until approximately 11:00 a.m. on July 9, 1755, when, at a distance of about seven miles south of Fort Duquesne, it collided with French forces on the banks of the Monongahela.

The advanced guard of about 300 men, including the two grenadier companies, under the command Lieutenant Colonel Thomas Gage were the first to engage the enemy. The small French force of 72 *Troupes de la marine,* 146 Canadian militia, and 637 Native Americans, led by Liénard de Beaujeu were marching to establish an ambush on the banks of the Monongahela and were just as surprised as the British.[43] Upon seeing the enemy, Beaujeu waved his hat in the air signaling for the Native Americans to move out on flanks. Gage's men fired a few orderly volleys in which Beaujeu was killed. The French wavered but were rallied by Captain Jean-Daniel Dumas,[44] who took command after the death of Beaujeu. Meanwhile, Native American warriors had overwhelmed the British flanking parties and occupied a strategic hill on the right. Within fifteen minutes after the first shot was fired, Gage's men wavered and began to fall back in disorder.

Jean-Daniel Dumas (1712–1792). Second-in-Command of French forces at the Battle of Monongahela. He served as commandant of Fort Duquesne, 1755–1756. Shown here later in life as Governor of the island of Mauritius off the coast of Madagascar in the Indian Ocean. Public Archives of Canada.

Approximately 100 yards behind the advanced guard was the working party of provincial carpenters and rangers under the command of Deputy Quartermaster General Lieutenant Colonel Sir John St. Clair. Their task was to clear a path for the wagons following behind with the main party. Gage's retreating men collided with St. Clair's party causing even more confusion. Both parties now fell back.[45] Meanwhile, at the first sound of gunfire, Braddock, who was at the head of the main body several hundred yards to the rear, sent them forward under the command Lieutenant Colonel Ralph Burton. They had advanced approximately ¼ mile when they collided with the fleeing parties of Gage and St. Clair.

The entire army was now a mass of confusion and completely disordered. Indian marksmen fired from three sides from behind trees and boulders, picking off the officers. The British soldiers, hysterical with fear, fired wildly, shooting many of their own men in the back. Those officers still fit for command, Braddock among them, tried in vain to rally the men and form some type of firing line.

Throughout the battle, George Washington and the Virginians fought courageously in the wilderness style, using the woods as protection. They suffered heavily, losing nearly all of their officers.

Around 3:00 p.m., the British made a last concerted effort to take the main French position on the hill to their right. Burton, with about 150 men including grenadiers attempted to advance up the slope but the French concentrated their fire on them and Burton was forced back.[46]

Shortly thereafter, realizing his position was hopeless, Braddock ordered a withdrawal. It soon turned into a rout after he received a mortal wound through the lung. The wounded general was carried off the field in his sash. The army fled in panic across the Monongahela River with the French and Indians on their tails. A small body of about 200 men maintained order and formed a rear guard that allowed many of wounded, including the general, to escape. The British left all of their artillery and about 30 wagons on the battlefield as plunder for the Indians, who soon swooped down to take scalps and strip the bodies. Braddock's war chest and all of his papers were also captured.

The British casualties were staggering. It is estimated that about 500 men were killed and another 500 wounded out of the approximately 1400 who fought in the battle.[47] The officer corps was hit especially hard with

24

63 out of the 86 who fought in the battle being either killed or wounded.[48] In contrast, the French casualties were incredibly light with only 3 officers including Beaujeu killed and 4 wounded along with 9 wounded French and Canadians. 27 Indians were killed or wounded.[49]

The remnants of the defeated army slowly staggered back to Dunbar's Camp near Jumonville Glen, where Braddock arrived on July 11. The remaining horses were required to transport the wounded and the two guns with Dunbar. With no way to transport the provisions and ordnance, Braddock ordered most of them destroyed.[50]

Braddock ordered a general retreat and the army began to fall back toward Fort Cumberland on July 13. They had not traveled far when the general died of his wounds near the Great Meadows. He was buried in the middle of the road he had built and soldiers marched over his grave to conceal its location. Dunbar and most of the army arrived at Fort Cumberland on July 20. Deeming further offensive measures impossible, Dunbar began his retreat to Philadelphia to go into winter quarters on August 2.[51] Thus ended the Ohio Expedition of 1755.

The copies of the "Orderly Book of General Edward Braddock" printed herein were made by Washington from the official orderly books kept by another of the general's aides, Captain Robert Dobson. They chronicle the general orders given to the army from its arrival in Virginia until June 17, 1755. This was the day before Braddock divided his forces and marched forward with a small elite advanced division. Forced to remain behind due to a bout of dysentery, Washington was unable to rejoin Braddock until July 8, the day before the Battle of Monongahela. All of Braddock's papers were lost on the battlefield, thus Washington was never able to complete his copy of the orderly books.[52]

Braddock's Orderly Books are held by the Library of Congress as part of the George Washington Papers. The Library of Congress obtained it as part of the collection of Peter Force, purchased by an Act of Congress in 1867. They were first published in 1878 by William H. Lowdermilk as an appendix to his *History of Cumberland.*

Our original plan for this edition was merely to issue a reprint of Lowdermilk with additional editorial remarks. However, when compared to the original manuscript, viewable on the internet through the Library of Congress American Memory Collection at www.memory.loc.gov, it became apparent that Lowdermilk's version was in many ways deficient. It contained numerous transcription errors and mistakes, including entire sections that were placed in the wrong locations.

At first, an attempt was made to maintain Lowdermilk's original transcription and note the differences in the manuscript by using endnotes. The corrections quickly became so numerous it was determined to include them directly into the text. In the end, Lowdermilk's errors were referenced in the notes.

The most significant corrections, notably changes in the wording and location of blocks of text, have been addressed in the endnotes. However, numerous minor corrections such as capitalization, punctuation, abbreviations, and the use of ampersands versus the word "and," have not been noted. The use of small capitals used prevalently by Lowdermilk has also been abandoned. Throughout, an attempt has been made to make this edition more closely reflect the text as it appears in the manuscript. However, most of the superscripts found in the manuscript and in Lowdermilk have been brought down in order to make the text more readable. Punctuation at the end of sentences has also been added. The bracketed numbers throughout the text represent the numbers given to the corresponding folios as found on the American Memory website.

Access to the manuscript has been provided courtesy of the Library of Congress.

Notes:

[1] Daniel-Hyacinthe-Marie Liénard de Beaujeu (1711–1755) had long served in the western posts, at various times commanding the forts at Niagara, Detroit, and Michilimackinac. He had recently been sent to the Ohio to take over command at Fort Duquesne. He was killed in the opening minutes of the battle.

[2] Memeskia (d. 1752) was commonly called Old Britain by the British and La Desmoiselle by the French.

[3] Near present-day Fort Wayne, IN.

[4] Located at the mouth of Loramie Creek at present-day Piqua, OH.

[5] Charles-Michel Mouet de Langlade (1729–circa 1801) was the son of a prominent fur trader at Michilimackinac and an Ottawa woman. He served with his Native American followers on the Ohio in 1755–1756 and in the Lake Champlain theater in 1757. He was serving at Fort Michilimackinac in 1758 but was at Quebec during the siege of 1759. He served the British in the Indian Department after the war and died at Green Bay, WI during the winter of 1800–1801.

[6] See "Antoine Louis Rouillé, Comte de Jouy to Ange Duquesne de Menneville, Marquis Duquense, July 9, 1752," in Theodore Calvin Pease and Ernestine Jenison, eds., *Illinois on the Eve of the Seven Years' War, 1747–1755,* Collections of the Illinois State Historical Library, Vol. XXX, Springfield, IL: Trustees of the State Historical Library, 1940, pp. 645–51.

[7] Paul Marin de la Malgue (1692–1753) had long served in the western posts. He was commissioned an ensign in the *Troupes de la marine* on May 26, 1722. Marin served as commandant at Baie des puants (Green Bay, WI) prior to taking command of the Ohio expedition.

[8] Fort Presqu'Isle was at present-day Erie, PA, and Fort Rivière aux Boeufs was at Waterford, PA.

[9] George Washington, *The Diaries of George Washington.* 6 Vols. Edited by Donald Jackson and Dorothy Twohig, Charlottesville, VA: University Press of Virginia, 1976–1979, 1:147.

[10] Jacques Legardeur de Saint-Pierre (1701–1755) was another long-time veteran of the French forces in the west. He had been sent to the Ohio to relieve Marin, who had died before his arrival at Fort Rivière aux Boeufs on December 3 (see "Ange Duquesne de Menneville, Marquis Duquesne à Jacques Legardeur de Saint-Pierre, December 25, 1755," in Fernand Grenier, ed., *Papiers Contrecoeur et autres documents concernant le conflit anglo-français sur l'Ohio de 1745 à 1756,* Quebec: Les Presses Universites Laval, 1952, p. 87–88). Legardeur was killed at the Battle of Lake George on September 8, 1755.

[11] "Robert Dinwiddie to George Washington, June 4, 1754," in W. W. Abbott, Dorothy Twohig, et. al., eds. *The Papers of George Washington: Colonial Series.* 10 Vols. Charlottesville, VA: University Press of Virginia, 1983–95, 1:126–27. Hereafter cited as *PGW.*

[12] James Mackay (d. 1785) had served as an officer in Oglethorpe's Regiment in Georgia during King George's War, rising to the rank of captain in 1745. The regiment was disbanded after the war and Mackay was appointed captain of the South Carolina Independent Company in 1749. He resigned his commission in the autumn of 1754 and returned to his lands in Georgia where he remained active in politics.

[13] Joseph Coulon de Villiers de Jumonville (1718–1754) was commissioned an ensign in 1741.

[14] Captain Louis Coulon de Villiers (1710–1757), Jumonville's brother, had served in Acadia during King George's War. In 1755–1756 he served on Lake Ontario and participated in the Siege of Oswego. In 1757 he served in the Siege of Fort William Henry. Coulon de Villiers died of small pox on November 2, 1757.

[15] Fred Anderson, *The Crucible of War: The Seven Years' War and the Fate of Empire in British North America, 1754–1766.* New York: Alfred A. Knopf, 2000, pp. 68–70.

[16] For Braddock's early career see Lee McCardell, *Ill-Starred General: Braddock of the Coldstream Guards.* Pittsburgh: University of Pittsburgh Press, 1958; reprint, 1986.

[17] See "Robert Orme's Journal," in Winthrop Sargent, ed., *A History of an Expedition Against Fort Duquesne in 1755; Under Major General Edward Braddock,* Philadelphia: Lippincott, Grambo & Co., 1855; repr., New York: Arno Press, 1971, p. 283.

[18] See "Sketch of an Order About the Rank &c. of the Provincial Troops in North America," in Stanley M. Pargellis, ed., *Military Affairs in North America, 1748–1765,* New York: D. Appleton-Century Company, 1936, pp. 43–44.

[19] Douglas S. Freeman, *George Washington: A Biography,* 7 vols., New York: Charles Scribner's Sons, 1948, 1:441.

[20] See the exchange of correspondence between George Washington and Robert Orme, pp. 135–39.

[21] See Braddock's orders of February 26, 1755, pp. 37–38.

[22] Sargent, "Robert Orme's Journal," p. 307.

[23] See the "Seaman's Journal," in Sargent, p. 368.

[24] Benjamin Franklin, *The Autobiography and other Writings,* Edited by L. Jessie Lemisch, New York: Signet Classics, second printing; 1963, pp. 146–149.

[25] Freeman, *George Washington,* 2:31.

[26] McCardell, *Ill-Starred General,* pp. 179–80.

[27] Sargent, "Robert Orme's Journal, p. 309.

[28] George Croghan (circa 1720–1782) was a well-known trader with great influence among the Ohio Indians. He was trading at Cuyahoga, present-day Cleveland, OH, as early as 1747. He later became deputy superintendent of Indian Affairs under Sir William Johnson and was heavily involved in western land claims. He lost most of his fortune and land claims during the War of American Independence.

[29] "George Croghan to William Johnson, May 15, 1755," in James Sullivan, et. al., eds. *The Papers of Sir William Johnson.* 10 Vols. Albany: University of the State of New York, 1921–1939, 1:496–97. Hereafter cited at *PWJ.*

[30] See p. 72.

[31] McCardell, *Ill-Starred General,* p. 188.

[32] Anderson, *Crucible of War*, pp. 94–96.

[33] McCardell, *Ill-Starred General,* p. 208.

[34] Sargent, "Robert Orme's Journal," p. 323.

[35] Sargent, "Seaman's Journal," p. 381.

[36] See p. 91.

[37] See "Memorandum," p. 169.

[38] Sargent, "Robert Orme's Journal," p. 331–32.

[39] See pp. 110–11, fn. 128.

[40] See pp. 121–22.

[41] See "George Washington to John Augustine Washington, June 28–July 2, 1755," pp. 179–83.

[42] Sargent, "Robert Orme's Journal," p. 346. This camp was located near present-day Madison, PA.

[43] Paul E. Kopperman, *Braddock at the Monongahela.* 2d printing. Pittsburgh: University of Pittsburgh Press, 1992, p. 51.

[44] Jean-Daniel Dumas (1712–1792) had served in the Regiment Agnais during the War of Austrian Succession. He transferred to the *Troupes de la Marine* and was stationed in Canada in 1750. Dumas later served as commandant of Fort Duquesne, 1755–56. He was promoted to Major General Inspector of the Canadian Troops in 1759, and commanded militia brigades at the Battles of Quebec and Ste. Foy. He later served as governor of Mauritius in 1766 and was promoted to the rank of major general in 1780.

[45] Kopperman, p. 192.

[46] Ibid., p. 164–65.

[47] Ibid., p. 91.

[48] Francis Parkman, *Montcalm and Wolfe,* 2 Vols., *France and England in North America: A Series of Historical Narratives, Part Seventh.* Boston: Little, Brown, and Company, 1891, 1:219–20.

[49] Parkman, *Montcalm and Wolfe,* 1:223.

[50] McCardell, *Ill-Starred General,* p. 264.

[51] William H. Lowdermilk, *History of Cumberland, (Maryland) from the Time of the Indian Town, Caiuctucuc, in 1728, up to the Present Day, Embracing an Account of Washington's First Campaign, and Battle of Fort Necessity, Together with a History of Braddock's Expedition,* Washington, DC, 1878, p. 185.

[52] See below, "George Washington to Robert Orme, July 28, 1755," and "Roger Morris to George Washington, November 3, 1755," pp. 196–99. "Halkett's Orderly Book," kept by Ensign Daniel Disney, did survive the battle and can be used to fill in many of the gaps found in Washington's copy. It has been printed in Charles Hamilton, ed., *Braddock's Defeat,* Norman, OK: Oklahoma University Press, 1959.

Part I

Major General
Edward Braddock's
Orderly Books

From
February 26 to June 17, 1755.

———

From the Originals
in the
Congressional Library.

Originally Edited by
William H. Lowdermilk

This Edition Edited by
James A. Harris

George Washington's Introductory Remarks

What immediately follows, is the Orders of his Excellency General Braddock from his arrival in Virginia until the 17th of June following, when Indisposition obliged the writer, or copier[1], thereof to seperate from him and remain (until he was in a condition to move forward again) with the rear division of the Army. Rejoining in a low & enfeebled state, only the day before the Action of Monnongahela (which happened on the 9th of July) there was not *time* even if he had been *able* to enter the orders that had issued during his seperation; which is more to be regretted [f. 5][2] as it is probable the Order of Battle, & many other important Orders were among them.

He did however, as may be seen by a letter of[3] to Captn Orme[4], dated the 28th day of July—Request a copy of these orders, but as they never were sent, they cannot be inserted.[f. 6]

[General Braddock's Orderly Books are two in number, the first embracing the orders issued from the 26th of February to the 11th of June, 1755; and the second from the 12th to the 17th of June, 1755. On a page preceding the orders appears the above extract, in Washington's own handwriting, and it is presumed that the books were kept under his direction. These books were transferred to the Congressional Library from the library of the late Peter Force, after the death of that eminent man, whose collection of manuscripts concerning American history was undoubtedly the most complete in existence.][5]

Notes:

[1] Washington fell ill of dysentery on June 17, 1755, while Braddock's Army was encamped at the Little Meadows. He remained ill in camp with Dunbar's division when Braddock marched with the advanced division on June 17, 1755. Washington recovered and marched forward on July 3 with a supply column commanded by Captain Adam Stephen. They arrived at Braddock's camp two miles east of the Monongahela near present-day Stewartsville, PA on July 8.

[2] The first page of the manuscript contains the title, "NO. 1." The next three pages are blank.

[3] The words "of his" were originally written and then crossed out of the manuscript.

[4] See "George Washington to Sir Robert Orme, July 28, 1755" below, p. 196. Sir Robert Orme (d. 1781) entered the Coldstream Guards as an ensign in September 16, 1745. On April 24, 1751 he was commissioned a lieutenant giving him the equivalent of a captain in the regiments of the line. He was one of Braddock's small family of favorites and served as his first aide-de-camp. He was severely wounded in the thigh at the Battle of the Monongahela, July 9, 1755. Orme was considered by many of the officers in the line regiments to be imperious and insubordinate. He returned to England in late 1755 after recovering from his wound and resigned his commission in October, 1756. He later married Audrey Townshend, sister of George Townshend, Wolfe's second-in-command at Quebec in 1759, and Charles Townshend, future Chancellor of the Exchequer and author of the Townshend Acts. Orme remained a steadfast defender of Braddock's honor and reputation against those critics who blamed him for the defeat at Monongahela.

[5] This is Lowdermilk's original editorial remark. Peter Force (1790–1868) was a printer and archivist from Washington DC who gathered a massive collection of rare colonial manuscripts and pamphlets that he eventually sold to the Library of Congress for $100,000. See Ralph V. Harlow, "Peter Force," *Dictionary of American Biography.*

General Braddock's Orderly Book, No. 1

His Excellency General Braddock[1] orders that the Commanding Officer of each ship upon their arrival in Hampton Road[2] shall imediately send a Return inclos'd to Mr. Hunter[3] at Hampton, specifying the number of their Sick, the time of their illness and the nature of them. And that every commanding Officer shall with the utmost dispatch apply to Mr. Hunter for Boats to carry the sick on Shore wch shall be executed with all imaginable care & expedition, and that a Subaltern Officer of each ship shall see their men safely conveyed to the place appointed at Hampton for their Reception, which Mr. Hunter will shew them; And that The Surgeons or Mates of the two Regiments and Train shall attend the sick of their own Corps. Every commanding Officer is to take particular care that as soon as their Sick are sent ashore[f. 7][4] all the Hatchways be uncovered scuttles opened and the Platform thoroughly washd and clean'd: No Officer or Soldier except the Sick to lie on shore upon any acct. The Hospital to continue on board till the Generals further Orders.[5]

Williamsburg Feby. 26th. 1755.

To the companies of Rangers and Carpenters

His Excellency General Braddock Orders ye Commandg Officer of each Company or Troop to send a weekly Return to the head Quarter's agreeable to the Form annexd; and duplicates of the Returns are to be Remitted weekly to His Excellency Governor Dinwiddie.[6] The Return for Genl. Braddock to be directed to me at the head Quarters.

Williamsburg, Feby. 26th. 1755.

35

Major General Edward Braddock (1694–1755). Commander-in-Chief of British forces in North America. This is a 19th Century engraving. Note the artist has pictured him wearing an American military uniform from that period. Reproduced from Cyrus Townsend Brady, *Colonial Fights and Fighters,* New York, 1901.

By His Excellency Edward Braddock, Esq.
Whereas, an act of Parliament was passd in England the last Session to subject all Troops raised in the Colonies to the Regulations and Orders of the Articles of War,[7] I therefore think it expedient and Order that upon forming the four Companies of Rangers, the Company of Carpenters and the Troop of light Horse, and whatever Troops are or shall be raizd for the Service of the present Expedition,[8] That the Articles of War be publickly Read to the Officers and Men, and that every man severaly shall take the Oath of Allegiance and Supremacy: and in consequence of these Articles

they are to obey from time to time any orders they shall receive from me or any of their superior Officers.

E Braddock

By His Excel'ys Com'd.
Feb'y. 26th, 1755.
Wilm Shirley Secrety. [f. 9]⁹

By His Excellency Edward Braddock, Esq., Genl. and Commander in Chief of His Majt Forces in North America. — Quarters of Sir Peter Halkets Regimt:¹⁰

Orderd, That it proceed to Alexandria in the Transports; five companies to remain in the Town wth the Company of Artillery and Stores of all kinds.

One company at Dumfries, two days march from Alexandria, thirty miles; to Halt the first Night after they cross the Ferry of Occoquan: One Company at Bladensburg, one Days march, they cross the Potomack at Alexandria. One company at upper Marlborough two days march, first Night at Bladensburg: Two companys at Frederick; These three last Cantonments in Maryland: Upon application to Major Carlyle¹¹ Magistrate of Alexandria, the whole will be furnishd with Guards¹² Quarter's of one Regiment. The Transports wch have them on board to stop in the River Potomack [f. 10] as near Fredericksburg as they can. These and an half Companys at Winchester, six days march from Fredericksburg, half a Company at Conogogee¹³ eight days from Winchester; Six Companys at Fredericksburg and Falmouth on the other side the River of Rappahannock.¹⁴

The five Companys of the Regiment that disembarks at Alexandria which are to be cantond to be landed first and to begin their march before the other five debark.

The Engineers and other Officer's, not immediately wanted to be at hand, may be conveniently lodgd on the Maryland side of the Potomack, leaving a direction where they lodge.

Application is to be made to the several Magistrats for Carriages to convey the stores, Baggage and Tents of the cantond Company's Receipts¹⁵ to be given by the commanding Officer's for the numbers employ'd. [f. 11]

The Regiment whose head Quarters are at Fredericksburg, will have[16] abt 15 miles from place of disembarking. Waggons will be orderd to attend them. Those[17] companys which are to march to Winchester and Conogogee, are to march first to Fredericksburg. The compa. Quarterd at Falmouth need not cross the Rappa. Waggon's to each Compa. to be assertained, a field Officer to go with each of the five compas and every Officer to go with his Compas.

Given under my hand at Williamsburg, this 26th of Febry, 1755.

E. Braddock — [f. 13][18]

Camp at Alexandria Thursday 27th March, 1755

Parole Williamsburg. —

Captn. Robert Orme of the Coldstream Regt. of Guards, and Captn. Roger Morris[19] of Colo. Dunbars[20] Regiment of Foot, are appointed aids de Camp to His Excellency Genl. Braddock.

His Majesty has been pleased to appoint Captn. Halket, of Sir Peter Halkets Regiment; Brigade Major.[21]

As the Troops have taken the Field His Excely. Genl Braddock is desirous the Officers and men should be informed of the Duties he requires of them, and of some Regulations he thinks beneficial to the Service: And as the two Regiments now employd have Servd under the Command of His Royal Highness[22] and are well [f. 12] acquainted with military discipline, His Excellency expects their conduct will be so conformable to order as to set the most soldier like example to the new Service of this Country; & the General orders that the Articles of War be immediately and frequently Read, and that every body may be informed all neglects or disobedience of them or of any Orders will not be forgiven.

Any Soldier who shall desert tho' he return again will be hangd without mercy.

As an Incouragement to the men, and to promote their diligence and activity every man will be allowed daily as much of fresh or salt Provisions and of Bread, or Flower without any stoppages for the same as long and

Captain Sir Robert Orme (d. 1781) of the Coldstream Guards. Aide-de-Camp to General Braddock. Courtesy of the National Gallery.

in as great proportion's as it will be possible to provide them unless any man shall be found drunk, negligent, or disobedient, in such case his gratuity [f. 14] shall be stopd.

All Orders relating to the men are constantly to be read to them by an Officer of the Company.

The eldest Captains Company of each Regt. is always[23] to act as a second Grenadiers Company and to be posted upon the left of the Battalion, leaving the same Interval, as the Grenadiers upon the Right; This company is to be kept compleat of Officer's and two of them as well as of the other Grenadier Company are to be posted in the Front and the other in the Rear.

The eight Battalian Companies are to form so many Firings and to be commanded by their respective Officer's. The commanding Officer of each Company is to give the word, the Second is to be posted in the center of the Front Rank and the Remaining Subaltorn Officer's of the Regiment after this disposition are to divide the ground equally: [f. 15] These Firings are to begin by the Colonel's Company Second by the Lieut. Colo.[24] and continued from Right to left as fast as possibly, but the two Captns. of Grenadiers are to take particular care never to give their Fire till the Company's upon the Right and left are loaded.

To avoid confusion if the Regiment should be ordered to wheel or fire by Platoons, every Officer commanding a Company is to tell it off in two division's and to post the second Commission'd Officer and non Commissioned Officer's and when the Regiment decamps or are to form, the Commanding Officer of the Company is to inspect[25] his mens Arms, compleat the Files, Post the Officer's and see his men loaded that they may wheel up and ye Battalion be instantly formed.

The Officer's upon a march are to remain in the same Order with their Companies, and [f. 16] Those Officers who were placed in the Rear are to march as posted which will consequently be upon the Flank as the Regiment moves by Files they are therefore required to keep the Soldiers in their Files, and if any lag behind one or more of these Officers is to bring them up.

Every Officer leaving his company upon a march will be Cashierd, and every commanding Officer will be answerable for the men of his Company left behind; and the Commanding Officer of the Regiments are ordered to punish with the utmost severity any Soldier who leaves his File but in cases of sickness.

Commanding Officers of Companies are to have their Arms in constant good order, and every man to be provided with a Brush, Picker two good spare Flints and 24 Cartridges.

The Roll of each Company to be calld by a commission'd Officer, morning, Noon & Night [f. 17] and a Return of the absent, or disorderly men to be given to the Commanding Officer of the Regiment who is to order proper punishment.

The Women of each Regiment are to march with the Provost[26] and none upon any acct are to appear with the men when under Arms.

Each Regiment is to Mount a Piquet Guard consisting of one captn. and three Subalterns and 100 men to be paraded at the Retreat they are to report to the Field Officer of the Day.

The two Regiments are to find the Genls Guard alternately consisting of one Lieut. & thirty Private and to Report to an aid de camp. The Regiment which finds the Guard finds also the adjutant of the day.

All Guards are to be reliev'd[27] at 8 oclock all Guards to be told of in two Division's Tho' ever so small. [f. 18]

Guards orderd at Orderly time are to remain for that duty and a new detachment is to be made for any orderd afterwards.

All Returns are to be signed by the Commanding Officers of Regiments. Reports of all Guards except the Generals are to be made to the Field Officer of the Day who is to visit them once at least and to go the piquet Rounds.

All remarkable occurrances in Camp to be reported to an aid de Camp.

Returns of all Commands to be made to the Brigade Major, and every Regiment, Company Troop, &c., are to make a daily Return to him specifying the Numbers wanting to compleat, who is to make one Generl. Return to his Excellency. [f. 19]

A daily return of the Sick is to be made to the Genl. thro' an aid de Camp.

As the Nature of the Country make it impossible to provide magazines of Forage, and as it is apprehended the Quantity will be very small, uncertain, and difficult to be procurd His Excellency recommends it to all the Officers to take no more baggage than they find absolute occasion for.

Commanding Officers of Regiments are directed by His Excellency to inform their men not to suffer themselves to be alarmd upon a march by any stragling Fires from the Indians in the woods they being of no consequence nor liable to any inconveniences but what arise from their misbehaviour.

Any Soldier by leaving his Company, or by words or Gestures expressing Fear shall suffer death and the Genl. will greatly approve & [f. 20] properly reward those men who by their Coolness and good Discipline treat the attempts of these Fellows with the contempt they deserve.

The Sergeants of the Two Regiments are to be provided with Firelocks and Bayonets, but to wear their Swords—They are to leave at Winchester under the care of the Train their Halberds[28] and all the private men their Swords. His Excellency likewise recommends it to all the Officers to provide themselves if possible with Fuzeis[29] as Espontoons will be extreamly inconvenient and useless in the Woods.

As the good of the Service renders the presence of all the Officer's absolutely necessary His Excellency cannot suffer any commissiond Officer to act as paymaster the General therefore desires the Colonels and Captains will agree as soon as possible for a proper person for that purpose. [f. 21]

The Line is to find one Field Officer daily to be reliev'd at 10 oclock, this duty to be done by the two Lieut. Colos. and two Majors[30] the Field Officer is to visit all Guards except the Generals and to go the Rounds of the Picquet which as well as other Guards and Posts are to report to the Field Officer and he is to make his report of ye whole at nine o'clock every morning to the Gen and in case of any alarm the Field Officer is to repair to the place of Alarm with all expedition and to send for all necessary assistance to the two Regiments who are immediately to comply with his Orders.

All reports and returns to be made before nine oclock. All out Posts are to receive the Genl with shoulderd Arms and without beat of Drum or Salute.

Upon any application from Sr. Jno. St Clair[31] Quarter Master Genl. for Men the Regiments are immediately to furnish them.

Sir Peter Halket is to be applied to for all Regulations of Provisions and his Orders are [f. 22] to be strictly complied with.

All Guards are to Rest and beat two Ruffles to his Honour Governor Dinwiddie.

Robert Dinwiddie (1693–1770), Lieutenant Governor of Virginia 1751–1758. Reproduced from R. A. Brock, ed., *The Official Records of Robert Dinwiddie,* Richmond, 1883.

The Regiments are to hold themselves in Readiness for a muster, each Company is to provide their Rolls, one of them of Parchment[32] and those Officers with new Commissions are to have them in their Pockets. After the muster the Genl. will receive the two Regiments by Companys the Officers to be in Boots & the men in Brown Gaters.

The Adjutants of the two Regiments and artillery, and also the Adjutant of the Rangers, to be at the Major of Brigades Tent, every day at eleven o'clock to receive Order's.

A Sergeant from the two Regiments Artillery and Rangers to attend the Major of Brigade as Orderly, and to be reliev'd every day at Guard Mounting. [f. 23]

The Gentlemen of the Hospital, and their Servants are to receive to morrow three Days Provisions.

Field Officers for the Day Lieut Colo. Gage.[33]

Alexandria March 28th, 1755.

Parole Albemarle.

The Generals Guard to be mounted in Brown Gater's, and the Officers in Boots.

Sir Peter Halkets Colo. Dunbar's & the Royal Regiment of Artillery[34] are to be musterd, on Monday Morning at seven o'clock, and afterwards they will be receivd by Genl. Braddock.

Robert Webster of Sir Peter Halkets Regimt. is appointed Provost Marshall and he is to be obeyd accordingly. [f. 24]

One Sergeant; one Corporal, and twelve men to mount as a Guard for the Provost Marshal and to be relievd every 48 Hours.

The Adjutant who does not send in his Return to the Major of Brigade, by seven oclock in the morning will be orderd under an Arrest.

The Quarter Master of the Corps which is to receive provisions is to give to the Commissary[35] a signed Return of the Number he is to draw Provisions for every Saturday at six in the Afternoon. The Quarter masters of the different Corps are to give in to Sir Peter Halkett a return of the Provisions they deliver'd out that week distinguishing the quantitys deliverd each Corps. In this return he's to have Column's for the quantitys of each Species of Provisions he has receivd that Week and a Column for the quantitys remaining in Store.

To morrow at Orderly time the Adjutants are to deliver in a return of the number of Servt.[36] [f. 25] who are not Soldiers and for whom Provision's are to be drawn for.[37]

44

The Commissarys[38] are to make two Copy's of this return, one for Genl. Braddock, the other for Sir Peter Halkett.

Field Officer to morrow Lieut. Colo. Burton.[39]

For the Genls. Guard 48th Regiment[40] one of the Orderly Sergeants or the Major of Brigade is to carry the Orders to Sir John St. Clair.

A General Court Martial, consisting of one Field Officer, Six Captains, and Six Subalterns, to sit tomorrow morning at 8 o'clock.

Lt Colo Gage, President.

Sir Peter Halkett gives 3 Captns and 3 Subalterns
Colo Dunbar's ....&c ....&c
Mr. Shirley Judge Advocate [f. 26]

The Picquet to consist of one Captn. two Subalterns and fifty men till further Orders.

No Officer Soldier or any other Person to Fire a Gun within a Mile Round the Camp. [41]

——————————————

Camp at Alexandria March 29th, 1755. —

Parole Boston,

For the General Guard 44th Regiment.

The alarm Post for all the Virginian Troops Quarterd in the Town of Alexandria to be before the march.

When any man is sent to the General Hospital he is to bring a Certificate signed by an Officer, of his name, Regiment and Company, to what day he is subsisted, and what Arms and acoutrements he brings with him.— The Arms and accoutrements to be bundled up, and markd, with the mans name and Company. [f. 27]

Colo. Dunbar's Regiment to morrow to receive three days provisions.

On Sundays every Regiment in Camp is to have divine service at the Head of their Colours.

After Orders —

Each Regiment to send to the Train for twenty Thousand Flints out of which number, they are to pick five thousand, and to send the Remainder back again; The Commanding Officers giving their receipts for what number's they receive.

All the Virginia Troops that are Quartered in Alexandria to be under Arms, to morrow morng. at half an hour after Seven o'clock.

The Officers that were formerly appointed Paymasters, to continue so till further Orders and are to Issue out in payment to the Troops, each a Dollar at 4^e | 9^e shil'g.

When either Regiment have occasion for Ammunition, or any Military Stores the Commanding [f. 28] Officers are to send to the Artillery where[42] they will be supplied giving their receipts accordingly.

The General Court Martial whereof Lieut. Colo Gage was President is dissolv'd, and James Anderson of Colo Dunbar's Regiment who was tryed by ye General Court Martial is order'd 1,000 lashes with a Cat and Nine Tails which he is to receive[43] in such manner as the Commanding Officer shall think proper.

Field Officer for tomorrow Lt. Colo. Gage.

———————————

Camp at Alexandria 30th March, 1755. —

Parole Chichester.

The two Regiments are to be musterd to morrow morning at seven Oclock but the General will not receive the Troops till further Order's.

The two Regiments from Ireland are to acct for their men for their Sea pay giving them credit for their Subsistance to the first of March and for their Arms to the 24th of Feb'y. The Captains [f. 29] are to take credit for their Watch Coats, Blankets, & Flannell waistcoats brought from Great Britain for their Companys.

The Men listed or incorporated into Sir Peter Halketts, and Colo. Dunbar's Regiment are to have Credit for twenty Shillings and to be chargd with the above mention'd necessarys. His Excellency order's this to be taken from the Recruiting Fund, and gives it to those Men for their Incouragement that they may do their duty like good Soldiers.[44]

The first Company of Carpenter's[45] are to march tomorrow Morning to Sir John St Clair for further Order's.

A Return to be sent to morrow Morning to Sir Jno St Clair from Sir Peter Halketts and Colo. Dunbars Regiments of the Number of Draughts they have receiv'd by whom they were enlisted and from what companys draughted. [f. 30]

Camp at Alexandria 31st of March 1755.—

Parole Darlington.

Field Officer for to morrow, Lt Colo. Burton.

For the Generals Guard 44th Regiment.

All Casualties or occurrances that happen in Camp to be reported immediately to the Genl. through an aid de Camp.

Whenever Sir John St. Clair has occasion for Artificers Tools, or Implements, he is to apply to the Commissary of the Train, who will supply him with what he demands taking his, or his assistants Receipts for the same.

The Officers to provide themselves with Bat Horses[46] as soon as possible.

The Artillery to have their men upon the Wharf every morning at 6 Oclock precisely to Land[47] their Stores &c. and care must be taken that they have their Waggons at the Wharf [f. 31] exactly at the same time that their may be no delay one Sergeant and 12 Men from the two Regiments to march immediately to the Wharf in order to assist the Artillery in the Landing of their Stores this party to be reliev'd every Morning and to be on the Wharf precisely at 6 Oclock.

Sir Peter Halkets Regiment Receives three days provisions tomorrow.

Camp at Alexandria April lst. 1755

Parole Essex,

Field Officer for tomorrow [48]
For the Generals Guard 48th Regiment.
Colo. Dunbars Regiment to receive three Days Provisions.
The two Regts. are to send to ye artily. for 1 Dozn. of carts. made up
with Ball in order to try if they will fit the men's Firelocks. [f. 32]

Camp at Alexandria April 2d. 1755.—

Parole Farnham.

Field Officer for tomorrow Majr. Chapman.[49]
For the Generals Guard 44th Regiment.
The Artillery and Hospital receive three days provision tomorrow.
The two Regiments are to apply to the Train for Paper Powder and
Ball sufficient to compleat every man with 24 rounds which are to be
made up and distributed as soon as possible.
The commanding Officers of Companys are desird to give particular
directions to their men to be careful of their Ammunition and to inform
them they will be very severely punished for any abuse or neglect of it.
And the Officer's of Company's who calld the Evening Rolls are to inspect
the Ammunition of their several Companys and to Report the defficiencys
to the Commanding Officers of the Regiments who are desird by his
Excellency to keep them compleat with 24 Rounds. [f. 33]
His Excellency General Braddock Orders that the Soldiers should be
told that any man who upon a march by fastening his Tent Pole, or by any
other means incumber's his Firelock, shall be immediately and most
severely punished.
One Corporal and eight men of the Line to attend at 6 Oclock every
Morning; to assist the Engineer's in Surveying.
The Artillery, Hospital and Engineers to receive three days provisions
tomorrow.

After Orders

One Sergeant one Corporal, and twenty men of the Line without Arms to March to the Wharf immediately to assist in disembarking the Artillery.

The Virginia Troops as appointed to the particular Regiments.

Sir Peter Halketts.

Captn. Stephen[50] ...	1st	Company
Captn. Peyronny[51] ...	4[52]	of
Captn. Cock[53] ...	6	Ranger's [f. 34]

Colo. Dunbars Regt.

Captn. Waggoner[54] ...	3	Company
Captn. Hogg[55]	5th	of Rangers
Captn. Polson[56] ...	2d	Compa. of Artificers

Sir Peter Halketts and Colo Dunbar's Regiments to find three Corporals one for each Company of Rangers to assist Lieut. Allayne[57] in the disciplining these Troops.

Camp at Alexandria April 3d. 1755.

Parole Canterbury.

Field Officer tomorrow Lt. Colo. Burton.
For the Generals Guard 48th Regimt.
The Generals Guard is this Day reduced to a Corporal and nine men and the Corporal is to report to the Officer of the Main Guard.
Sir Peter Halkets Regiment to receive three days Provisions Tomorrow.
[f. 35]

Camp at Alexandria, 4th of April, 1755.

Parole Dorsett

Field Officer tomorrow Major Sparke.[58]
For the Generals Guard 44th Regimt.
Colo. Dunbar's Regiment to have one Corporal and Six Men ready to March tomorrow at 6'oclock from Alexandria to Frederick with the Hospital Stores they are to carry six days Provision's with them and to take the Arms and accoutremts. with which they are to take the Field. Each Man to have his Blanket and 24[59] rounds of Ammunt.
Colo. Dunbar's Regiment to have three days provisions tomorrow.

Alexandria Saturday April 5th 1755.

Parole London,

Field Officer tomorrow Lt. Colo. Burton.
For the Generals Guard 48th Regimt.
The Tents and cloathing for the Virginia Companys to be brought on Shore as soon as possible, Their tents are to be pitched the first fair Day after they are on Shore.
The Artillery Hospital and Engineers to receive three days provisions to morrow. [f. 37]

Alexandria April 6th 1755.

Parole Kinsale,

Field Officer for to morrow Majr. Chapman.
For the Generals Guard 44th Regiment.
All Detachments[60] for Duty of every Nature what ever are to parade at the Grand Parade and to March from thence, Detachments from different Corps to draw up by Seniority.
The Grand Parade for this Camp is appointed to be at the head of Sir Peter Halketts Regiment.

A Report to be made every morning to Sir Peter Halket, of the Sergeants Corporals, Drummers and Private Men who are Drunk upon Duty, the Sergeants of the Companies they belong to, to keep an exact Roll of their names. Sir Peter Halkett being determined to put a stop to any more Provns. being drawn for such men. [f. 38][61]

Sergeants, Corporals, Drummers, and Private men who appear Drunk in Camp tho they are not upon duty will have their provision's stop'd for one week.

Sir Peter Halketts Regiment to receive three days Provision's Tomorrow.

The Detachments from the Ordinary Dutys of Camp to change from Right to left every Day.

After Orders.

One Sergeant, one Corporal, and thirty men are tomorrow at 6 o'clock in the morning, to go to Alexandria to assist the Officer's of the Artillery in loading the Waggons for Winchester and Shipping of Stores for Rock Creek[62] One Officer and thirty men from Colo. Dunbar's Regiment to March tomorrow for Rock Creek The Officer to call this Night upon Sir Peter Halkett who will give him his Instructions. [f. 39]

Alexandria Monday April 7th 1755. —

Parole Dublin,

Field Officer for tomorrow Lt. Colo. Burton.

For the Generals Guard 48th Regimt.

One Officer one Sergeant and 20 men of Sir Peter Halketts Regiment to hold themselves in Readiness to morrow morning to march to Winchester the Officer at Retreat beating to call upon Sir Peter Halkett for his Instruction's; They are to take six days provisions with them, subsistence to the 24th of this month and every thing with which they are to take the Field.

Every Party ordered to march from Camp is to have 24 Rounds per man.

A Greater number of Women having been brought over than those allowd by the Government sufficient for washing with a view that the Hospital might be servd; And Complaint being made that a concert is enterd into not to serve without exorbitant Wages a Return will be calld for of those who shall refuse to serve for six pence [f. 40] per day and their Provisions that they may be turnd out of Camp and other's got in their places.

Colo. Dunbar's Regt. is to rec. 3 Days Provn. tomorrow.[63]

———————————

Alexandria Tuesday, Apl 8th 1755.

Parole Guilford.

Field Officer for tomorrow Majr. Sparke.

For the Generals Guard 44th Regimt.

The Quarter Master's of Sir Peter Halketts and Colo. Dunbar's Regiments to meet Mr. Leslie[64] assistant Quarter Master General this afternoon at 4 Oclock who will show them their Regimental Store Houses. The Commanding Officer's of each of the Regimt. as soon as their Regimental Store Houses are fix'd are to order their Officer's baggage and their mens Stores to be immediately lodgd.

The Soldiers are to leave their Shoulder Belts, Waist Belts and hangers behind and only to [f. 41] take with them to the Field one spare shirt, one spare pair of stockings, one spare pair of Shoes and one pair of Brown Gater's.

For the future the Generals own and all other Guards are to beat a March to him and the Line is always to turn out when the General passes. As a mistake has happend in regard to the Commissions of the youngest Subalterns of the Rangers. The Commissions of Second Lieuts being deliverd to them instead of Ensigns are to be immediately changd to avoid any Inconveniency,[65] which may arise from disputes[66] of Rank.

His Excellency Genl. Braddock Orders that all Ensigns bearing Commissions in any of his Majestys Regiments shall take post of the third Officer in any of the Companys of Ranger's.

Sir Peter Halkett (1695–1755), Colonel of the 44th Regiment. Killed at the Battle of Monongahela, July 9, 1755. Reproduced from Francis Parkman, *Montcalm and Wolfe,* Boston: Little, Brown, and Company, 1901.

After Order's

Six Companys of Sir Peter Halketts Regiment are to march for Winchester at 6 o'clock on thursday [f. 42] Morning;[67] Eight[68] Waggons will be orderd to be at the head of that Regiment on Wednesday Night for the Tents, Baggage, etc. of those Companys application is to be made to Mr. Leslie assistant Quarter Master for a proper Guide. — Every man is to receive 8 Days Provision's to carry with hm. The Lt. Colo. is to be left with the 8 Remaining Companies till further Order's.

All the sick are to be left in the General Hospital.

The Regiments find the Generals guard as usual and the proportion of Duty is to be made up by Colo. Dunbar's Regiment in the Town & other Guards.

March Rout of Sir Peter Halketts Regiment from the Camp at Alexandria to Winchester.

	Miles
To ye old Court House[69]	18
To Mr. Colemans on Sugar Land Run where there is Indian Corn, &c[70]	12
To Mr. Miners[71]	15
To Mr. Thompson ye Quaker wh ye is 3000 wt Corn[72].	12
To Mr. Key's 17 ye Ferry of Shanh 12[73]	17
From Mr. Key's to Winchester	23
	97 [f. 43]

If the Bridge should not be laid over the Opeckon Canves will be provided for the Troops.

As soon as the Artillery arrives at Winchester a Detachment of their Regiment and what ever part you shall judge proper of the Ranger's must be orderd to march with the Artillery to Wills Creek.

But if the road should be cut from the bridge on ye Opeckon to Bear Garden and is made passable for ye Artillery, it is then to go along that Road and not by Winchester[74] and your Detachment from Winchester must join them at Henry Enoch's.[75] A Report will be made to you whether this road is passable or not.

As the Removal of the Troops from Winchester to Wills Creek must depend upon the Quantity of Flower that is to be sent from Pennsylvania, when a proper Quantity is arrivd you shall receive advice of it. [f. 44][76]

Alexandria Wednesday April the 9th 1755.

Parole Henly.[77]

Field Officer for tomorrow Lt. Colo. Gage

For the Genls. Guard 48th Regiment.

Colo. Dunbar's Regiment to send this Forenoon two Sergeants and twenty men to Rock Creek to Reinforce the Officer there.

A Return to be given in this Day of the two Regiments specifying all extraordinarys that have happend since their embarking in Ireland.— A monthly Return of the Two Regiments to be given in to General Braddock every first Day of the month.— The Companys of Ranger's, Artificer's and the Troop of light Horse[78] are to give in a Monthly return at the same time: They are to apply to the Major of Brigade, who will shew them the proper form.

The Officers to see that their men are providd as soon as possible with Bladder or thin Leather [f. 45] to put between the Lining and Crown of their Hatts to guard against the Heat of the Sun.

One Subaltern Officer of Dunbar's Regiment to march to morrow morning to Frederick in Maryland who upon his arrival is immediately to take upon him the Command of the several Detachments of the Regiment that are now there or may arrive and he is to see yt they are properly providd & Subsisted.

Alexandria Thursday, 10th April, 1755.—

Parole Winchester.

A Detachment from the two Regiments of a Subaltern, two Sergeants, two Corporals and 20 men is to remain at Alexandria as a guard for the Hospital and to march with it to Frederick.

The Generals Guard is to be taken off on Friday.— A Sergeant and twelve men of Colo Dunbars Regiment to mount as the Generals [f. 46] Baggage Guard and to March with it.[79]

The Provost Marshall is to March with Colo Dunbar's Regiment and to have a guard of a Sergeant and ten men who is to make the Rear of the whole.

Two Officer's and forty men of the four remaining companies of Sir Peter Halketts Regem is to mount the Town Guard till further Orders.

Colo Dunbar's Regiment is to march at 5 Oclock on Saturday Morning for Rock Creek.[80]

Waggons will be orderd on Friday to carry the baggage and whatever Tents may be struck to the Boats destind for their Transportation and at Day break on Saturday morning Waggon's will attend at the head of the Regiment for the mens Tents &c.

A Subaltern Officer with three Sergeants three Corporals and thirty men are to be sent on board the Boats as a baggage Guard, and this Guard is [f. 47] to assist in conveying the Tents &c to the Boats and to help in putting them on board.

All the Boats upon that part of the River near Rock Creek are orderd to attend to cary the Troop over.

The Sick men that are not able to March with the Regiment, to be left in the General Hospital.

After Orders

As Colo. Dunbar's Regimt is to march on Saturday, they are to receive Tomorrow nine Days Provisions one for to morrows use, and the remaining 8 Days the men are to carry with them.[81]

The four companys of Sir Peter Halketts Regimt the Royal Regt of Artillery Engineer's and the Hospital are to continue to receive their Provisions as usual till further Order's.[82] [f. 48]

March Rout of Colo. Dunbar's Regiment from the Camp at Alexandria to Frederick in Maryland.

	Miles
To Rock Creek	—
To Owen's Ordinary[83]	15
To Dowden's Ordinary[84]	15
To Frederick	<u>15</u>
	45

Within a few miles of the Minocasy—[85] cross the Minocasy in a Float.—[86]

Upon your arrival at Rock Creek you are either to Encamp or lodge your Men as you shall find most convenient and as fast as the Waggon's arrive you are to employ them in the Service of ye Regiment and Regulate your Detachments accordingly and to be particularly careful not to use any more Waggons than are absolutely necessary.[87]

You are to leave at Rock Creek an Officer and 30 men who is to remain there till all the Stores of [f. 49] the Train and Hospital are put into the Waggons is then to march and form the Rear Guard of the whole.[88]

You are also to leave at Rock Creek a Subaltern and 20 men who are to wait there till the arrival of Mr. Johnston[89] the Paymaster and to Escort him to Frederick.

You will be joined at Rock Creek by an Officer and 30 Seamen[90] who you are to take under your command and give them your Orders and Regulations as they will want some conveyance for their baggage you will dispose of it, as you find most convenient.

Upon your arrival at Frederick you are to encamp your men the Troops to Remain there till further Orders except a Captn, two Subalterns and 50 men who are to be sent immediately on to Conogogee[91] as a covering Party for the magazines & you are to direct the Commanding Officer of this Detacht to stop all Waggons which shall brg in Flower, &c. from Pennsylvania and to send a Daily to you of the number's which return you are to remit [f. 50] to me unless you should see Sir Jno St. Clair and that he should have securd a sufficient number for Transporting the Stores from Frederick to Wills Creek[92] in such case the Waggons are to be dismissd.

You will find provisions at Frederick which you are to issue to your men in the same proportions as at Alexandria and to begin upon it as soon as you have expended the Provisions card with you.

You are to direct your Officers to provide themselves as soon as possible with Bat-Horses as no more Waggons will be allowd after they get to Frederick.[93] [f. 51]

Alexandria Friday, Apl. the 11th 1755.

Parole Kendall.

The Officer of the Town Guard to make his Report to the General through an Aid de Camp.

After Orders

Colo Dunbar's Regiment to hold themselves in Readiness but not to march till further Orders.

They are to give their Proportion of men for the Guards to morrow.[94]

One Sergeant, one Corporal and 12 men to Parade immediately at the Town Guard of Colo Dunbar's Regiment.

They are to take their Knapsacks, Haversacks, and Provision's with them; when they come to the Town Guard the Sergeant is to enquire for Mr. Leslie assistant Quarter Master who will give him Orders. [f. 52]

No Person whatever to press or employ any Waggons without an order from General Braddock the Quarter Master Genl. or his assistant.

This Order to be read not only to the Soldiers but to the Officer's, Servants, and followers of the Army, as any one who shall be found guilty of disobeying it will be severely punish'd.—

After Order's

As there are Boats provided to carry Colo Dunbar's Regiments Baggage to Rock Creek the former orders relative to their march to be obeyd. [f. 53]

58

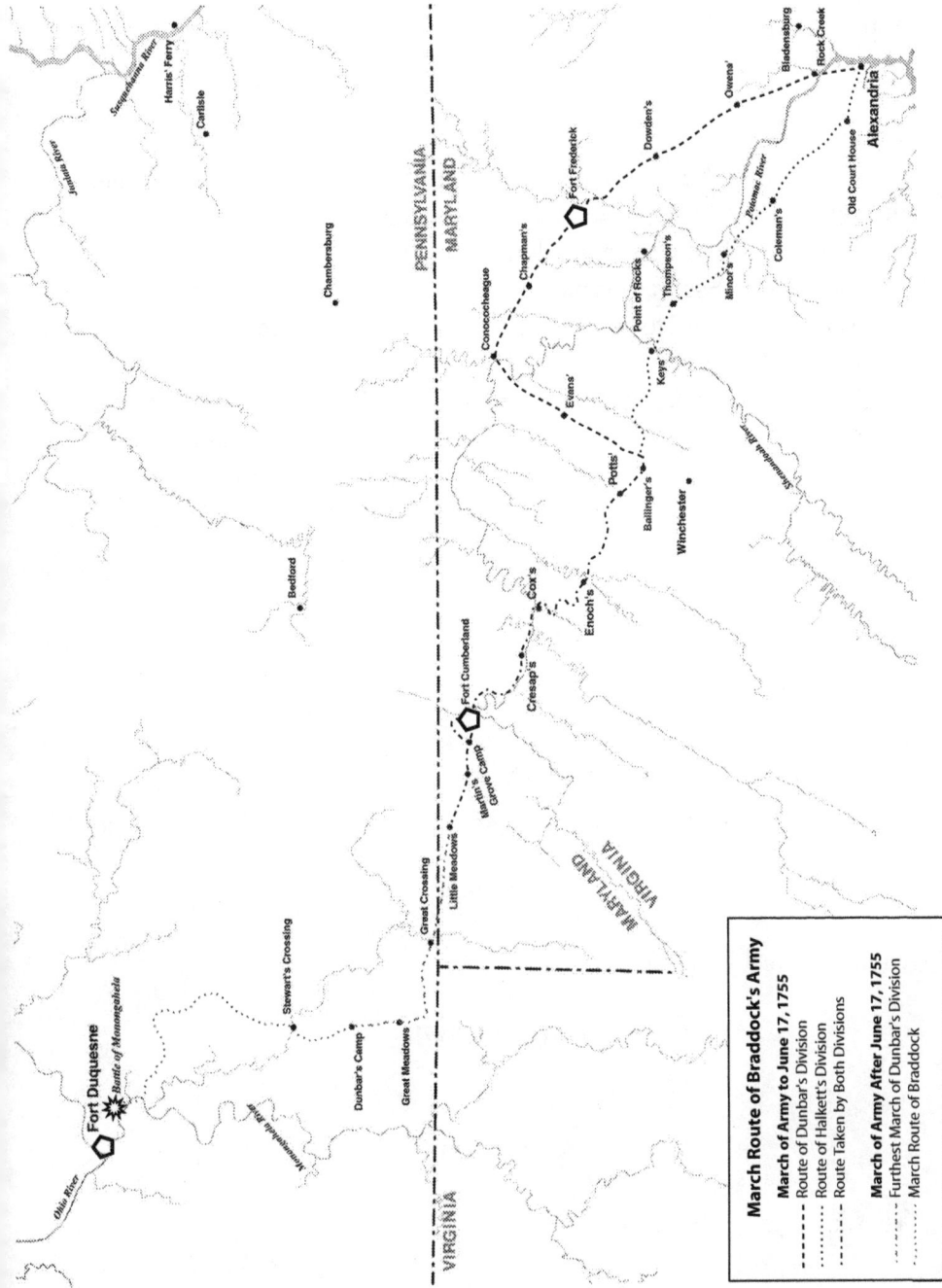

Fort Duquesne

Battle of Monongahela

Ohio River

Monongahela River

Stewart's Crossing

Dunbar's Camp

Great Meadows

Great Crossing

Little Meadows

Grove Camp

Martin's Camp

Fort Cumberland

Cresap's

Cox's

Enoch's

Bedford

Juniata River

Susquehanna River

Harris' Ferry

Carlisle

Chambersburg

PENNSYLVANIA

MARYLAND

Conococheague

Chapman's

Fort Frederick

Evans

Potts

Ballinger's

Winchester

Keys

Point of Rocks

Thompson's

Minor's

Shenandoah River

Potomac River

Coleman's

Old Court House

Dowden's

Owens'

Bladensburg

Rock Creek

Alexandria

VIRGINIA

MARYLAND

VIRGINIA

March Route of Braddock's Army

March of Army to June 17, 1755

- – – – Route of Dunbar's Division
- ········· Route of Halkett's Division
- – · – Route Taken by Both Divisions

March of Army After June 17, 1755

- – – – Furthest March of Dunbar's Division
- ········· March Route of Braddock

Alexandria

Saturday April 12th 1755.

Parole Leicester.—

One Company of Sir Peter Halketts Regimt to March to morrow Morning, they are to Parade opposite to the town Guard at 6 oclock where they will be joind by five Waggons belonging to the Artillery, which they are to take under their Escort to Winchester.

The Town Guard to be reduced to morrow morning to one Subaltorn Officer and thirty men.

Mr Leslie will take care that there shall be at Sir Peter Halketts Quarter Guard this afternoon 3 Waggons, one for the Companys Tents and Baggage and the other two are to carry ye Regiments spare Arms and Stores.

The Men are to take eight Days Provisions with them. [f. 54]

Alexandria

Sunday April 13th 1755

Parole Marlborough.

Alexandria

Monday April 14th 1755

Parole Oxford

Alexandria

Tuesday April 15th 1755

Parole Petersborough

Alexandria

Wednesday April 16th 1755

Parole Rochester [f. 55]

Thursday April 17th 1755.

Parole Queen Town

Friday April 18th 1755

Parole Salisbury

Saturday April 19th 1755

Parole Tamworth.

The commanding Officer of the Artillery[95] to apply to Mr. Leslie for a Store House to lodge their new cloathing in, and the Officers are to see that their men comply with the Order's of the 8th of Apl. (viz) to leave their Shoulder Belts waist Belts and Hanger's behind, and are only to take with them to the field one spare shirt one spare pair of stockings one spare pair of shoes and one pair of brown Gater's. [f. 56]

Frederick

Monday April 21st 1755—

Parole Dunbar.—

Frederick

Tuesday, April 22^d 1755.—

Parole Westminster

One Sergeant one Corporal and 12 men to parade immediately at the Town Guard to March with the Waggons laden with Artillery Stores to Conogogee and to return back with the. Waggon's to Frederick as soon as they are unloaded.[96]

Frederick

Wednesday April 23[d] 1755

Parole Exeter.

The commanding Officers of Regiments to order [f. 57] their Officers to provide themselves as soon as possible with Bat men out of such Recruits & Levies, as are unfit to the Duty *to do the*[97] of solder and such men are to be enlisted as can act as Bat men and are to be taken for any Term and to be allowd as effectives; and according to the number settled in Flanders 3 Men to each Company and 4 to the staff.[98]

You are to go immediately to that part of the Antietum[99] that lies in the road to Connogogee and press such Boats or Canoes as you shall meet with upon the River, agreeable to the Orders you shall receive from Governor Sharpe.[100] If you shall find any difficulty in the execution of this Order, you are to send an express to me and you shall be immediately supplied with a party of men to inforce it sending word when they shall join you, and you are to collect all the Boats &c at that pass by the 28th of this Month. [f. 58]

Frederick

Thursday April 24th 1755—

Parole Yarmouth.

Horatio Sharpe (1718–1790) Lieutenant Governor of Maryland, 1753–1763. 19th Century Engraving from J. T. Scharf, *History of Maryland,* 1879.

Frederick

Friday April 25th 1755

Parole Appleby—

Colo. Dunbars Regiment to hold themselves in readiness to March by the 29th.

After Order's

One Corporal and four men to March to morrow Morning to Rock Creek with four Waggons that came up this Evening; when the party comes to Rock Creek they are to put themselves under the command of Ensign French.[101] [f. 59]

Frederick

Saturday April 26th 1755.—

Parole Bedford.

Colo. Dunbar's Regiment to furnish 3 Officers for a Court Martial, to try some prisoners of the Independant Company; Captn Gates[102] Presidt the report to be made to General Braddock.

Frederick

Sunday April 27th 1755.

Parole Chester

Colo. Dunbar's Regiment is to march ye 29th and to proceed to Wills Creek agreeable to the following Route [f. 60]

64

	miles
29th From Fredk. on ye Road to Conogogee[103]	17
30th From that halting place to Congogee	18
1st From Conogogee to John Even's[104]	16
2^d Rest	
3^d To the Widow Baringers[105]	18
4th To George Polls[106]	9
5th To Henry Enoch's[107]	15
6th Rest	
7th To Cox's[108] at ye Mouth of little Cacapn[109]	12
8th To Colo. Cresaps[110]	8
9th To Wills Creek	<u>16</u>
	Total 129

The men are to take from this place three Days provision's, at Conogogee they will have more.

At the Widow Baringers 5 Days

At Colo Cresaps one or more Days.

And at all these places Oats or Indian Corn must be had for the Horses but no Hay. [f. 61][111]

At Conogogee the Troops cross the Potomack in a Float.

When the Troops have marchd 14 miles from Jno. Evans they are to make the new road to their Right, which leads from Opechon Bridge.[112]

When the Troops have marchd 14 miles from George Polls's they come to the great Cacapehon they are to pass that River in a Float. After passing they take the road to the Right.[113]

If the water in the little Cacapehon is high the Troops must Encamp opposite to Cox's.

At the mouth of the little Cacapehon the Potomack is to be crossd in a Float—Four miles be yond this they cross Town Creek, if the Float shoud not be finishd Canoes[114] will be provided.—

If the Bridges are not finishd over Wills Creek and Evan's Creek, Waggons will be orderd to carry the men over. It will be propr to get 2 D. Prvns at Colo. Cresaps ye whole shd. not arrive till ye 10th.— [f. 62]

CRESAP'S FORT.

Cresap's Fort at present day Oldtown, Maryland. Reproduced from William H. Lowdermilk, *History of Cumberland,* Washington D.C., 1878.

A Subalturn and thirty men are to be left behind with a proper number of Tents which will be carried for them; these men are to have six Days Provision's.

The Generals Guard is not to be relievd to morrow but proper Centrys are to be found from the 30 Men orderd to remain.—

Frederick

Monday April 28th 1755.—

Parole Daventry.

The Detachment of Sailors, and the Provos Marshall's Guard, consisting of one Sergeant, one Corporal and 10 men to March with Colo. Dunbars Regiment to morrow morning, and to make the Rear Guard. [f. 63]

To Captn. Gates   28th April 1755

You are directed by His Excellency Genl. Braddock to proceed with your Company to Conogogee, where you are to act as a covering party for the Magazines, and you are to remain there till further Order's unless all the Stores Ammunition, &c, should be come up from Rock Creek and forwarded to Wills Creek, in that case you are to joyn the General at Wills Creek as soon as possible.—

You are to give all possible assistance and use your utmost endeavours in transporting the several Stores, Ammunition, Provision, &c to Wills Creek with the utmost expedition.

Whilst you remain at Conogogee you are to send a Sergant, or Corporal, with such of your men as are to be trusted with all the Waggon's which arrive at that place from Rock Creek allowing one man to each Waggon and you are to send them immediately back to Rock [f. 64] Creek for more Stores till you shall be informd from the Officers there, that every thing is sent up.

Horatio Gates (1728–1806), commissioned captain of a New York Independent Company, 1754–1759. A 19th Century engraving from an original portrait by Stuart. From C. H. Jones, *Conquest of Canada in 1776,* Philadelphia, 1882.

To Ensign French at Rock Creek   28ᵗʰ Apl. 1755

You are orderd by his Excellency Genl. Braddock to forward with
all Expedition the Ammunition Stores &c at Rock Creek to Mr.
Cresaps at Conogogee taking care to send the Ammunition Train
Stores &c first, then the Hospital Stores and Salt Fish.¹¹⁵
   You are not to wait for the Beeves but as soon as the
aforemention'd things are gone up you will move with your party
and join the Regiment at Wills Creek agreeable to the followg March
Route; as you will find Provisions very scarce on the Road you
must take with you as many Days of salt Provisions, as the Men
can carry.— [f. 65]

From Rock creek to Owen's Ordy	15 Miles
To Dowdens	15
To Frederick	15
On the Road to Conogogee	17
To Conogogee	18
To John Evans	16
To Widow Baringers	18
To George Polls's	9
To Henry Enochs	15
To Mr. Cox's	12
To Colo Cresap's	8
To Wills Creek	16
	Total— 174

You must if you shoud find it necessary, take with you Guides from
place to place, and make such halts as you shall find absolutely
necessary being careful not to loose any time.
   If the Waggons shoud come in very slowly make your
application to the Civil Officers [f. 66] and if that shoud not succeed
send Parties to fetch in any Waggons you shall hear off. Inform
Lieut Breerton¹¹⁶ of the March Route, and tell him it is the Generals
Orders that he make all imaginable dispatch.

Camp at Fort Cumberland

Saturday May 10th 1755.

Parole Connecticut.

Mr. Washington[117] is appointed Aid de Camp to His Excellency General Braddock.—

Field Officer for to morrow Majr Spark.

The Articles of War to be read to morrow morning at which time the Servants women & followers of the Army are to attend with the Respective Corps and Companies that they belong to.—

The two Independent Companies and Rangers to receive three Days provisions tomorrow.

For the Generals Guard 48th Regiment.

Colo. Dunbar's Regiment to relieve the Fort Guard immediately, and the Fort Guard is to march to Fraziers[118] as a Grass Guard and to be relievd every 48 hours. Capn. Polson's[119] Company of Carpenters is to send one corporal and 6 men with their tools [f. 68] and to make such fences as the Officer of the Grass Guard shall think proper.

The Virginia and Maryland Rangers and the Company of Carpenters to settle their men's accts immediately giving them credit for what arrears &c are due and they are for the future, to be subsisted regularly twice a week as the Rest of the troops are.

A Return to be given in to morrow morning of the Strength of each of the Regiments by Companys the return to be signd by the commanding Officer of each Corps. The Independent Companys, Virginia and Maryland Rangers and the Troop of Light Horse are also to send in a Return to morrow morning of their strength which return is to be signed by the Captain, or Officer commanding each Company, and to be given in separately.

The General has fixd the Hour for his Levy from ten till eleven in the forenoon every Day. [f. 69]

George Washington (1732–1799), Aide-de-Camp to General Braddock. Depicted at age 25. Reproduced from Cyrus Townsend Brady, *Colonial Fights and Fighters,* New York, 1901.

Camp at Fort Cumberland

Sunday May 11th 1755.—

Parole Albany.

Field Officer to morrow Lt. Colo. Burton.
The Generals Guard —44th Regimt.

A Return to be sent in of the numbers of men who understand the springing of Rocks those men that are fitt are to be told that they will receive proper Encouragement.[120]

All the Troops are to begin their Field Days. Powder may be had from the Train by applying for it and each man is to have 12 Rounds for every field Day.—

A Return to be given in tomorrow morng at Orderly time of the Recruits of the whole Army setting forth their age, Size Country and occupation.[121]

One Sergeant and 6 men from piquet to attend during the time of marketting to prevent [f. 71] Disputes and if any should happen he is to apply to the captn of the Picquet he belongs to. This duty to be done alternately.—

All Provisions brought into Camp to be settled according to a settled Rule a copy of which will be given to the Troops by the Major of Brigade and no Persons bringing provisions shall presume to ask more nor shall any body offer less for good and wholesome meat.—

The 48th Regiment is to receive their Day provisions tomorrow at 10 oclock.

After Orders

All the out Guards to be relievd to morrow morng and parade at 5 Oclock.—

Evening Orders

It is His Excellencys General Braddocks Orders that no Officer soldier or others give the Indians, Men, Women or children any Rum other Liquor or money upon any acct. whatever.—[122] [f. 71]

Camp at Fort Cumberland

Monday, May 12th 1755.—

Parole Boston—

Field Officer tomorrow— Majr Sparke
The Generals Guard— 48 Regimt.

Whereas Captn. Polson of one of the Virginia Company of Carpenters desird a Court Martial to enquire into his Character, having been accusd of being in Arms in the late Rebellion in Scotland. His Excellency has been informd that the accusations is scandalous and groundless; if therefor any Person whatever can prove Captn. Polson to have been in the late Rebellion they are desird immediately to send their accusation to the Genl. If not His Excellency intirely frees him from any Imputation of that kind and desires that no Reflections for the future may be thrown on Captn. Polson on that accd.—[123] [f. 72]

After Orders

A General Court Martial to sit immediately at the Presidents Tent, it is to consist of one field Officer, 6 Captns. and 6 Subalterns.

Maj[r] Sparke ….. President.
Mr Shirley …… Judge Advocate

His Excellency has thought proper to Brigade the Army in the following manner and they are for the future to Encamp accordingly.
    The first Brigade to be commanded by Sir Peter Halkett and to consist of the 44th Regmt, Captn Rutherford,[124] and Captn Gates's Companys of New York, Captn. Polsons Company of ye Virginia Carpenter's, Captn. Peyrouney, Captn. Waggeners of the Virginia Rangers and Captn. Dagworthy's Company of Maryland Rangers.[125]

The Second Brigade to be Commanded by Colo. Dunbar and to consist of the 48th Regimnt. [f. 73] The Detachment from South Carolina Commanded by Captn. Demere[126] The Company from North Carolina Commanded by Captn. Dobbs,[127] Captn. Mercer's Company of Virginia Carpenters, Captn. Stephen's Captn. Hoggs and Captn. Cock's Companys of Virginia Ranger's and the Detachment of Seamen to Encamp with the 48th Regimt.

The Troop of Light Horse to Encamp by themselves.[128]

Any Soldier or follower of the Army who shall stop any one bringing in Provisions or Forage to the camp shall immediately suffer Death.

No out Post to march from or to Camp with beat of Drum nor is any *beat of* drum to beat before the Troop unless when any of the Troops are out at exercise, and of which they are to acquaint the Genl. the Night before thro' one of His Aid de Camps. [129][f. 74]

The Companies in each Brigade exclusive of the Regiments are to Mount a Picquet consisting of one Captn. 2 Subalturns 2 Sergeants 2 Corporals and 48 Centinals and to parade at the head of the Companies in each Brdigade; and when any Detachment is demanded from any of these Companys they are to parade there and then to order them to be marchd to the Genl. Parade.

Camp at Fort Cumberland.

Tuesday 13th May 1755—

Parole Charles Town—[130]

Field Officer for tomorrow .... L Colo. Burton.
The Generals Guard ....44th Regt.

The Quarter Masters, Camp colour men, and Pioneers of the two Regiments with two men of the Independent Companies with proper Tools [f. 75] for clearing the Ground in the Front to parade att five Oclock in the Evening at the head of the 48th Regiment and to remain there for the Field Officer of the Day's Order's.

The Picquets are to lay advanced and to remain att their Parade till they receive the Field Officer's Orders. Each of the two Regim to send 6 Tents to the Companies in each Brigade and also to send six tents each for the men of their advanced Picquets. The Centrys on the advanced Picquet are not to suffer any body to pass unexamined[131] after Sun sett.

The Picquett Returns at 6 oclock in the morning.

The Quarter Guard of Sir Peter Halkets Regiment for the future to be posted on the Right Flank. [f. 76]

Camp at Fort Cumberland.

Wednesday 14th May 1755.—

Parole Dumfries—

Field Officer tomorrow .... Lt Col Burton
The Generals Guard .... 48th Regit.

The Genl. Court Martial is Dissolved. Luke Woodward Soldier in the 48th Regimt commanded by Colo Dunbar having been tryed for Desertion by a Genl Court Martial whereof Maj Wm Sparke was president, is by sentence of that Genl. Court Martial adjudged to suffer Death. His Excellency, Genl Braddock has approved of the Sentence but has been pleasd to Pardon him.

Thomas Conelly, Jas Fitzgerald and James Hughes soldier's in the 48th Regimt. and tryed for theft by the said Court Martial whereof Major Sparke was president are by the Sentence of the sd Court Martial adjudged to suffer the following punishments: [f. 77]

Thomas Conelly one thousd. ....   Lashes att the
Jas Fitzgerald, eight hundd. ....   Head
Jamess Hughes eight hundd..........   of the Line.

Also that they be oblig'd to make satisfaction for the Kegg of Beer stolen by them to the value of thirty three shilgs. Maryland Cury., and that proper stopages be made out of their Pay by their Officers for that purpose; His Excellency has approvd the sentence, but has been pleased to remit one hundred lashes from the punishment of Conelly and two hundred from each of the other two. Conelly is to receive 900 lashes at 3 different times 300 lashes each time. Jas Fitzgerald and Jas Hughes are to receive 600 lashes each at two different times, 300 lashes each time. The 48th Regiment to send the Drummers to the head of ye line, to put the Sentence in execution the first time of punishment to be tomorrow morning at Troop beating. The two Picquets formd from the Independant Companies Virginia and Maryland Rangers, to consist of one [f. 78] Captn. 2 Subaltorns 2 Sargeants, 2 Corporals and 38 Centinals.

Camp at Fort Cumberland

Thursday 15th May 1755

Parole Portsmouth.

Field Officer to morrow .... Majr Sparke
For the Generals Guard .... 44th Regimt.

The Officers who were orderd to get themselves in Readiness to go with the Paymaster, are countd.

One Subaltern, one sergt. 1 Corpl and 30 cent'l to march this Eveng to Mr. Martins[132] where the Troop of light Horse Graze the men to take Tents with them and Provisions for three Days the Officer to receive his Orders from Captn. Stuart[133] of the light Horse, this Guard to be relievd every 3d Day.

One Sergt. one Corpl & 12 men to parade att the Fort Guard this Day at 12 Oclock; The [f. 79] Sergeant will receive his Orders from Capt Orme.[134]

Fort Cumberland 1755 from the Foot of Nobley. Reproduced from William H. Lowdermilk, *History of Cumberland.*

After Orders—

The Subaltern's Guard that was orderd to march to Martin's is countermanded.—

Camp at Fort Cumberland

Friday 16th May, 1755.

Parole Winchester.

Field Officer tomorrow .... Lt Colo. Gage.
For the Generals Guard .... 44th Regimt.

Any Indian Trader, Soldier or follower of the Army who shall dare to give Liquor to any of the Indian's or shall receive or purchase from them any of their presents made to them by His Majesty thro' his Excellency Genl Braddock, shall suffer the severest punishment a Court Martial can Inflict.
There will be a public Congress of the Indians tomorrow at 12 Oclock at the Genlss Tent. [f. 80]

Camp at Fort Cumberland

Saturday 17th of May, 1755—

Parole Eskaw

The Congress of Indians mentiond in Yesterdays Orders, is putt off.

Field officer tomorrow .... Lt. Colo. Burton.
For the Generals Guard .... 48th Regit.

The Two Regiments, the Independant Compys. the Company's of Carpenter's, the Virginia & Mary land Companys of Rangers and the Troop of Light Horse are to send immediately to Mr. Lake, Commissary of Provision's a separate Return of the number of Persons they each of them draw Provision's for; this Return to be signed by the Commanders of the two Regts. and by the Captn. or Officers Commanding each of the Independent Companys &c. The form of this Return is sent to the Brigade Major and [f. 81] is to be given in regularly every eight Days.

His Excellency expects that this Order will be punctually obey'd as the Commissary will not be able to provide a proper quantity of Provisions for the Army unless he has the above Return sent to him regularly.

One Subaltern one Sergt. 1 Corporal, & 30 Men to mount as a Guard on the Artillery. They are to parade this afternoon at 5 Oclock and to be Reliev'd every 48 hours.

Camp at Fort Cumberland

Sunday May 18th 1755—

Parole Farnham—

There will be a publick congress of the Ind. this Day at 12 Oclock at the Genls Tent.

Field Officer tomorrow .... Majr. Sparke.
For the Genls Guard .... 44th Regt. [f. 82]

One Corpl. & 8 Men of the Line to attend the Engineers in Surveying; they are to parade at 9 Oclock.

Each Regiment, Independant Company &c in the making up of their Cartridges are to allow 36 round of Ball to 1 lb. of Powder, and for Field Days or Exercise they are to allow 46 with or without Ball.

Six Women per Company are allowd to each of the two Regimts. and the Independent Companys; Four Women to each of the Companys of Carpenters Virginia and Maryland Rangers five Women to the Troop of Light Horse as many to the Detachment of Seamen, and 5 to the Detachment of Artillery.

His Excellency expect that this order is[135] punctually complied with as no more Provns. will be allowd to be drawn for than for the above number of women.

One Subaltern 1 Sergt. 1 Corpl. & 50 Centy. To parade tomorrow morning at 6 Oclock. They are to [f. 83] take three Days provisions with them and the Officer of this to receive his Orders from Sir Jno. St. Clair.[136]

Camp at Fort Cumberland

Monday 19th of May 1755.—

Parole Guilford.

Field officer tomorrow .... Lt. Colo. Gage.
For the Genls Guard .... 44th Regt.—

Each Brigade to send a man to the Gen'1 Hospital as orderly, who are to receve and obey the directions of Doctr. Napper[137] *Director of the sd. Hospital.*[138]

All the Troops are to acct with the Director of the Hospital once in three months or as soon after as can be for stoppages at the rate of 5 pence stirl'g per Day, for every Man that is admitted in the Gen1. Hospital; This stoppage to commence from the 24th of May Ensuing. [f. 84]

As soon as the Retreat has been beat this night the Drum Majr. of each of the two Regiments are to March with the Drummers and Drums[139] to the Head of the Artillery where they will receive Orders.

After Orders—

A Return to be given into the Brigade Major, to morrow at orderly time of the number of Smiths and Carpenters that are in the two Reg. Independant Companies &c.

Camp at Fort Cumberland

Tuesday May the 20th 1755—

Parole—Hindon.

Field Officer tomorrow .... Lt. Colo. Burton.
For the Genls. Guard .... 48th Regt.

One Subaltern, 1 Sergt, 1 Corpl & 24 men to parade to morrow morning at 5 O'clock. They are to have three Days Provns [f. 85] with them and the Officer is this night to recieve his Order's from Sir Jno. St. Clair.[140]

Camp at Fort Cumberland.

Wednesday 21st of May 1755.

Parole Ilchester.

Field Officer tomorrow .... Majr. Chapman
For the Generals Guard .... 44th Regt.—

No Soldier that is employd as a Baker by Mr Lake Commissary of Provisions, is to be put upon any Duty whatever till further orders.—
It is his Excellency's Order's that no Sutler give any liquor to the Indian's on any acct. if any one does he will be severely punished.

The provost is to go his Round every Day through all the Roads leading to the Camp Every Soldier or woman that he shall meet with on the other side of the River, or beyond the advanced Picquets without a pass from the Regiment or from the Officer Commanding the Company to [f. 86] which they belong He is to order his Executioner to tye them up and give them fifty Lashes and to march them Prisoners thro' the camp to expose them.—

One Gill of Spirits mixed with three Gils of Water may be allowd each Man per Day which the Officers of the Picquet are to see deliver'd out every Day at Eleven Oclock, any sutler[141] that shall sell any Spirits to the Soldiers without an Officer being present shall be sent to the Provosts.

Camp at Fort Cumberland

Thursday 22^d May 1755.[142]

Parole Kensington.

Field Officer tomorrow .... Majr. Sparke
For the Generals Guard .... 48th Regt.—

Camp at Fort Cumberland

Friday May 23^d 1755—

Parole Lincoln [f. 87]

Field Officer tomorrow ....Majr. Chapman.
For the Genls. Guard ....44th Regimt.

A General Court Martial to sitt tomorrow morning at 8 Oclock at the Genls. Tent to consist of one Field Officer, 6 Captns 6 Subalterns.

Lt. Colo. Gage .... President.
Mr. Shirley .... Judge Advocate

If any Officer Soldier or follower of the Army shall dare to give, any strong liquor, or money to the Indian Men or Women, if an Officer he shall be brought to a General Court Martial for disobedience of Orders if a non Commission Officer, Soldier; or follower of the Army he shall receive 200[143] lashes witht. a Ct Mart1.

Camp at Fort Cumberland.—

Saturday 24th of May 1755—

Parole Monmouth [f. 88]

Field Officer tomorrow .... Lt. Colo. Burton
For the Generals Guard .... 48th Regiment

Six Men of the Line without Arms to be at the head of the Artillery to Morrow morning at 5 Oclock and to receive their Order from Captn. Ord.[144]

Camp at Fort Cumberland

Sunday, May 25th 1755.—

Parole Norwich.

Field Officer tomorrow .... Majr Sparke.
For the Generals Guard .... 44th Regimt.

If any Non Commission'd Officer or Soldier belonging to the Army is found Gaming he shall immediately receive three hundd. Lashes without being brought to Court Martial, and all Standers by or lookers on shall be deemd principals and punishd as such.— [f. 89]

An exact Return to be given in to the Genl. as soon as possible of the strength of the Army; the Return of the two Regiments to be signd by the Commandg Officer's of each Corps and that of the Artillery Independent Companys &c. by their Captns. Or Officers Commanding the Companys.

Evening Orders

A Return to be given in to the Genl tomorrow at 12 Oclock from the two Regiments, Artillery, Independent Companys the Companys of Carpenr. Virginia and Maryland Rangers the light Troop of Horse and Detachment of Seamen of the number of Person's that each of them draw Provns. For Daily.

Mr. Lake the Comy. is also to give in att the same time a Return of the number of Guides, Indians, Workmen &c. that draw Provns. Daily. And Mr. Scott Waggon Master Genl. is to give in a Return at the same time of the number of Waggoner's and Horse that draw Provisions. [f. 90]

His Excellency expects that the Commanding Offrs. Of Corps Companys &c. will be very particular and exact in this Return.[145]

One Captn. 1 Lt. 1 Ensign and 70 men of the 2 brigades to parade immediately att the Fort.— They are to take Tents and 10 days Provns. with them. The Captn. is to receive his Orders from Sir Jno St. Clair.[146] A Genl. Court Martial of the Line to sit to morrow to try Lt. McLead[147] of the Royal Regt. of Artillery confind by Genl. Braddock. To consist of one Colo. 2 Field Officers & 10 Captns.—

Sir Peter Halkett .... President
Mr. Shirley .... Judge Advoce.

To sit at the Presidents Tent and to meet at 12 Oclock.

A Return to be given into Sir Jno. St. Clair by the Quarter Masters of each Brigade and Artillery of the quantity of Provisions drawn from the [f. 91] Commissarys.— A Return likewise to be given in to Sir Jno. St. Clair every Monday Morning of the Provisions drawn for the preceeding Week.[148]

Camp at Fort Cumberland

Monday 26th May 1755.

Parole Oxford

Field Officer tomorrow .... Lt. Colo. Gage
For the Genls. Guard .... 48th Regt.

The Genl. Court Martial whereof Lt Colo. Gage was President is dissolvd.— His Excellency havg approvd of the several sentences allotted them.

John Nugent of the 44th Regiment having been tryed for theft, and found Guilty of the crime laid to his charge as an accomplice in receiving a share of the Money that was Stole, is adjudgd to receive one Thousand Lashes, and to be drum'd out of the Regt. Thro' the Line with a Halter about his Neck. [f. 92]

Saml. Draumer, of the 44th Regimt. and George Darty of Captn. Demere's Independent Company havg been tryed for Desertion are adjudgd each of them to receive two hund'd Lashes.

Henry Dalton of the 48th Regt. havg been tryed for Shooting Henry Pelkington, soldr. in the said Regiment the Court Martial[149] is of Opinion that the said Dalton did not Shoot the said Pelkington with design but that it was done by accident therefore His Excellency Genl Braddock has orderd him to be Releasd, and to be sent back to his Regt.[150]

If any soldier is seen Drunk in Camp He is to be sent immediately to the Quarter Guard of the Regmt. he belongs to, and the next morning he is to receive two hundred Lashes without a Court Martial.— [f. 93]

Camp at Fort Cumberland.—

Tuesday May 27th 1755.—

Parole Petersfield

Field Officer tomorrow ……………………….. Lt. Colo. Burton
For the Genls. Guard …………………………….. 44th Regimt.

The Genl. Court Martial whereof Sir Peter Halkett was President is Dissolvd.—[151]
The Party of the Picquets that lay advanced to load with running[152] ball, the Rest of the Picquets to load with Powder, and to have their Ball in their Pockets.
The following Detachment to March on Thursday[153] morning to Parade at Reveille beatg. The Men to be provided with two Days Provisns ready dressd.—
The 44th & 48th Regts. are to furnish 1 Field Officer, 4 captns. 12 subalterns 12 sergeants and 250 Rank and File. [f. 94]
Captn. Rutherford's Captn. Demere's Independent Companys Captn. Waggener's Captn. Peyrouney's Companies of Virginia Rangers and Captn. Polson's Company of Carpenter's are also to March with this Detachment who are to take with them their Camp Equipage and Baggage.—
Major Chapman Field Officer for the Detachment.[154]
The Independant Company and Companys of Virga. Rangers orderd for this Detachment to furnish no Men for the Guards tomorrow and any Men that they may have upon the out Guards are to be relievd immediately. Particular care is to be taken that the Men's Arms are in good Order & that each Man is provided with ten Flints and compleated to 24 rounds of Ammunition.
The Tools and Tomahawks of the 2d Brigade are to be given out at Gun firing this evng to the Quarter Master General at his Tent and a demd to be made to morrow mg. at 6 o'clock of ye numr. of Tools each Brigade will want; the Quarter Master to attend.— [f. 95]

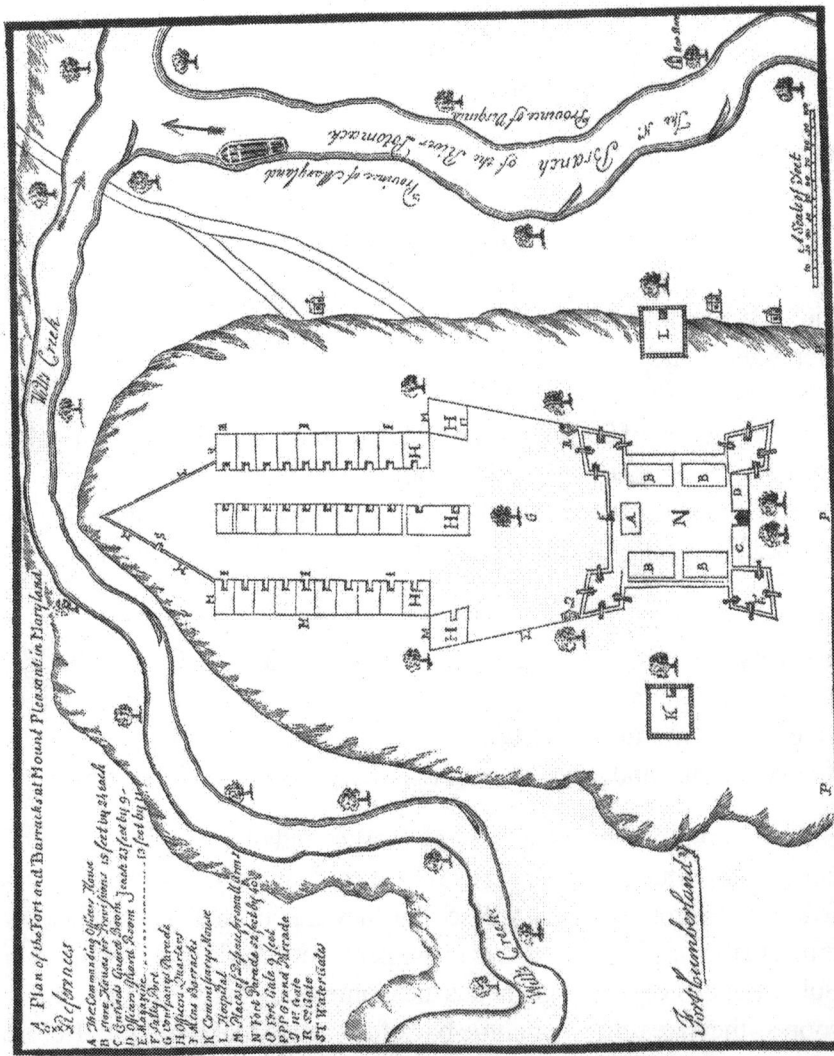

A. Plan of the Fort and Barracks at Mound Pleasant in Maryland

References

A The Commanding Officers House
B of Provisions is feet by 24 each
C Carlands Guard Room
D Officers Guard Room Jack 32 feet by 9
E Magazine .... 13 feet by
F Sally Port
G Company Parade
H Officers Quarters
J Mens Barracks
K Commissary House
L Hospital
M Places of Safety from the
N Fort Roads 22 feet by 60
O Fort Gale 9 feet
P P P Grand Parade
Q H Gate
R S. Gale
S T Waterfalls

Fort Cumberland

Plan of Fort Cumberland 1755
from the King's MSS. Library
of the British Museum.

Reproduced from William H.
Lowdermilk, *History of
Cumberland.*

Camp at Fort Cumberland

Wednesday May 28th 1755.—

Parole Quarendon.

Field Officer tomorrow ……………………….. Maj Sparke
Generals Guard ……………………………… 48th Regt.

The Regulation of Stoppages with the Director of the Genl. Hospital to commence from the 24th of this month.

As it is necessary to employ the Soldiers in mg. and amendg. the Roads His Excelly. has been pleasd to appt. the followg. Allowances

	s	d	
To every Sub: Officer ………………………	3	0	Sterlg.
To every Sergeant …………………………..	1		per
To every Corporal …………………………..		9	Day
To every Drum and private Centinal …………...		6	[f. 96]

But as at present there is no publick market and of course the Men will have no opportunity of making use of the ready money, His Excellency is so kind as to promise that he will see that they are punctually paid whatever is due to them; when they arrive in Winter Quarters. Therefore whatever Subaltern Officer or Sergeant has the Command of any workg. Party as soon as they are relievd or come back they are to make an exact Return of the number of Men of their Party and give it in to the Quarter Master Genl.

But if hereafter there should be any publick market or that the money will be found to be of use to the men, upon a proper application His Excellency will give Order's for their being paid.

The Companies of Rangers are for the Future to furnish their proportion of men for Duty with the Rest of the Line. [f. 97]

As there will be an express going in a few days, any Officers that have *any* Letters to send to Great Britain are desird to give them to either of the Genls. Aid de Camps or to Mr. Shirley.¹⁵⁵

After Order's

The men of the Detachment that march to morrow to be commanded by the Officers of their own Corps or Company.

Sixteen Men from Line to be appointed to the Guns to morrow that March and to be under the Direction of the Officer of ye Artillery.

The Independant company and Rangers of the two Brigades to Mount but one Picquet.

Camp at Fort Cumberland

Thursday 29th May 1755

Parole Queensbury

Field officer to morrow ....Lt. Colo. Gage.
The Genlss Guard ....44th Regt. [f. 98]

Camp at Fort Cumberland

Friday 30th of May, 1755.—

Parole Rochester

Field Officer tomorrow .... Lt. Colo. Burton
Generals Guard .... 48th Regt.

The Troops to hold themselves in Ready to March at 24 hours warning.

Whatever Barrells the Regiments & Comp. have got belonging to the Artillery are to be sent back immediately with their Troops to the Foreman of the Train.

Camp at Fort Cumberland

Saturday, 31st of May 1755—

Parole—

Field Officer tomorrow .... Majr. Sparke.
Generals Guard .... 44th Regt. [f. 99]

Camp at Fort Cumberland

Sunday 1st of June 1755—

Parole Tamworth—

Field Officer tomorrow .... Lt. Colo. Gage
Genls Guard .... 48th Regt.

Camp at Fort Cumberland

Monday 2d of June 1795.

Parole Weybridge

Field Officer tomorrow .... Lt. Colo. Burton
Generals Guard .... 44th Regimt.

The Hatchett Men of the two Regiments & one man per Company from the Rest of the Line to Parade this Afternoon att 3 Oclock at Mr Gordon[156] Engineer's Tent.

Four Sergeants 2 Corporals & 100 Men with Arms, 1 Subaltern, 1 Sergeant, 1 Corpl. and 30 Men with [f. 100] Arms to Parade tomorrow morning at Revielle beating at the Head of the Line and to receive their orders from Mr Gordon Engineer.

His Excellency has been pleasd to appoint Colo. Innis Governor of Fort Cumberland.[157]

Monday Evening

Three Subaltern Officers to march with the detachment of 100 Men without Arms which is to parade tomorrow morning at Reveille Beatg.

Camp at Fort Cumberland

Tuesday June 3^d 1755.

Parole Yarmouth

A General Court Martial of the Line consisting of 6 captns & 6 Subalterns, to sitt to morrow morning at 8 o'clock att the President's Tent.

Majr. Sparke .... President
Mr. Shirley .... Judge Advocate
[f. 101]

Field Officer tomorrow .... Lt. Colo. Burton
Generals Guard ....48th Regimt.

Four Subalterns, 5 Sergts, 5 Corpls, and 150 Men without Arms to parade tomorrow morning at ye head of the Line at Reveille Beating.

One Subaltern 1 Sergt. 1 Corpl, and 30 Men with Arms to parade at the same time and act as a covering Party; they are to receive their Order from Mr. Gordon Engineer.—

Camp at Fort Cumberland

Wednesday 4th June, 1755—

Parole Doncaster.

Field Officer tomorrow .... Lt. Colo. Burton
For the Genls. Guard .... 44th Regt.

The 44th Regiment and Captn. Mercer's Comp. of Virginia carpenters to hold themselves in Readiness to march in an hour's warning. The Workg [f. 102] Party to be relievd tomorrow morning, and by the same number.

Camp at Fort Cumberland

Thursday June 5th 1755

Parole Boston.

Field Officer tomorrow ....Majr. Sparke.
For the Generals Guard ....48th Regt.

The Working Party to be relievd tomorrow morning and by the same number of men.—

Camp at Fort Cumberland—

Friday June 6th 1755—

Parole

Field Officer to morrow ....Lt. Colo. Burton

Sir Peter Halketts Regiment to march to morrow morning. The Sick of the Regimt. unable to march to be sent to the Genl Hospital. One Subaltern officer to be left behind with them. [f. 103]

The Men of Sir Peter Halketts Regiment now upon Guard when they are relievd or orderd to come off are to be Assembled together and marchd Regularly to the Regiment by an Officer.

Captn. Gates's Independant Company & all ye remaining Companies of provincial Troops to march on Sunday Morning with the whole Park of Artillery.

No more women are allowd to march with each Regimt. & Company than the number allowed of by His Excellency in the Orders of the 18th May.

Any Soldier, Sutler, Woman or other person whatever who shall be detected in Stealing, purloining or wasting of any Provisions shall suffer Dth.

The Genl Court Martial whereof Majr. Sparke's was President is dissolvd.

Michael Shelton and Caleb Sary Soldier's belonging to Captn. Edward Brice Dobbs's Company of Americans tryd for Desertion [f. 104] are by the Sentence of the Court Martial found guilty and adjudgd to receive 1000 Lashes each.

John Igo a Convict Servant, accusd of theft is by the Sentence of the Court Martial found guilty of receiving and concealing Goods the property of soldiers in his Majestys Service and is adjudgd to receive 500 Lashes with a cat and Nine Tails by the hands of the common hangman.

John McDonald Soldier in Sir Peter Halketts Regiment accused of being an accomplice and concernd with John Igo is acquitted.

The Guards advanced up Wills Creek the Potomack and the Flatts* to be taken off tomorrow Morning, and to join their Several Corps the other Guards to remain and to be relievd as usual.

---

* The Flats were on the East side of Will's Creek.

Captn. Gates's Independt. Company and ye remaing Companies of the Provincial Troops, to furnish their Proportion for the Guards tomorrow and when they [f. 105] are relieved they are to join their Companys in the same manner as those of Sir Peter Halkett's Regimt are directed to do in this Days Orders.

No Soldiers wife to be suffered to march from this Ground with a Horse as their own.

Camp at Fort Cumberland

Saturday June 7th 1755.—

Parole Doncaster

Capt Gates's[158] Independant Companies & the Remaining Companies of Provincial Troops & ye whole Park of Artillery to march to morrow Morning and to be under the Command of Lt. Colo. Burton.

The Artillery & Companies that march to morrow to receive this Afternoon Provisions to compleat them to the 11th Inclusive & ye Women to ye 17th.

The 48th Regiment to take all the Guards tomorrow the men of the 48th Regt. now upon [f. 106] Train Guard are to join their Corps to morrow morning when the Artillery Marches off & that Guard to be mounted by the Companies that march to morrow.

The 48th Regt. to hold themselves in Readiness to march on Monday next.

After Orders

The Generals Guard is to be reduced to morrow to 1 Sergt. 1 Corpol and 12 Men who are not to be relieved but to remain with the Genls Baggage.

Camp at Fort Cumberland

Sunday June 8th 1755—

Parole Essex.

Captn. Gates's Independant Company and the remaining Companies of the Provincial Troops and Artillery are to March to morrow.

The 48th Regt. to march on Tuesday [f. 107] As Colo. Dunbar's Regt. is not to march to morrow the Genls. Guard to be relievd to morrow morning.

The Companies that march tomorrow to send immediately 1 Sergeant Corporal & 12 men to assist Mr. Lake Commissary of Provisions at the Fort.

A Return to be sent immediately from Colo. Dunbar's Regt. Captn. Gates's Company & the American Troops of the number of men they have fitt for Waggoners or Horse Drivers.

In the return of Colo. Dunbar's Regt. they are only to include those men that have joind the Regiment since they have been landed in America.—

Camp at Fort Cumberland

Monday June 9th 1755

Parole Fallmouth

Col Dunbars Regiment to send their Sick [f. 108] unable to march to the Genl Hospital and to leave a Subaltern Officer behind with them.

One Sergt. 1 Corpl. and 24 men without Arms to parade tomorrow morning at Day break to assist Mr. Lake Commissary of Provisions in loadg. of ye waggon's.

Camp at Fort Cumberland

Tuesday, June the 10th 1755—

The Fort Guard to join their Regimt. as soon as Governor Innis has taken possession of it and placed his Centrys.—

Camp at the Grove, first Camp from Fort Cumberland.[159]

Parole Gainsborough.

Field Officer tomorrow .... [f. 109]

All the Officers of the Line, to be at the Genls. Tent tomorrow Morning at 11 o'clock.

No Fires to be made upon any acct. whatever within 150 yards of the Road on either side any person acting contrary to this order shall be very severely punished.

All the Waggon's to be drawn up tomorrow morning as close as possible and as soon as the waggons belonging to the Detachment under the Commd. of Majr. Chapman have closd up to the Rear of the Artillery; that Detachment then to join their respective Corps.

Colo. Dunbars Regiment to Encamp to morrow morning upon the left of the whole, according to the Line of Encampment.

Camp at the Grove

Wednesday June 11th 1755

Parole Hartford.

Captn. Rutherford and Captn. Gates's Indep [f. 110] Companys and all the Americans Troops to be under Arms immediately att the head of their respective Encampments.

Any person whatsoever that is detected in Stealing shall be immediately hangd witht. being brought to a Court Martial.

One Subaltern Officer 1 Sergt. 1 Corporal & 40 men witht. Arms from each of ye two Regemt. to parade immediately at ye hd. of the Artillery.

One Sub 1 Sergt. 1 Dr & 30 Men of the Line to Parade in the Rear of Colo. Dunbar's Regt. as soon as they have come to their proper ground. The Officer is to receive his Order's from Majr. Sparkes.

Whatever number of Horses are furnishd by the Officers are to be paraded as soon as possible in the Rear of Colo. Dunbars Regimt. and to be reviewd by Majr. Sparke. [f. 111]

The Officers are desird to acquaint Majr. Sparkes which of their Horses for carrying *Horses* and which are for Draught and to be so good as to send with the carrying Horses, Bat-Saddles &c. if they have them.

The Commandg Officers of the two Regts. & the Captns. of the Independt. and Provincial Troops to send in a Return to the Genl. of the number of Horses furnish'd by their respective Officers, and opposite to the Officer's names, The number of Horses furnishd by each Officer; that the Genl. may be able to inform His Majesty of the Inclination and Readiness of the particular Officers in carrying on the Service.—

After Orders

No more than two Women per Company to be allowd to march from the Camp a List of the names of those that are to be sent back to be given into Captn. Morris that there may be an Order sent to Colo. Innis at Fort Cumberland [f. 112] to Victual them.— A List of the names of the women that are allowd to stay with the troops to be given in to the Majr. of Brigade and any woman that is found in Camp and whose name is not in that List will for the first time be Severely punishd and for the Second suffer Death.[160]

After Orders

Colo. Dunbar's Regt. is immediately to furnish a Sergt. & 12 Men as a Guard for the Provisions on their Left and the Sergt. is to receive his Orders from Mr. Lake Comy. of Prons.

The Line is to furnish two Sergts. & 30 Men witht Arms who are to attend Mr. Lake Comy. of Prons. tomorrow morng at Day break & assist in loading the Horses.—

It is the Genls. Orders yt. Mr. Lake Comy. of Prons. with his People & ye Party yt is allowd him begin weighg out ye Flour & othr Prns. for back Lds[161] tomorrw mg by Day bk. & his Excellency yt every thg. will be in readiness by 1 O'clock in ye Afternoon. [f.113][162]

Notes:

[1] Braddock and his staff arrived at Hampton, VA on February 20. They proceeded to Williamsburg to consult with Governors Robert Dinwiddie of Virginia and Horatio Sharpe of Maryland on February 23. See "Robert Orme's Journal," p. 283–85.

[2] Hampton Roads off present-day Hampton, VA, was the first point of landing for the transports carrying the 44th and 48th Regiments from Ireland. A fleet of 13 transports, three ordnance ships, and two frigates left Cork on January 15. The fleet arrived at Hampton Roads between March 2 and March 15. See Lawrence Henry Gipson, *The British Empire Before the American Revolution, Volume VI. The Great War for Empire: The Years of Defeat, 1754–1757.* New York: Alfred A. Knopf, 1946, p. 64.

[3] Colonel John Hunter was a Justice of Elizabeth City County Court and a colonel of Virginia militia. He served as agent for the Thomlinson Hanbury merchant firm of London which was used by the Government to transfer funds to the forces in North America. In December, 1754, he was named Resident Agent and Paymaster of British forces for the 1755 campaign. He sold out his interest in the firm and moved to England, 1766.

[4] Lowdermilk transcribed this as "on shore."

[5] This is a reference to the general hospital directed by Dr. James Napier. In addition to the general hospital, each regiment had its own surgeon and at least one surgeon's mate.

[6] Robert Dinwiddie (1693–1770) was appointed lieutenant governor of Virginia, July 20, 1751. He arrived in Virginia in November, 1751 and quickly took the lead in pursuing British interests in the Ohio Valley. This inevitably propelled him into the forefront of the growing conflict with the French, who considered the Ohio country theirs by right of exploration. The son of a Glasgow merchant, he had begun his career as a clerk in the Customs Office in Bermuda in 1721, eventually rising to Collector of Customs for Bermuda and Surveyor General of Customs for the Southern Colonies in 1738. It was Dinwiddie who commissioned George Washington to deliver his warning to the French in 1753, and he was the primary organizer of the expedition of 1754 which resulted in Washington's defeat at the Battle of Great Meadows on July 3, 1754. Dinwiddie was recalled to England in January, 1758.

[7] On November 12, 1754 Royal orders were issued that all provincial field officers, when serving with regulars, would rank below that of the youngest British captain. See "Sketch of an Order About the Rank &c. of the Provincial Troops in North America," in Pargellis, *Military Affairs in North America,* pp. 43–44.

[8] Upon his arrival in Virginia, Braddock divided the colony's forces into two companies of carpenters, six companies of rangers, and a troop of light horse, see Sargent "Robert Orme's Journal," 284–85.

[9] William Shirley (1721–1755) was the eldest son of Governor William Shirley of Massachusetts. He had served as a colonial naval officer in Boston in 1741. He later went to England to attend to family affairs. While in England, he was appointed Secretary to General Braddock without rank, in the fall of 1754. Shirley was shot in the head and killed at the Battle of Monongahela, July 9, 1755.

[10] Sir Peter Halkett (1695–1755) was colonel of the 44th Regiment. Halkett was serving as a major in the Scots Fusiliers in 1739. He was commissioned lieutenant colonel of the 44th Regiment in 1741. He had made a name for himself at the Battle of Prestonpans in September, 1745 when he held a group of five officers and fourteen men together until offered terms of surrender while the remainder of the regiment fled the field. He was a Scottish Baronet and served as MP for Inverkeithen. Halkett was promoted to colonel of the 44th Regiment on February 26, 1751. He commanded the rearguard of Braddock's Division and was killed at the Battle of Monongahela, July 9, 1755.

[11] Major John Carlyle (1720–1780) was a merchant born in Dumfrieshire, Scotland. He was the son-in-law of William Fairfax, agent to his brother Lord Fairfax, the proprietor of the Northern Neck of Virginia. He was also brother-in-law to Lawrence Washington, older brother of George Washington, who had died in 1752. Carlyle had served as commissary for the expedition of 1754. Braddock used his home as his headquarters while in camp at Alexandria.

[12] Lowdermilk transcribed this as "Guides."

[13] Conococheague was at the mouth of the river of the same name near present-day Williamsport, Maryland. Thomas Cresap (c. 1695–1790) owned a storehouse there. He had been contracted to provide provisions for the army. Thomas Swearingen operated a ferry on his land near Shepherdstown, VA that was used to transport men and provisions across the Potomac.

[14] Dumfries and Occoquan are both in Prince William County, Virginia. Bladensburg and Upper Marlboro are both in Prince Georges County, Maryland. These orders were based on a plan submitted by Sir John St. Clair to disperse the companies in various small camps. Commodore Augustus Keppel objected to the plan and the decision was made to encamp the entire army outside of Alexandria. Ross Netherton, *Braddock's Campaign and the Potomac Route to the West,* Falls Church, VA: Higher Education Publications, Inc., 1989, p. 5. For St. Clair's plan see "Sir John St. Clair to Robert Napier, February 10, 1755," in Pargellis, *Military Affairs in North America,* pp. 58–66.

[15] Lowdermilk omitted this word.

[16] Lowdermilk transcribed "halt."

[17] Lowdermilk transcribed "Three."

[18] In the manuscript, this paragraph is on a separate page numbered 13 in the American Memories Collection on the Library of Congress internet site. The paragraph below is found before it on the page numbered 12. Lowdermilk appears to have been correct in placing the text in this order, although he appears to have misdated it as February 28th, 1755.

[19]Captain Roger Morris (1727–1794), from Yorkshire, was commissioned a captain in the 17th Regiment in September, 1745. He was serving in the 48th Regiment when Braddock appointed him an aide-de-camp. Morris was wounded in the nose at the Battle of the Monongahela, July 9, 1755. He was later appointed lieutenant colonel of the 47th Regiment May 19, 1760. He resigned his commission in 1764. After the war, Morris settled on the Hudson River and served on the Council of New York. He was condemned as a loyalist during the War of American Independence and had his property confiscated. After the war he returned to his home in Yorkshire.

[20] Thomas Dunbar (d. 1767) was colonel of the 48th Regiment of Foot. He had served in the 18th Regiment for 25 years and had risen to the rank of lieutenant colonel by 1745, when he was present at the Battle of Culloden. He was commissioned colonel of the 48th Regiment on April 29, 1752. Dunbar was placed in command of the second division of Braddock's army. He was much criticized when he took command after Braddock's death and withdrew to winter quarters in Philadelphia in August, 1755. He resigned his commission on November 11, 1755 and returned to England. In 1758 he was appointed Lieutenant Governor of Gibraltar. Dunbar later reentered the military service and eventually rose to the rank of lieutenant general.

[21] Captain Francis Halkett was the eldest son of Colonel Peter Halkett, and a captain in the 44th Regiment. He later served as an aide-de-camp to Brigadier General John Forbes during his expedition to the Ohio in 1758. The brigade major was in charge of the organization of the army's camp.

[22] This is a reference to William Augustus, Duke of Cumberland (1721–1765), son of King George II. Both the 44th and 48th Regiments had served under the direct command of the Duke during the Scottish Rebellion of 1745. Cumberland was Captain General of the British Army 1745–1757.

[23] Lowdermilk omitted this word.

[24] The lieutenant colonels were Sir Thomas Gage of the 44th Regiment and Sir Ralph Burton of the 48th Regiment.

[25] Lowdermilk transcribed "instruct."

[26] Captain Robert Webster of the 44th Regiment was appointed Provost Marshall on March 28, 1755, see page 44. Webster served in Dunbar's division and therefore did not participate in the Battle of the Monongahela.

[27] Lowdermilk transcribed "retird."

[28] Lowdermilk transcribed "Halters."

[29] "Fuzee" was a short musket sometimes carried by officers. The manuscript reads "Fuzeis."

[30] The majors were Russell Chapman of the 44th Regiment and William Sparke of the 48th Regiment.

[31] Lieutenant Colonel John St. Clair (d. 1767) was named deputy quartermaster general of the British Army in Pennsylvania on October 15, 1754, and served in that capacity until 1767. He became third Baronet St. Clair in 1726 and was

commissioned major in 22nd Regiment. He had served under Field Marshall Maxillian von Browne in Italy during the War of the Austrian Succession. St. Clair served with a local commission of lieutenant colonel in North America and arrived in Virginia ahead of Braddock on January 9, 1755. He was in charge preparing the roads and encampments for Braddock's Army and commanded the working party at the Battle of Monongahela, where he was severely wounded in the early stages of the fight. He received a commission as lieutenant colonel in the 60th Regiment on March 20, 1756 and rose to the rank of colonel in North America in January, 1758.

[32] Lowdermilk transcribed "one of Parchment."

[33] Lieutenant Colonel Sir Thomas Gage (1726–1787) had entered the army sometime between 1736 and 1740. He had participated in the Battles of Fontenoy and Culloden, and was commissioned lieutenant colonel of the 44th Regiment of Foot March 24, 1751. Gage commanded the advanced guard at the Battle of Monongahela where he was wounded in the belly. In 1758 he became colonel of the 80th Light Infantry Regiment. He was promoted to brigadier general and was second-in-command under Abercromby at the Battle of Ticonderoga, July 9, 1758. He was named commander in the West in the Fall of that year. He then served as commander of the rearguard during Amherst's advance toward Montreal in 1760. After the French surrender of Canada, Gage served as Governor of Montreal from October 1760 until he was promoted to Major General and given overall command of British forces in North America, November 16, 1763. He remained in that position until the outbreak of the War of American Independence in 1775.

[34] A company of Royal Artillery under the command of Captain Thomas Orde accompanied Braddock along with four 12-pounders, six 6-pounders, four howitzers, and fifteen coehorn mortars, Gipson, *The Years of Defeat,* p. 64.

[35] Robert Leake was commissary of provisions. He later served as major in the Second Battalion, King's Royal Regiment of New York, during the War of American Independence. His lands in Albany County were confiscated by the State of New York in 1779.

[36] Lowdermilk transcribed this as "servd."

[37] Lowdermilk did not break the paragraph at this point.

[38] Lowdermilk transcribed "Commissary."

[39] Sir Ralph Burton, (d. 1768) was lieutenant colonel of the 48th Regiment. He had exchanged his commission as major in the Second troop of Horse Grenadiers for the lieutenant colonelcy in the 48th Regiment in 1754. He served with distinction and was wounded in the hip at Battle of Monongahela while leading a charge on the French position. He served with the 48th Regiment throughout the war and commanded the reserve battalion at Battle of Quebec, September 13, 1759. After the conquest of Canada he was named Governor of Trois Rivières. Burton was promoted to major general, July 10, 1762 and became Colonel of the 3rd Regiment of Foot, November 22, 1764. Burton was appointed commander-in-chief of British forces in Quebec and the Upper Great Lakes in 1764. He subsequently retired to Yorkshire in 1766 where he died two years later.

[40] Lowdermilk included a paragraph break at this point.

[41] Beginning with "Lt. Colo. Gage," Lowdermilk had transcribed the above text as one paragraph. The structure has been changed to reflect the manuscript.

[42] Lowdermilk transcribed "when."

[43] Hamilton transcribed this as "revew" See "Halkett's Orderly Book" in Hamilton, *Braddock's Defeat*, p. 7.

[44] This is a reference to the men recruited into the two regiments once they reached North America. The regiments had sailed from Ireland with compliments of 500 men each. Braddock had orders to recruit them to 700 men each once he arrived in America. Stanley McCrory Pargellis, *Lord Loudoun in North America,* Yale University Press, 1933; repr. New York: Archon Books, 1968, pp. 31–33.

[45] Captain George Mercer (1733–1784) commanded the 1st Company of Virginia Carpenters. He had enlisted as a lieutenant in the Virginia Regiment on February 25, 1754, was promoted to captain on June 4, and fought at the Battle of the Great Meadows, July 4, 1754, where he was wounded. His company was in the working party under St. Clair at the Battle of Monongahela. He later became George Washington's aide-de-camp in September, 1755 and served through most of 1756 at Fort Loudoun in Winchester. In 1757, he served in the contingent of Virginia troops sent to Charleston, SC. He was appointed lieutenant colonel of 2nd Virginia Regiment in 1758 and served in the Forbes expedition to the Ohio. In 1763 he was sent to London as agent for the Ohio Company. Mercer briefly returned to Virginia in 1766 as Stamp Agent for the colony of Virginia, but he was forced to destroy the stamps by an angry mob. After that, he returned to London and eventually died there in 1784. Alfred Procter James, *George Mercer of the Ohio Company: A Study in Frustration,* Pittsburgh: University of Pittsburgh Press, 1963.

[46] Bat horses were horses used to carry the goods and supplies of officers.

[47] Lowdermilk transcribed "send."

[48] Lowdermilk placed a long dash here that does not appear in the manuscript.

[49] Major Russell Chapman had been commissioned a captain in the 44th Regiment in 1741. He was promoted to major in 1751. He served as second-in-command of Dunbar's Division and thus was not present at the Battle of the Monongahela. He was commissioned a lieutenant colonel in the 60th Regiment on January 5, 1756. Chapman resigned his commission in 1757.

[50] Captain Adam Stephen (c. 1718–1791) had been lieutenant colonel of the Virginia Regiment and had Fought at the Battle of Great Meadows on July 3, 1754. When the regiment was disbanded in October of that year Stephen became captain of one of the independent companies formed in its place. He was a native of Scotland who had earned a degree as a surgeon from the University of Edinburgh and briefly pursued a career in the British Navy before immigrating to Fredrick, Maryland in 1745. Stephen fought at the Battle of the Monongahela where he was wounded. He later commanded the Virginia troops garrisoned at Fort Cumberland from 1755 until June, 1757, when he was placed in command of the Virginian contingent sent to Charleston. He served in Forbes's expedition to the Ohio in 1758.

Stephen was colonel of the Virginia Regiment raised in 1761 and also commanded regiments raised to participate in Pontiac's Rebellion in 1764. He was appointed colonel of the 4th Virginia Regiment in 1776 and was promoted to brigadier general in September, 1777. He fought at Battle of Brandywine but was later dismissed by Washington and court-martialed in November, 1777 for being drunk and missing the Battle of Germantown. Stephen later settled in Berkeley County (now West Virginia), became a member of the House of Burgesses, and a member of the Virginia Convention to ratify the U.S. Constitution in 1788.

[51] Captain William la Péronie, (d. 1755) was a French Huguenot who immigrated to Virginia around 1750. He was commissioned an ensign in the Virginia Regiment in 1754 and was named adjutant in June of that year. He was wounded at the Battle of Great Meadows, July 3, 1754. Péronie was promoted to captain on August 25, 1754 and commanded a company of Virginia rangers at the Battle of the Monongahela on July 9, 1755, where he was killed and scalped.

[52] Lowdermilk transcribed "A," but it is actually the number "4."

[53] Captain Thomas Cocke was commissioned a captain in the Virginia forces in December, 1754. His company of rangers served with Dunbar's division and was not present at Monongahela. He lost his captaincy in the reorganization of the Virginia Regiment and resigned in June 1757. He was later commissioned a captain in the 2nd Virginia Regiment in June, 1758, and served on the Forbes Expedition of that year.

[54] Captain Thomas Waggener (d. 1760) had served as an officer in the aborted expedition against Canada in 1746. He was commissioned a lieutenant in the Virginia Regiment on February 26, 1754. Waggener was wounded in the Skirmish at Jumonville Glen on May 28, 1754, and was also present at the Battle of the Great Meadows on July 3 of that year. He was promoted to captain on July 20, 1754. He commanded his company of rangers at the Battle of Monongahela. He later served on the Virginia frontier along the South Branch of the Potomac from Autumn, 1755 until 1758, when he served in Forbes expedition. He served in the garrison at Fort Pitt from December, 1758 until September, 1759.

[55] Captain Peter Hogg (1703–1782) was a native of Edinburgh who had settled in Augusta County, VA in 1745. He was commissioned a captain in the Virginia Regiment on March 9, 1754 and had fought at the Battle of the Great Meadows on July 3, 1754. Braddock dispatched his company to protect workers on the road being built between Shippenberg, PA, and Turkeyfoot, at present-day Confluence, PA. In September, 1755 he was sent to Augusta County and was placed in charge of building the various fortifications along the frontier in that section of the colony. Washington dismissed him in June, 1757 for failing to complete those forts. He remained in Augusta County after his dismissal and was licensed to practice law in 1759 and was appointed prosecuting attorney for Dunmore County in 1772. At the time of his death in 1782 he held extensive lands in Virginia and Kentucky.

[56] Captain William Poulson (d. 1755) was a Scot who had been commissioned a lieutenant in the Virginia Regiment on February 28, 1754, and fought at the Battle

of Great Meadows, July 3, 1754. He was promoted to captain, July 21, 1754. He commanded a company of artificers at the Battle of Monongahela, where he was shot through the heart.

[57] Lieutenant James Allen (d. 1755) of the 44th Regiment was ordered by Braddock to instruct the Virginia troops in field maneuvers. He was killed at the Battle of the Monongahela.

[58] William Sparke (c. 1698–1777) was commissioned an ensign in the 48th Regiment in 1734 and was serving as a captain in 1740. He was commissioned major of the 48th Regiment in June 3, 1752. He was wounded at the Battle of Monongahela and served in North America until 1758, when he sold his commission and returned to England.

[59] Lowdermilk transcribed "29 Rounds." The manuscript appears to read "24."

[60] Lowdermilk transcribed "Departments."

[61] Lowdermilk did not break the paragraph here.

[62] Braddock's plan at this time was for the 44th Regiment to advance overland through Virginia from Alexandria to Winchester and from there to Fort Cumberland. The 48th Regiment was to march to Frederick, Maryland and from there proceed to Fort Cumberland along the north bank of the Potomac River. Goods and provisions bound for the march across Maryland were unloaded at the mouth of Rock Creek in the present-day District of Columbia. Braddock had thought that he would find better roads and more forage in Maryland than in Virginia. See Netherton, *Braddock's Campaign*, pp. 12–13.

[63] At this point, the manuscript goes directly to the orders issued on April 8. Lowdermilk has incorrectly inserted the section beginning with the sentence "Colo Dunbar's Regiment is to march at 5 Oclock on Saturday Morning for Rock Creek," through the marching orders for Dunbar's Regiment ending with the sentence "Within a few miles of the Minocasy cross the Minocasy in a Float." These orders were actually issued on April 10. The text in this edition has been placed in its correct location.

[64] Lieutenant Matthew Leslie of the 44th Regiment served as assistant deputy quartermaster general under St. Clair. He was wounded at the Battle of the Monongahela. Leslie was promoted to captain on September 29, 1760.

[65] Lowdermilk had transcribed "Subaltern," "Ensign," and "Lieut" as singular. All are clearly plural in the manuscript.

[66] Lowdermilk transcribed "disrules." The manuscript clearly reads "disputes." This coincides with "Halkett's Orderly Book," which reads "Dispuits." See Hamilton, *Braddock's Defeat*, p. 77.

[67] Halkett's Brigade left camp at Alexandria at 6:00 a.m. on April 10.

[68] At this point Lowdermilk is again incorrect. He had placed the orders from the sentence beginning with "Eight" through the sentence ending with "you shall receive advice of it," at note 81 with the after orders for April 11.

[69] The first court house for Fairfax County, VA was located near Tysons Corner in present day Vienna, VA. The court house was moved to Alexandria in 1752.

[70] Richard Coleman (d. 1763) operated an ordinary on Sugarland Run approximately one mile west of present-day Dranesville, VA.

[71] Nicholas Minor operated an inn at the site of present-day Leesburg, Virginia.

[72] Edward Thompson's inn was at present-day Hillsboro, Virginia.

[73] Lowdermilk transcribed "They's," but the manuscript reads "Keys." This is a reference to the home of Gersham Keyes, on the west-bank of the Shenandoah River. John Vestal operated a ferry over the Shenandoah about six miles east of present-day Charlestown, WV.

[74] The Opequon River flows north through the Shenandoah Valley to the Potomac just east of Winchester. St. Clair and Patrick MacKellar had built a bridge across the Opequon at Carter's Fort and cut a road north of Winchester that cut several miles off the march. Final repairs on the road from Winchester to Fort Cumberland were completed on May 1.

[75] Henry Enoch's homestead was on the Cacapon River near present-day Forks of Cacapon, WV.

[76] Lowdermilk had placed the above text, from the sentence beginning "Eight waggons" to this point with the After Orders for April 11. These orders were actually written for 44th Regiment on April 8.

[77] Lowdermilk transcribed "Henry." The parole is clearly "Henly." This corresponds to "Halkett's Orderly Book." See *Braddock's Defeat,* p. 78.

[78] At Braddock's request, Virginia provided a troop of about thirty light horse under the Command of Captain Robert Stewart.

[79] Braddock's departure from Alexandria was delayed by the arrival of Governors William Shirley of Massachusetts, James De Lancey of New York, and Robert Hunter Morris of Pennsylvania. After holding council on April 14, The governors departed Alexandria on April 17, and Braddock left for Frederick on April 19. He arrived at Frederick on April 21. See Sargent, "Robert Orme's Journal," pp. 300-7.

[80] The 48th Regiment crossed the Potomac into Maryland at Rock Creek on April 12. It arrived at Frederick on April 17.

[81] Lowdermilk has mistakenly placed the text beginning with this paragraph through the sentence ending with "cross the Minocasy in a Float," as the After Orders for April 7. The text has been inserted here in its correct location as part of the After Orders for April 10.

[82] Gage was to remain behind at Alexandria with four companies of the 44th Regiment and the artillery train while the rest of Halkett's Division marched to Fort Cumberland.

[83] Lawrence Owens operated an inn about fifteen miles west of Rock Creek and eight miles below the Falls of the Potomac in present-day Rockville, MD.

[84] Michael Dowden's Ordinary was located in present-day Clarksburg, MD.

[85] The Monocacy River flows into the Potomac southeast of Frederick.

[86] Here marks the end of the section of orders that Lowdermilk mistakenly placed under the After Orders for April 7. He also misplaced the text beginning

below through the sentence ending, "no more Waggons will be allowd after they get to Frederick." Lowdermilk included these with the After Orders for April 8. They are actually a continuation of the orders issued to Dunbar's Regiment on April 10.

[87] These orders and those subsequent are meant for Dunbar's Division, which was to march to Rock Creek and then to Maryland on April 12.

[88] This officer was probably Ensign French. French was in command of the detachment at Rock Creek on April 25.

[89] William Johnston was deputy paymaster. He arrived in Virginia in March, 1755. He accompanied Dunbar's brigade during the advance on Fort Duquesne. Johnston later served under Lord Loudoun in Albany.

[90] At Braddock's request, Admiral Keppel dispatched a party of thirty seamen under the command of Lieutenant Charles Spendelowe. They played an important role in Braddock's Army ferrying provisions and stores across the various waterways, and also transporting the artillery train, which included a few naval guns, across the mountains. The detachment was present at the Battle of the Monongahela where it suffered heavy casualties.

[91] Thomas Cresap's store house at Conococheague served as the rendezvous point for supplies being transported from Pennsylvania. From there the provisions were ferried across the Potomac to Virginia then brought overland to Fort Cumberland.

[92] Wills Creek flowed into the Potomac River at the site of present-day Cumberland, Maryland. The Ohio Company had operated a storehouse there since 1751. It served as the starting point for Washington's expedition of 1754 as well as Braddock's expedition in 1755. Fort Cumberland was erected on the west bank of the creek in 1754.

[93] Here the text mistakenly placed under After Orders for April 8 referred to in note 91 ends.

[94] Lowdermilk did not break the paragraph here.

[95] Captain Thomas Ord of the Royal Regiment of Artillery was in command of the siege train. He was commissioned a captain in March 1, 1746. Ord fought at the Battle of Monongahela where his gunners suffered heavy casualties. He served in North America throughout the war and was promoted to lieutenant colonel of Royal Artillery in 1760.

[96] Once Braddock determined there was no way to cut a road across Western Maryland from Fort Frederick and Fort Cumberland, he made the decision to cross back over to Virginia at Conococheague See Netherton, *Braddock's Campaign,* pp. 12–13.

[97] This phrase is underlined in the manuscript.

[98] Lowdermilk transcribed "3 men to each company." Also, he did not begin a new paragraph here.

[99] Antietam Creek in Maryland.

[100] Horatio Sharpe (1718–1790) was lieutenant governor of Maryland. Born in Yorkshire, he had served as a captain of marines. He was appointed lieutenant

governor by the colony's proprietor and arrived in Maryland on August 10, 1753. Sharpe was commissioned lieutenant colonel and named acting commander in chief of the Fort Duquesne Expedition on October 19, 1754. He relinquished his command upon General Braddock's arrival in February.

[101] General Braddock had requested that Commodore Keppel send a naval detachment to the mouth of Rock Creek to transport supplies to the north shore of the Potomac River. Ensign French was in command of this detachment. Rock Creek flowed into the Potomac in present-day Washington, D.C. See "Orme's Journal," in Sargent, *History of an Expedition to Against Fort Duquesne,* p. 299.

[102] Captain Horatio Gates (1728–1806) came from a connected family in England and was the godson of Horace Walpole. He served as a lieutenant in Nova Scotia from 1749 to 1754. Gates was commissioned captain of a New York Independent Company in September, 1754 and served in that capacity until 1759. He fought in the van under Gage and was wounded at the Battle of Monongahela. He later became a major general in the Continental Army during the War of American Independence.

[103] The camp "on the road to Conogogee" was located in the wilderness near present-day Boonesboro, MD. Cholmley's Batman referred to it as Chapman's Ordinary. Walter Hough believe this may have been in honor of Major Russell Chapman of the 48th Regiment. See Hough, *Braddock's Road,* p. 74 (Taped into the rear of this editor's personal copy of the book is a seven page appendix numbered pages 71–77. It was apparently printed by the author and inserted after publication).

[104] John Evans settled in present-day Martinsburg, WV.

[105] Mary Wright Ballinger (1708–1800), the widow of Josiah Ballinger (d. 1748) resided near the present intersection of Virginia Routes 672 and 739. See Netherton, p. 15. The residence was abandoned shortly after Braddock's defeat when Indians began to raid the area.

[106] George Poll's, or Potts, was located on a hill just outside of present-day Gainesboro, VA, Netherton, p. 15.

[107] Lowdermilk transcribed "Enocks" at this point as well as in the marching orders for the party of Ensign French below. In both cases the manuscript reads "Enochs."

[108] Friend Cox's homestead was located along north bank of the Potomac River across from the mouth of the Little Cacapon River. Cox's Fort was later built on his land in 1756.

[109] Lowdermilk transcribed "Cacaph."

[110] Colonel Thomas Cresap (c. 1695–1790) was born in Yorkshire and immigrated to Maryland. He had a long and successful career as an Indian trader and was a partner in the Ohio Company. He built his home at Shawnee Old Town, later Oldtown, MD in 1736. He was known as "Big Spoon" by the Native Americans for the large ladle used to pour the soup that was available to all who came to his home. It was he along with the Delaware chief, Nemacolin, who had blazed the original trail from Wills Creek to the forks of the Ohio in 1751. He served as a commissary in Virginia

in 1754 for the colony of Maryland and was contracted by Braddock to supply goods for the army. Braddock used his storehouse at Conococheague as supply depot.

[111] Lowdermilk transcribed the above as one paragraph. It appears in the form of a list as above in the manuscript.

[112] Lowdermilk transcribed "Opeckon."

[113] Lowdermilk transcribed "Polle's." Here and below he transcribed either "Cacapekon," or "Cacapepon." The manuscript appears to read "Capcapehon" throughout.

[114] Lowdermilk transcribed "Canves." The manuscript clearly reads "canoes."

[115] Thomas Cresap owned a storehouse at the mouth of the Conococheague River that Braddock used to hold supplies.

[116] Lieutenant Percival Brereton, or Brierton (d. 1755), was an officer in the 48th Regiment and was killed at the Battle of Monongahela. It would appear that he was in command of a detachment, probably at Alexandria, that was forwarding supplies to Rock Creek.

[117] Washington left Mount Vernon to meet up with Braddock on either April 24 or 25. He joined Braddock in Frederick on May 1. See "George Washington to William Fairfax, April 23, 1755," p. 146, and Freeman, *George Washington*, 2:31.

[118] John Frazier was a well-known Indian trader, blacksmith, and gunsmith. He had lived on the Allegheny at the mouth of French Creek from 1741 until the French drove him out in 1753. He then built a storehouse along the Monongahela River at the mouth of Turtle Creek but the French drove him from that spot as well when they occupied the forks of the Ohio in April 1754. He was living near Fort Cumberland at this time.

[119] Lowdermilk transcribed "Pilsons." This is a reference to Captain William Poulson of the Virginia troops.

[120] Lowdermilk did not have a new paragraph at this point.

[121] Lowdermilk did not have a new paragraph at this point.

[122] When Braddock arrived at Fort Cumberland on May 10, he found George Croghan present with 100 friendly Indians, mostly women and children, waiting for him. Braddock's relations with the Indians quickly went sour. By the end of the month only five scouts led by Scarroyady, remained.

[123] Poulson had immigrated from Scotland to Virginia sometime after 1745. Someone had apparently accused him of being a Jacobite.

[124] Captain John Rutherford (1712–1758) had served as the captain of a New York Independent Company since the early 1740s. He was in England when his company arrived in Virginia in 1754. He served with his company in the garrison at Fort Cumberland from the time of his return to North America in September, 1754 until the departure of Braddock's expedition. Rutherford served in Dunbar's Division and did not participate in the Battle of the Monongahela. Rutherford returned to England in January, 1756 and was promoted to major of the 60th Regiment. He was killed at the Battle of Ticonderoga, July 8, 1758.

[125] Captain John Dagworthy had received a royal commission as captain in 1746 when he raised a New Jersey Company for the aborted expedition against Canada. He moved to Maryland in 1754 and was given command of Maryland troops. He served with Dunbar's column and did not participate in the Battle of Monongahela. Dagworthy later served in the garrison of Fort Cumberland. He was promoted to lieutenant colonel and commanded the Maryland Regiment that served on Forbes Expedition, 1758.

[126] Paul Demeré (d. 1760) was commissioned captain of the South Carolina Independent Company serving garrison duty at Fort Cumberland in November, 1754. They served in Braddock's Army in 1755. Demeré later commanded Fort Loudoun on the Tennessee River during the Cherokee Uprising of 1760. He was captured and tortured to death by the Cherokee at Ball Play Creek on August 10, 1760.

[127] Captain Edward Brice Dobbs (1729–1803) was the son of Governor Arthur Dobbs of North Carolina. He had served as a lieutenant in the regular army prior to accompanying his father to North America in 1754. He was placed in command of the North Carolina company serving under Braddock. He contracted an ailment while at Fort Cumberland that impaired his eyesight and prevented him from accompanying the expedition.

[128] Here Lowdermilk deviated from the manuscript. He omitted the three paragraphs above and instead inserted a table of the two brigades that included a return of the troops. He made no mention of the light horse. Lowdermilk's table is below:

The first Brigade to be commanded by Sir Peter Halket

		Compliment.	Effective.
44th Regiment of Foot		700	700
Captⁿ Rutherford's	Independent Compy	100	95
Captⁿ Gates	of New York		
Capt. Polson's	Carpenters	50	48
Capt. Peronnee's	Virginia Rangers	50	47
Capt. Wagner's	Virginia Rangers	50	45
Capt. Dagworthy's	Maryland Rangers	50	49

Second Brigade, Commanded by Colonel Dunbar.

		Compliment.	Effective.
48th Regiment of Foot		700	650
Captn Demerie's	South Carolina Detacht	100	95
Capt. Dobb's	North Carolina Rangers	100	97
Capt. Mercer's	Company of Carpenters	50	35
Capt. Stevens's	Virginia Rangers	50	48
Capt. Hogg's	Virginia Rangers	50	40
Capt. Cox's	Virginia Rangers	50	43

[129] The text from this point through the end of the orders for this date was omitted by Lowdermilk.

[130] Lowdermilk transcribed "Charleston."

[131] Lowdermilk transcribed "unquestioned."

[132] Martin's Plantation was located on a ridge near the upper reaches of George's Creek overlooking present day Frostburg, MD.

[133] Captain Robert Stewart (d. 1809) commanded the Troop of Virginia Light Horse. He had fought and was wounded at the Battle of Great Meadows, July 3, 1754. He was promoted to captain, November 11, 1754. The light horse served as a guard for General Braddock throughout the campaign and were present at the Battle of the Monongahela. He served in the Virginia Regiment through 1762 and eventually rose to the rank of lieutenant colonel. Stewart maintained a regular correspondence with Washington for several years after the war.

[134] Lowdermilk made each of the last two sentences a new paragraph. They would appear to be one paragraph in the manuscript.

[135] Lowdermilk transcribed "will be."

[136] Lowdermilk omitted this paragraph. The manuscript is difficult to read so this transcription may be incorrect.

[137] Dr. James Napier (d. circa 1799) was director of the general hospital. He remained on active duty through the War of American Independence. He is found on the half-pay lists through 1799.

[138] Lowdermilk transcribed "2d Hospital." Also, the italicized text is underlined in the manuscript.

[139] Lowdermilk transcribed "Drummers and Drumers."

[140] St. Clair was overseeing improvements on the defenses at Fort Cumberland. See "The Seaman's Journal," in Sargent.

[141] Lowdermilk transcribed "settler."

[142] Lowdermilk transcribed "Tuesday."

[143] Lowdermilk transcribed "250 lashes," but it appears to be 200.

[144] The above paragraph was omitted from Lowdermilk. The name of the captain is difficult to make out but would appear to be Captain Thomas Ord of the artillery.

[145] Lowdermilk omitted all of folio 90 as well as the first paragraph on folio 91 above.

[146] St. Clair was cutting a wagon road over Wills Mountain west of Fort Cumberland.

[147] Lieutenant William McCleod, or McCloud, of the Royal Artillery fought at the Battle of the Monongahela. Two of the three printed lists of casualties listed him as wounded. See Hamilton, *Braddock's Defeat*, p. 57.

[148] The above paragraph was omitted by Lowdermilk.

[149] Lowdermilk transcribed "Marshal."

[150] Lowdermilk transcribed "duty."

[151] Lowdermilk omitted this sentence.

[152] Lowdermilk transcribed "raming."

[153] Lowdermilk transcribed "Tuesday morning."

[154] St. Clair and Chapman led an advance party to the Little Meadows just east of Casselmans River where they were to construct a fortified camp. They arrived on June 5.

[155] Lowdermilk omitted "of," which changes the sense of the sentence somewhat.

[156] Harry Gordon (d. 1787) had joined the Royal Engineers in 1742 and served under Cumberland in Flanders in 1745 and again in 1747–1748. He was personally recommended for the expedition by Cumberland and was considered a road-building specialist. Gordon was wounded in the forearm during the battle. He was promoted Engineer in Ordinary and Captain on January 4, 1758 and served under Forbes during his successful expedition to capture Fort Duquesne later that year. He eventually rose to the rank of lieutenant colonel in the line in 1777. This detachment was being sent out to construct a road up Wills Creek and around Wills Mountain on the north. The original road that crossed the summit of the mountain had proved extremely difficult for the wagons. On June 2, Lieutenant Charles Spendelowe had discovered this alternate route that came to be known at "Spendelowe's Road." The road was completed on June 6.

[157] Colonel James Innes (d. 1759) was born in Scotland and immigrated to North Carolina sometime after 1733. He had served in the American Regiment at the Siege of Cartagena in 1741 as the captain of the Cape Fear, NC Company. Innes was a successful planter and became colonel of the New Hanover County, NC militia. He was named commanded the North Carolina Regiment sent to serve in the expedition of 1754. He served off and on as commander of Fort Cumberland from June, 1754 until June, 1756, when he returned to North Carolina on personal business.

[158] Lowdermilk transcribed "Yates's."

[159] The Camp at the Grove, also known as Spendelowe's Camp, was on the western side of Wills Mountain, where Spendelowe's Road rejoined the main wagon route. It was at a grove sometimes called Wills Glade near present-day

Allegheny Grove, MD. Halkett's Brigade had marched to this location on June 7 and Braddock arrived here along with Dunbar's Brigade on June 8.

[160] Braddock held a council of war on June 11. It had taken two days for the army to travel the five miles to Wills Glade. It was decided to lighten the load to "all such baggage as was not absolutely necessary." The heaviest wagons were returned to Fort Cumberland along with all of the women but two per company. The detachment, escorted by Captain Peter Hogg's Virginia Company, returned to Fort Cumberland on June 12. See Sargent, "Robert Orme's Journal," 331–32.

[161] Lowdermilk transcribed "2ds" here. The manuscript is difficult to read but it would appear to be Lds.

[162] The first notebook ends here. Several blank pages follow and the second notebook begins with the orders for June 12, 1755 on folio 125.

General Braddock's Orderly Book, No. 2

Camp at the Grove

Thursday June 12ᵗʰ 1755.—

Parole Ilford

Field Officer of the Picquet .... Lt Col Gage.

The Picquet to load with Cartridges, and not with running Ball to challenge and demand the countersign till troop beating; and the Field officer and Picquet to be always receivd as Grand Rounds as often as he thinks proper to visit the out Posts, by Night or Day.

The advanced Corporals and Centries to have their Bayonets fixd; the Detachd partys from the Sergeants Guard to have Corporals with them; the advanced Centrys not to suffer anybody to come within ten paces of their arms without demanding the Countersign.

The advancd Parties not to build any bowers, upon pain of severest punishment; those already built to be immediately destroyed.—

These Orders to be read to the Men, by the Officer of ye Piqt before the out Guards are posted. [f. 125]

Whatever communications from Sergeants Guards to Sergts Guards, & from Corpls Guards to Corp guards are not yet opend to be done immediately.

This to be a standing Order and to be observd by ye Troops in all Camps no Person whatever to fire their Arms within a mile of ye Camp but in case of an alarm or their being attackd.

These Orders to be read to the men by the commandg. Officer of each Company, and the Orders relative to the men of the Picquet to be read to them before they are detachd on ye out Guards by the Officers of ye Picquet.

The Captns. of ye several Picquets to be at ye Field Officer of ye Picquet's Tent an hour before retreat beating in order to receive the Countersign from him.

All the Troops to be compleated this afternoon with provisions to the 16ᵗʰ Inclusive and the waggoners and Horse Drivers to the 26ᵗʰ.

After Orders

Sir Peter Halkett's Grenadiers and the Battalion Companys of that Regt. to March immediately to the crossing of the new and old Road, a little beyond [f. 126] where the Detachment of Sea Men are now Encampd.[1] They are to Encamp there; the Grenadiers Camp across the Road and the Battalion Compys accordg. to the present line of Encampment covering the advanced wagons. The commanding Officers to take care to advance Picquets in the same manner & proportion of numbers as orderd in the Disposition of march and to take care that his advanced Picquets comply with the Orders of this Day.

The Detachment of Sea Men commanded by Mr. Spendelowe,[2] to be disposd of in such parts of the Line as he shall think proper and their Arms and accoutrements are to be carried in whatever Waggons he shall appt.

Three hatchet Men of ye Line with their Tools to remain constantly with the Detachment of Seamen and to receive their Orders from Mr Spendelowe.

One Tumbrel with Tools to March in the Front immediately after Captn. Polsons Company of Carpenters and another Tumbrel of Tools to March in the Centre of the Carriages. [f. 127]

One Engineer to March with Captn. Polson's Compy of Carpenters and another Engineer is to March in the Center of ye Carriages.

The Pioneers of every Company of ye Line with their Tools except those three that are orderd to ye Detacht. of Seamen to march constantly in ye centre of ye Carriages, and to be under the Directions ye Engineer who marches in the Centre.

The troops to March to morrow and the Genl. to beat at four oclock in ye morning.—

116

Colonial teamster and British infantry hauling artillery through the wilderness. 19th Century engraving from the Normal Warfare Collection.

Camp at

Friday 13th June 1765

Parole Hertford.

Field Officer tomorrow .... Majr. Chapmn

The Line is not to march tomorrow.³ [f. 128]

Camp at Martin's

Saturday June 14th 1755.

Parole Leicester

Field Officer tomorrow .... Lt. Colo. Burton

Upon the beatg. of the Genl which is to be taken from Sir Peter Halketts Regt. all ye Troops are to accoutre, turn out and form two Deep at ye head of their respective Encampments and there wait for further Orders and no Soldier's Tent to be suffered to be struck till orderd by the Genl.

As soon as the Tents are struck they are to be immediately loaded, as also the Officers Baggage and then the Troops are to lay upon their Arms till they receive an order to march and upon the beating of ye March the whole to Face to the Right and Left.

The Field Officers are not to be particularly Posted excepting the one who marches at ye head of ye Van Guard.

The number of Carriages to be equally divided & Sir Peter Halkett and his Field Officers with the Troops of his Brigade are to take under their care half of [f. 129] Carriages and see that their Officer's order their men to assist the waggoners upon any Point or Difficulty that may happen.

Colo. Dunbar and his Field Officers with ye troops of the 2ᵈ Brigade to act in the same manner with the remaining number of Carriages.

118

Braddock's Route as drawn by Middleton and corrected by William H. Lowdermilk. From Lowdermilk, *History of Cumberland.*

In case any Waggon should break down in such a manner as to be unable to keep with the Line it is immediately to be drawn out on one side of ye Road and a report of it with what it is loaded to be sent to Mr. Scott[4] Waggon Master Genl who is to order it to be repaird or see that the Load is divided among the rest of ye Waggons as he shall think proper.

Upon any Halt, tho' ever so small the Comp are to form two Deep and face outwards.

Upon a March the Captns and Officers of ye Picquet to visit frequently their out Detachments and see that they keep at a proper distance from their Companies.

Upon ye firing of a Cannon either in ye front centre or Rear the whole Line to form face outwards and then wait for further Orders. [f. 130]

When the Troops come to Savage River[5] the Servants Bat Men Waggoners and Horse Drivers must take particular care to prevent their Horses from eating of Laurel as it is certain Death to them.

The General to beat tomorrow morning at 4 Oclock.[6]

After Orders

Upon the beating of the General tomorrow morning. two Companys from the Right of Sir Peter Halkett's Regt. to Strike their Tents and march as an Escort to the Carrying horses of ye army The Commanding Officer to apply to Captn. Morris to morrow Morning for his orders. [f. 131]

Note,

Here is an omission of two days orders which cannot be supplied, but a blank may be left in the records to show the chasm.—* [f. 132]

---

* This note is written in Washington's handwriting.

Camp at the Little Meadows[7]

Tuesday June 17th 1755

Parole Orford

Field Officer tomorrow ....Lt. Colo. Burton

A Detachment to march tomorrow morning att 4 oclock consisting of one Field officer 2 Captn. 6 Subns. 12 Sergn. & 150 Rank and File of ye two Regiments; Captn. Gates, 2 Subns. 2 Sergeants 2 Corporals and 50 private Men of his Independant Company, Captn. Waggoners and Captn. Perouney's Company's of Rangers.[8]

Lt. Colo. Gage to Command this Detacht. A Detachment to march on Thursday g at 4 Oclock consisting of one Colo. 1 Lt. Colo. 1 Majr. the two oldest Company's of Grenadiers 5 Captns. 20 Subns. 22 Sergts. and 550 Rank & File of ye two Regiments.

Sir Peter Halkett Lt. Colo. Burton & Maj. Sparke Field Officer's for this Detacht. The King's Colour of ye 44 Regt & ye second colour of ye 48th Regt. to be sent with this Det. [f. 133]

The Men of the two Regiments that are to march with the Detachment of tomorrow and Thursday to be taken out of those which landed from Ireland; The Commanding Officers of each Regiment to be answerable to His Excellency that this is punctually complied with.[9]

A Return to be sent in tomorrow morning to either of ye Aids de Camp signd by the Comg. Officers of ye Companys of ye two Regiments of ye Names and Countries of ye Men that are for ye above two Detachments their time of service and the Regiments they have servd in.

His Excellency has been pleasd to appoint the following Captn. and Subns. Officers for ye above Detachments and desires that they will take with them as little baggage as possible.

For ye Detacht. and Comd. of Lt. Colo. Gage[10]

Of ye 44 Regt.	Captn. Beckwith[11]	Of ye 48th R.	Captn. Morris[12]
	Lieut. Treby[13]		Lieut Hansard[14]
	Lieut. Littler[15]		Lieut Barbutt[16]
	Ensign Clarke[17]		Ensign Dunbar[18]

[f. 134]

For the Detacht that marches on Thursday

Of the 44th Regimt.   Of the 48th Regiment

Captn. Hobson[19]	Captn Dobson[20]
…….. Gethins[21]	……. Cholmley
Lieutt. Halkett[22]	……. Bowyer[23]
…….. Baily[24]	Lieutt. Walsam[25]
…….. Pottinger[26]	…….. Hathorn[27]
…….. Simpson[28]	…….. Edmonstone[29]
…….. Lock[30]	…….. Cope[31]
…….. Kennedy[32]	…….. Brierton[33]
…….. Townshend[34]	…….. Hurt[35]
Ensign Nortlow[36]	…….. Gladwin[37]
Pennington[38]	Ensign Cowart[39]
Preston[40]	…….. Harrison[41]
	…….. Crowe[42]
	…….. McMullen.[43]

The Surgeon's Mate of ye 48th Regiment to march with this Detachment.[44]
    Captn. Rutherfords Independent Company and Captn. Stephens Company of Rangers, to march to morrow morning with the detachmt. under ye command of Lt Col Gage and to return to camp at night. [f. 135]
    One Corporal & 4 light Horse to march tomorrow morning with the Detachment under Col Gages Comd. and to remain with him.

West Pennsylvania and Virginia 1755. From George Dallas Albert, *Frontier Forts of Pennsylvania*, Vol. 2, 1916.

A MAP OF PART OF THE PROVINCE OF PENNSYLVANIA WEST OF THE RIVER SUSQUAHANNAH

WEST PENNSYLVANIA AND VIRGINIA. 1755.

FROM MR. DARLINGTON'S FORT PITT.

COPIED FROM THE ORIGINAL IN THE PUBLIC RECORD OFFICE, LONDON,
FOR W.M. DARLINGTON ESQ. J.A. BURT. APRIL 1882.

LYCAMICR

BIG ISLAND

LYWASOCH

MUNSEY CR.

CHILLISQUAGUE CR.

WEST BRANCH

BUFFELOW CR.

OMGEPECKON

POST BRANCH

FALL SUGARKION

MUNCY CR.

JOHN PENNS CR.

PENNES CR.

FERNEY CASTLE

MIDDLE CR.

JUNIATA RIVER

PATTERS VALLEY

TUSCARORA

KISHIKOQUILLIS

SHAWMINGVERSON

CONOCOCHEAGUE

CUMBERLAND VALLEY

CARLISLE

SHIPPENSBURG

HARRIS FERRY

YELLOW BREECHES CR.

SOUTH MOUNTAIN

FT. GRANVILLE

FT. SHIRLEY

SPARNING STONE CR.

LITTLE JUNIATA

FRANKS T.

SIDELING HILL

RAYS TOWN BRANCH

RAYE HILL

PENDERGRASSES

RAYS TOWN

TOBYS

MILBURN RIVER

BEAR CAMP

LITTLE CONE

CROSSINGS

BROWN'S MILL

SOMBOOGHOR

SHAWNESE CABBINS

SHAWNESE CABBINS

MACGOR WITH JOHN BYRNE

BEAR CAMP RIVER

PORTOMAC RIVER

WELLS CR.

FT. CUMBERLAND

A BRANCH OF THE SOUTH BRANCH OF YOHIOGAIN.

BRADDOCK ROAD

ALLEGHANNY MOUNTAINS.

THREE FORKS OF YOHIOGAIN.

GREAT MEADOWS

GREAT CROSSING OF THE SOUTH BRANCH OF YOHIOGAIN.

NEW RIVER 100 MILES

FRENCH F. (DU QUESNE)

The Detachment of Seamen, and Captn. Stuart with 1 Subaltern & 18 light horse to march on Thursday morning.

No woman to be victualled upon the Detach. that march to morrow and Thursday.

After Orders

Each of the two Regits. as also Captn. Gates's Independant Company to send a sufft. numbr. of Tents for ye respective Detachts. that march to morrow under ye command of Lt Col Gage.

After Orders

His Excellency has been pleasd to appoint Lt. Buchanan[45] of ye Artillery to march with ye 2 Gun's to morrow morng. & Captn. Lt. Smith[46] and Lt. McLoud[47] of ye Artillery to march with ye Detacht. on Thursday morng. The men that march tomorrow & on Thursday mg. to be compleated to 24 Rounds of Ammunition. [f. 136]

*N. B.—After the orders in this, and the book preceding it, are transcribed, leave six pages blank for insertion of the commission of G. W_____n and the proceedings which intervened between the defeat of Gen. Braddock and the resumption of the command by G. W_____n.

Next, the Letters, Instructions, and orders, in the order they appear in the parchment covered book, are to be transcribed.[48] [f. 137]

This commission of George Washington as Colonel of the First Virginia Regiment and Commander in chief of the Virginia forces is missing from the Washington Papers.

The "parchment covered Book" is also missing. The whereabouts of the commission and the book are unknown to the Library of Congress.[49]

J.G.S.

[f. 139]

---

* The above appears in Washington's handwriting, on a page following the last of the recorded orders.

Notes:

¹ This is a reference to the intersection of Spendelowe's Road with the old road over Wills Mountain.

² Lieutenant Charles Spendelowe (d. 1755) was commissioned a lieutenant in the Royal Navy on May 1, 1752. He commanded the detachment of sailors serving under Braddock and is best known for the alternate route around Wills Mountain that bore his name. He was killed at the Battle of the Monongahela.

³ Braddock marched forward with Halkett's Brigade to Martin's Plantation on June 13. Dunbar's Brigade arrived on June 14. Martin's Plantation was located on a ridge near the upper reaches of George's Creek overlooking present day Frostburg, MD.

⁴ John Scott was the wagon master. The wagon master was responsible for maintaining the army's wagons.

⁵ The Savage River flows south from Savage Mountain into the Potomac. Braddock's Army crossed the Savage near present-day Frostburg, MD.

⁶ This is a reference to the general beating, or general. It was the drum beat used to call out the troops in the morning.

⁷ Braddock left Martin's Plantation with Halkett's Brigade on June 15 and arrived at Little Meadows on June 16. Dunbar's Division arrived at the Little Meadows on June 17.

⁸ Braddock held a council of war on June 17 in which it was decided to push forward with an advanced or "flying" division, leaving Dunbar in command of the second division to follow up with the wagons. Gage's detachment of approximately 350 men, representing the van of the advanced division, left Little Meadows on June 18.

⁹ The main body of Braddock's advance division marched from the Little Meadows on June 19. It consisted of the veteran soldiers from Ireland. Most of the men that remained behind with Dunbar were raw recruits who had joined the regiments when they arrived in North America. Lowdermilk omitted the word "punctually."

¹⁰ All of the officers listed below were still with the advanced division on July 9 and fought in the Battle of the Monongahela.

¹¹ Captain John Beckwith was named major of the 44th Regiment July 18, 1758 and rose to the rank of lieutenant colonel in the line, January 13, 1762. He resigned his commission and settled in Halifax after the war.

¹² This is a reference to Captain Roger Morris, who served as General Braddock's aide-de-camp.

¹³ Lieutenant John Treby of the 44th Regiment was wounded at the Battle of the Monongahela. He was later promoted to the rank of captain on September 15, 1758.

¹⁴ Lowdermilk transcribed "Harsard." Lieutenant Jonathan Hansard (d. 1755) was killed at the Battle of the Monongahela.

[15] Lowdermilk transcribed "Sittler." Lieutenant William Littler of the 44th Regiment was wounded at the Battle of the Monongahela.

[16] Lieutenant Theodore Barbutt of the 48th Regiment was wounded at the Battle of Monongahela.

[17] This is a reference to Ensign George Clarke, Clark, or Clerk of the 44th Regiment. He was promoted to lieutenant in 1755.

[18] This is a reference to Ensign Jonathan Dunbar of the 48th Regiment. He is not to be confused with Lieutenant William Dunbar of the 44th Regiment, who is not listed among the officers in Braddock's orders of June 17 but was also present at the Battle of the Monongahela.

[19] This is reference to Captain Samuel Hobson of the 44th Regiment. Hobson was commissioned captain in the 44th Regiment on December 25, 1747. Winthrop Sargent mistook him for Lieutenant Thomas Hobson, See Sargent, p. 361.

[20] Captain Robert Dobson was Senior Captain of the 48th Regiment. Braddock named him an additional aide-de-camp during the Battle of the Monongahela. He sold his commission and returned to England shortly after the battle in July, 1755.

[21] Lowdermilk transcribed "Gethius." Captain Richard Gethins (d. 1755) of the 44th Regiment was killed in the Battle of Monongahela.

[22] Lieutenant James Halkett (d. 1755) was the son of Colonel Peter Halkett and brother of Brigade-Major Captain Francis Halkett. He was killed at the Battle of the Monongahela while attempting to aid his fallen father.

[23] Captain Richard Bowyer of the 48th Regiment was wounded at the Battle of the Monongahela.

[24] This is a reference to Lieutenant Richard Bailey of the 44th Regiment.

[25] This is a reference to Lieutenant John Walsam, or Walsham, of the 48th Regiment.

[26] This is a reference to Lieutenant James Pottinger (d. 1758) of the 44th Regiment. He had served as a volunteer in Flanders and was then commissioned an ensign. He purchased his lieutenant's commission in 1752. He later became an alcoholic and was forced to sell his commission. He was appointed a cadet in Rogers' Rangers on September 14, 1757 and was commissioned 1st Lieutenant in Charles Bulkeley's Company on January 14, 1758. He was killed at Roger's Rock on March 12, 1759. For a short biographical sketch, See Burt Garfield Loescher, *The History of Rogers Rangers, Volume III: Officers and Non-Commissioned Officers*, Bowie, MD: Heritage Books, 2001, p. 33.

[27] This is a reference to Lieutenant Jonathan Hawthorn of the 48th Regiment.

[28] Lieutenant Andrew Simpson of the 44th Regiment was wounded at the Battle of the Monongahela.

[29] Lieutenant William Edmeston of the 48th Regiment was wounded at the Battle of the Monongahela. He was promoted to Captain on March 23, 1758 and eventually rose to the rank of lieutenant colonel. In 1770 he and his brother Robert were granted 10,000 acres of land at what is now the town of Edmeston, NY.

[30] Lieutenant Robert Lock was wounded at the Battle of the Monongahela. He served as a lieutenant in the 44th Regiment until 1764.

[31] This is a reference to Lieutenant Jonathan Cope of the 48th Regiment.

[32] Lieutenant Quintan Kennedy of the 44th Regiment was wounded at the Battle of the Monongahela. He later served under James Grant in his campaign against the Cherokee in 1761.

[33] Lieutenant Percival Brierton, or Brereton (d. 1755), of the 48th Regiment was killed at the Battle of Monongahela.

[34] Lieutenant Robert Townshend (d. 1755) of the 44th Regiment was killed in the Battle of the Monongahela.

[35] This is most likely Lieutenant John Hart (d. 1755) of the 48th Regiment. He was killed in the Battle of Monongahela.

[36] Ensign William Nortlow (d. 1755) of the 44th Regiment was killed at the Battle of Monongahela.

[37] Lieutenant Henry Gladwin (circa 1729–1791) of the 48th Regiment was wounded in the Battle of the Monongahela. He was commissioned a captain in the 80th Light Infantry on December 25, 1757, major of the 80th Regiment on June 20, 1759. He was serving as commander at Detroit during Pontiac's siege in 1763. Gladwin was promoted to lieutenant colonel on September 17, 1763 and Deputy Adjutant General in America. He eventually rose to the rank of major general.

[38] This is a reference to Ensign George Pennington of the 44th Regiment.

[39] This is a reference to Ensign Joseph Cowart of the 48th Regiment. A James Cowart was commissioned lieutenant in the 48th Regiment on November 6, 1755, and still on active duty in 1763

[40] This is a reference to Ensign William Preston (circa 1741–1812) of the 44th Regiment. His father purchased him an ensign's commission in the 25th Regiment at age 13. He held commissions with five different regiments during the period from 1754 until his retirement from the army in 1766. A short biographical sketch can be found at www.inglis.uk.com. The date of his commissions appear to be incorrect as the site states Preston was serving in the Scots Greys in 1755 and did not enter the 44th until 1756.

[41] This is a reference to Ensign Henry Harrison of the 48th Regiment.

[42] Ensign Richard Crowe of the 48th Regiment was wounded in the Battle of Monongahela. He was commissioned lieutenant on November 10, 1755 and was still serving with the regiment in 1763.

[43] Ensign Alexander McMullen of the 48th Regiment was wounded in the Battle of Monongahela.

[44] This was most likely surgeon's mate Jonathan Lee. See Hamilton, *Braddock's Defeat,* Norman, OK: University of Oklahoma Press, 1959, p. 56.

[45] Lieutenant Francis James Buchanan was wounded at the Battle of the Monongahela. He was promoted to captain in the Royal Regiment of Artillery on January 1, 1759.

[46] Captain Lieutenant Robert Smith of the Royal Regiment of Artillery died from wounds received in the Battle of Monongahela.

[47] This is a reference to William McLeod, or McCloud, of the Royal Regiment of Artillery. He was wounded in the Battle of Monongahela.

[48] The above notes were made by George Washington to his clerk.

[49] Following Washington's note, folio 138 is blank. The above note is found on folio 139. It was probably written by Jared Sparks (1789–1866), who edited *The Life and Writings of George Washington,* a twelve volume set printed from 1833–1837. It was the first major edition of George Washington's papers.

Part II

Selected Correspondence
of
George Washington

From
February 26 to June 17, 1755.

———

From the Originals
in the
Congressional Library

Edited
by
James A. Harris

Introduction

The following section consists mostly of selected correspondence to and from George Washington related to the Ohio Expedition of 1755. The manuscripts for all of the letters written by Washington can be found in Letterbook 2. The letters to George Washington are found in Series 4: General Correspondence. All of the original manuscripts are available for viewing on the American Memories page of the Library of Congress internet site.

At some point during the 1780s Washington edited his earlier Letterbooks, making changes in grammar and wording directly over the original letters. In many cases, the original text is nearly illegible. This edition has attempted to present the letters as they were originally written in 1755. In those instances where the original language may be in question, this edition has relied on the text as presented in John C. Fitzpatrick, *The Writings of George Washington from the Original Manuscript Sources.*

The letters have been printed in chronological order. Included in Letterbook 2 are several memorandums written by Washington to provide an historical background for the letters contained therein. Most modern printings of Washington's papers, Abbott and Twohig, and Fitzpatrick included, have subdivided those memorandums. This edition prints the memorandums as George Washington originally wrote them, in the appropriate order as found in Letterbook 2.

Selected Correspondence of George Washington

Robert Orme to George Washington[1]
March 2, 1755

A Copy
of Captn. Robt. Orme's first Letter to Washington.

Sir

The General having been informd that you expresd some desire to make the Campaigne, but that you declind it upon some disagreeableness that you thought might arise from the Regulation of Command,[2] has orderd me to acquaint you that he will be very glad of your Company in his Family; by which all inconveniences of that kind will be obviated.

I shall think myself very happy to form an acquaintance with a person so universally esteem'd and shall use every opportunity of assuring you how much I am

Sir

Williamsburgh   Your most Obedt. Servant,

Mard 2d. 1755   Robt. Orme, aid de Camp. [f. 1]

---

[1] This letter and all those that follow, unless otherwise noted, are taken from George Washington's Letterbook No. 2.

[2] This is a reference to the royal orders of November 12, 1754. See p. 99, fn. 7. Also, *PGW,* 1:242, fn. 2.

George Washington to Robert Orme
March 15, 1755

To Robert Orme Esq.

aid de Camp to the General,

Sir,

I was not favourd with your agreeable Letter (of ye 2d) till Yesterday; acquainting me with the notice his Excellency is pleased to honour me with by kindly desiring my Company in his Family.—Its true Sir, I have, ever since I declind a command in this Service expressd an Inclination to serve the Ensuing campaign as a Volunteer; and this believe me Sir, is not a little encreasd, since it is likely to be conducted by a Gentleman of the Generals great good Character.

But beside this, and the laudable desire I may have to serve, (with my poor abilitys) my King & Country, I must be ingenuous enough to confess, I am not a little biassd by selfish, and private views.— To be plain Sir, I wish for nothing more earnestly, than to attain a small degree of knowledge in the Military Art: and, believeing a more favourable opportunity cannot be wishd, than serving under a Gentleman of his Excellencys known ability and experience, it will, you must reasonably imagine not a little contribute to influence me me in my choice.

But, Sir, as I have taken the liberty so far to observe that freely, I shall beg your Indulgence yet a little longer, while I say, that the only bar that can check me in the pursuit of these my desires is the inconveniences that must necessarily arise on some proceedings in a late space—(I mean before the Generals arrival) had in some measure abated the edge of my Intentions and determined me to lead a life of greater inactivety, and into which I was just entering at no small expence, the business whereof must greatly suffer in my absence. [f. 2]

I shall do myself the pleasure of waiting upon his Excellency, so soon as I hear of his arrival at Alexandria, (and woud sooner was I certain where to find him)[1] till which I shall decline saying further on this head; begging you'll be kind enough to assure him, that I shall always retain a grateful Sense of the favour he was kindly pleasd to offer me, and that I should have embraced this opportunity of writing to him, had I not some little time ago wrote a congratulatory Letter on his safe arrival &c., and as I flatter myself you will favour me in communicating my Sentiments herein, it will need no other mentn. or reptition.

You do me a singular favour, in proposing an acquaintance which cannot but be attended with the most agreeable Intimacy on my side; as you may already experience by the familiarity and freedom with which I now assume to treat you; a freedom, which, even if disagreeable, you'll excuse, as I shall lay the whole blame at your door for encouraging me to throw of the formality which otherwise might have appeard in my deportmt. on this occasion.— The hope of shortly seeing you will be an excuse for my not adding more than that I shall endeavour to approve myself worthy of your friendship, and that I beg to be esteemd

Your most Obedient Servant

Mount Vernon
March 15th. 1755   Go. Washington [f. 3]

---

[1] "to find him" is written above the line. Fitzpatrick did not include it in his transcription, but it would appear to be in his original hand and not a later revision.

George Washington to Robert Orme
April 2, 1755

To Robert Orme Esqr.

Alexandria

Dear Sir,

The arrival of a good deal of Company (among whom is my Mother,—[1] alarmd with the report of my attending your Fortunes) prevents me the pleasure of waiting upon you to day as I intended; therefore I beg you'll be kind enough to make my compliments & excuse, to the Generl.; who I hope to hear is greatly recoverd from his indisposition; and recruited sufficiently to prosecute his Journy. to Annopolis.[2] I find myself much embarrassd with my Affairs; having no person in whom I can confide, to entrust the management with. Yet, under these disadvantages and circumstances, I am determined to do myself the honour of accompanying you with this proviso only—that the General will be kind enough to permit my return, so soon as the hurry off,[3] or grand Affair is over, (if desird). Or, if there should be any space of inaction long enough, to admit of a visit (for otherwise I coud by no means obtain my own consent, what ever private losses I might sustain) to endulge me therein and I need not add how much I should be oblig'd by joining at Wills Creek only, for this the General has kindly promised. These things Sir, however unwarrantable they may appear at first sight, I hope will not be taken amiss when its considerd how unprepard I am at present to quit a Family, & Estate scarcely settled, & in ye utmost confusion.[4]

I have inclosd you a Letter from Colo. Fairfax[5] to Governor Shirley, which with his Complts. he desird might be given to Mr. Shirley: He also sends his Blessing to you, and Desires you may be a good boy & deserve them, & entitle yourself to more[6] at present he entertains those pleasing, & sanguine hopes that a dutiful & worthy Son shoud expect from the most paternal fondness of an endulgent Father—this for your comfort.— I herewith send you a small Chart of ye back Country, which tho' imperfect, & roughly drawn (for want of proper utensils) may, not withstanding, give you a better knowledge of these parts than you have hitherto had an opportunity of acquiring.[7]

I shall do myself the honour of waiting upon the General as soon as I hear of His return from Annopolis—My Compliments attends him, Mr. Shirley &c. And I am Sir

Yr. Truly Obedt. Servt.

Mount Vernon

2d. of Apl. 1755   Go. Washington   [f.

4]

---

[1] Washington's mother, Mary Ball Washington (1706–1789), like any mother, was concerned about her son's going off to war.

[2] Braddock left for Annapolis, MD on April 3 to meet with Governors Robert Hunter Morris of Pennsylvania, James De Lancey of New York, and William Shirley of Massachusetts. When they failed to arrive, Braddock returned to Alexandria on April 7. See McCardell, *Ill-Starred General,* 162–63. The mention of recruiting refers to Braddock's attempts to recruit men in the colonies to complete his regiments.

[3] The text here is crossed out and Fitzpatrick considered it illegible. Abbott and Twohig have transcribed it as "hurry off."

[4] Washington was referring to the management of his estate at Mount Vernon, the former home of his brother Lawrence (1718–1752). Per his will, the home was bequeathed to his daughter Sarah Washington (1750–1754). However, when Sarah died, it reverted back to his wife Ann Fairfax Washington (d. 1761), who had since remarried to George Lee (1714–1761). Washington leased Mount Vernon from Ann Fairfax and George Lee on December 17, 1754, and was in the process of arranging the plantation at this time. See *GWP,* "Lease of Mount Vernon, December 17, 1754," 1:232–35. Washington became the owner of Mount Vernon on the death of Ann Fairfax in 1761.

[5] Colonel William Fairfax (1691–1757) was the cousin of Lord Fairfax and the manager of his estates in Virginia. He was a member of the Governor's council and a long-time friend of the Washington family. Ann Fairfax Washington was his daughter.

[6] Fitzpatrick found this illegible. "& entitle yourself to more," was taken from Abbott and Twohig.

[7] The map mentioned above has not been found.

Robert Orme to George Washington
April 3, 1755

An Answer to the foregoing

Dear Sir

I communicated your desire to the General who expresses the greatest satifaction in having you of our Party and Orders me to give his Compliments and to assure you his Wishes are to make it agreeable to yourself and consistant with your Affairs and therefore desire you will so settle your business at home as to join him at Wills Creek if more convenient for you and whenever you find it necessary to return he begs you will look upon yourself as entire Master, and judge of what is proper to be done.

Pray present my Duty to my Father and assure him if Filial Obedience and honour for a parent can secure his Affection I am extreamely safe.[1]

I long with impatience to have you of our Family that I may have frequent opportunity's to assure you with how much sincerety I am

Dr. Sir

Apl. ye 3d. 1755

Yr. Most obedt. Servant &

Mr. Shirley[2] desires
His Compliments

R Orme [f. 5]

---

[1] Orme is here referring to William Fairfax, who had referred to him as a son in Washington's letter of April 2.

[2] This is William Shirley the younger, secretary to General Braddock.

George Washington to William Byrd III
April 20, 1755

To The Honble William Bird Esqr.
Westover[1]

Dr Sir

I am sorry it was not in my power to wait upon you at Westover last Christmas—I had enjoy'd much real satisfaction in the thought when an unexpected accident put in intirely out of my power to comply either with my promise, or Inclination; both of which equally urg'd me to make the Visit.[2]

I am now preparing for, and shall in a few days sett off, to serve in the ensuing Campaigne; with different views from what I had before; for here, if I can gain any credit, or if I am entitled to the least countenance and esteem, it must be from serving my Country with a free, Voluntary Will; for I can very truly say I have my expectation of reward but the hope of meriting the love of my Country and friendly regard of my acquaintances; and as to any prospect of obtaining a Comn. I have none, and am pretty well assured it is not in Genl. Braddocks power to give such a one as I would accept off as I am told a Compa. Is the highest Comn. That is now vested in his gift.—[3] He desird my Company this Campaigne, has honour'd me with particular marks of Esteem, and kindly invited me into his Family; which will ease me of that expence, which otherwise, woud undoubtedly have accrued in furnishing a proper Camp Provision; where as the expence will now be easy, (comparitively speaking) as baggabe Horses, Tents & some other nesessarys will constitute the whole of the charge tho' I mean to say, to leave a Family just settling, and in the utmost confusion & disorder (as mine is in at present) will be the means of my using my private Fortune very greatly, but however this may happen, it shall be no hindrance to my making *this* Campaigne.— I am Sir with very gt esteem,

Your most Obt. Servt.

Mount Vernon
20th Apl. 1755   Go Washington [f. 6]

[1] William Byrd III (1728–1777) was a member of the Virginia Council. He served as an agent to the Cherokee and Catawba in 1754–1755 and as a volunteer under Lord Loudoun, 1756–57. In 1758 he was commissioned colonel of the 2nd Virginia Regiment in 1758 and succeeded Washington as colonel of the Virginia Regiment in 1759–1761. Westover, his plantation, is located in Charles City, VA.

[2] The nature of the accident Washington refers to here is unknown.

[3] Washington would not accept less than a field officer's commission.

George Washington to Carter Burwell[1]
April 20, 1755
[Extract][2]

To Carter Burwell, Esqr.—
Chairman of the Military Commee

Williamsburgh

... I am just ready to embark a 2d. time in ye Service of my Country; to merit whose regard and esteem is ye sole move that induces me to make this Campaigne; for I can very Truly say I have no views, either of profitting or Rising in the service and go a Volunteer witht. Rank or Pay, & am certain it is not in Genl. Braddocks power to give a Comn. That I wd. accept; I might further add —that so far from being serviceable I am throughly convinced it will prove very detrimental to my private Affairs, as I shall have a Family scarcely Settled, & in gt. Disorder; but however prejudicial this may be, it shall not stop me from going.— A happy Issue too all your Resolves is most sincerely wishd by

Sir yr. Most Obt. Servt.
Go Washington

Mount Vernon
20th Apl. 1755 [f. 7]

---

[1] Carter Burwell (1716–1756) was a leader in the House of Burgesses and chairman of the committee appointed to oversee military expenditures in the war with France.

[2] Washington wrote to Carter Burwell on April 20, 1755 seeking reimbursement for losses he sustained in the Campaign of 1754. The last paragraph of the letter relates to his plans to join Braddock's forces as a volunteer. It has been extracted and included herein.

George Washington to John Robinson, Jr.[1]
April 20, 1755
[Extract][2]

To Jno. Robinson Esqr.

Speaker of the House of Delegates Virginia[3]

Dear Sir

I little expected when I wrote you last that I should so soon engage in another Campaigne; but in this hope I may be allowd to claim some small share of merit; if it is consider'd that the sole motive wch. Envites me to the Field, is, the laudable desire of servg. My Country and not for the gratification of any lucrative ends; this, I flatter myself, will manifestly appear by my going a Volunteer, without expectation of reward, or prospect of attaining a Command; as I am confidently assur'd it is not in Genl. Braddocks power to give a Comn. That I woud accept.— Perhaps with any others the above declaration might be look'd upon as a piece of self sufficient merit, which, being unwilling to loose, I choose to proclaim it myself;—but by you Sir, I hope it will be taken in a different light, who seem'd to sympathize in my disappointments, and lent your friendly Aid to resinstate me in a suitable Command; which mark of your approbation was not lost upon one who is always sensible of and ready to acknowledge an obligation, and this is the Reason why I am so much more expressive in my Sentiments to you, than I shou'd choose to be to the World whose Censures, and Criticisms often place the best design's in the worst light; and give a different turn to the best of Actions; But to be ingenuous, I must confess I had other Intention's in writing and [f. 8] if there is any merit in going out upon such terms as I do I was unwilling to loose it among *my Friends,* who I did not doubt might be made to believe I had some advantageous offer's that engaged my Services, when in reality it is very far from it, for I expect to be a considerable looser in my private Affairs, by going.— Its true, I have been importuned to make this Campaigne by Genl. Braddock in his Family who I suppose, imagined the small knowledge

I have (had an opportunity of acquring) of the Country, Indians, &c. worthy of his notice; and therefore—thought I might be useful to him in the progress of this Expedition....

Yr. Most Obt. Servt.

Go Washington.

Mount Vernon
20th Apl. 1755. [f. 9]

[1] John Robinson, Jr. (1705–1766) was speaker of the House of Burgesses and treasurer of the colony from 1738–1766, and was one of the most influential men in Virginia. After his death in 1766 it was revealed that he had maintained much of his influence by providing illegal loans from the treasury to many Virginia politicians.

[2] Washington wrote this letter seeking reimbursement for losses suffered in the Campaign of 1754. He opened the letter with this statement of his purposes for joining the Braddock Expedition.

[3] The Virginia House of Delegates was not created until 1776.

George Washington to William Fairfax
April 23, 1755

To The Honble. Wm Fairfax Esqr.
Prest at Williamsburgh

Dear Sir,

I cannot think of quitting Fairfax[1] without embracing this last opportunity of bidding you farewell.

I this day set out for Wills Creek, where I expect to meet the Genl., and to stay—I fear too long, as our march must be regulated by the slow movements of the Train,[2] which I am sorry to say, I think will be tedious in advancing very tedious indeed—as answerable to the expectation I have long conceived, tho' few believ'd.—

Alexandria has been honourd with 5 Governors[3] in Consultation—A happy presage I hope, not only of the success of this Expedition, but for our little Town; for surely, such honours must have arisen from the Commodious, and pleasant situation of this place, the best constitutional qualitys for Popularity and encrease of a (now) flourishing Trade.—

I have had the Honour to be introduced to the Governors; and of being well receiv'd by them all, especially Mr. Shirley, whose Character and appearance has perfectly charmd me, as I think his every word, and every Action discovers something of the fine Gentn, and great Politician.— I heartily wish such unanimity amongst us, as appeard to Reign between him and his Assembly; when they, to expedite the Business, and forward his Journey here sat till eleven, and twelve o'clock at Nights.—

It will be needless as I know your punctuality requires no Repetition's to remind you of an Affair abt. Which I wrote sometime ago—therefore, I shall only beg my compliments to Mr. Nicholas and his Lady,[4] and to all Friends who think me worthy of their enquirys.

I am Dear Sir

Mount Vernon,   Yr. Most Obedient Servt.
23d of Apl. 1755

Go Washington [f. 10]

[1] George Washington lived in Fairfax County, Virginia.

[2] The first division of the artillery train did not leave Alexandria until April 27 and arrived at Fort Cumberland on May 15, McCardell, *Ill-Starred General,* 190.

[3] Braddock held council in Alexandria on April 14 with Governors Robert Dinwiddie of Virginia, Horatio Sharpe of Maryland, Robert Hunter Morris of Pennsylvania, James de Lancey of New York, and William Shirley of Massachusetts, Sargent, "Robert Orme's Journal," pp. 300–307

[1] Robert Carter Nicholas (1728–1780) Served in the House of Burgesses from 1756–1776 and succeeded John Robinson, Jr. as treasurer of the colony in 1766. He was appointed to the Court of Chancery in 1778. He married Ann Cary Nicholas in 1751.

George Washington to Sarah Cary Fairfax[1]
April 30, 1755

To Mrs. Fairfax —Belvoir[2]

Dear Madam

In order to engage your corrispondence, I think it expedient just to deserve it; which I shall endeavour to do, by embracing the earliest, and every opportunity, of writing to you.

It will be needless to exapatiate on the pleasures that a communication of this kind will afford me, as it shall suffice to say—a corrispondence with my Friends is the greatest satisfaction I expect to enjoy in the course of the Campaigne, and that none of my friends are able to convey more real delight than you can to whom I stand indebted for so many Obligations.

If an old Proverb can claim by belief, I am certainly [?][3] share of success—for surely no man ever made a worse beginning than I have: out of 4 Horses which we brought from home, one was killd outright, and the other3 renderd unfit for use; so that I have been detaind here three days already, and how much longer I may continue to be so,—the womb of time most discover.

I must beg my Compliments to Miss Hannah,[4] Miss Dent,[5] and any other's that think me worthy of their enquirys.

I am Madam

Bullskin[6] Apl.
The 30th 1755   Yr. Most Obedt. Servt.

Go Washington [f. 11]

148

¹ Sarah Cary Fairfax (c. 1730–1811) was the wife of Washington's good friend, George William Fairfax, son of William Fairfax, Sarah, or "Sally," was also the sister of Ann Cary Nicholas. Much has been made of Washington's infatuation with Sally.

² Belvoir was the Fairfax plantation located about four miles from Mount Vernon.

³ The original text has been erased and is illegible.

⁴ Hannah Fairfax (1742–1808), youngest daughter of William Fairfax. She later married Washington's cousin, Warner Washington.

⁵ Miss Dent is probably Elizabeth Dent (1727–1796) of Maryland, who was apparently visiting at Belvoir at this time, See *PGW*, 1:262, fn. 3.

⁶ Bullskin was Washington's land along Bullskin Creek near present-day Charleston, WV.

George Washington to William Fairfax
May 5, 1755

To the Honble. Wm. Fairfax Esqr.
Belvoir

Dear Sir

I overtook the General at Frederick Town in Maryld. and from thence we proceeded to this place,[1] where we shall remain till the arrival of the 2d. Division of the Train, (which we here left Alexandria on Tuesday last);[2] after that, we shall continue our march to Wills Creek, from whence it is imagined we shall not stir till the latter end of this Month, for want of Waggons, and other conveniences to Transports our Baggage &c., over the Mountn.

You will naturally conclude that to pass through Maryld (no business requir'd it) an uncommon, & extraordinary Rout for the Genl., and Colo. Dunbar's Regiment to this place; but at the same time the Reason, however, was obvious to say that those who promoted it had rather have the communication should be that way, than through Virginia; but I now believe the Imposition has to evidently appeared for the Imposer's to subject us to the same Inconvencies again.— Please to make compls. To Colo. G. to whom I shall write by the first opportunity, and excuse haste—I am Sir

Yr. Most Obedt. Servt.

Winchester
5th of May 1755

Go. Washington [f. 12]

---

[1] Washington had probably joined Braddock at Fort Frederick on May 1. Braddock and his aids crossed the Potomac at Swearingen's Ferry the next day and arrived at Winchester on May 3, *PGW*, 1:263, fn. 2. Thomas Swearingen (1708–1760) operated a ferry on the Potomac near present-day Shepherdstown, WV.

[2] The second division of artillery left Alexandria on April 29 and arrived at Wills Creek on May 17.

George Washington to Thomas, Lord Fairfax[1]
May 6, 1755

To the Right Honble.
The Lord Fairfax—Greenway Court[2]

My Lord

I have had the misfortune to loose 3 of my Horses since I left home; and not bringing money enough to buy others, and to answer all the contingent expences that may arise in the course of this Campaigne, I have made bold to sollicit your Lordships assistance which will infinitely oblige me.—

About 40 or 50 £ will supply my wants, and for which I shou'd gladly pay your Lordship Interest, beside many thanks for the favour, as I am greatly distress'd at this present, not being able to proceed well with't.

The Genl. sets out to morrow, and proceeds directly to Wills Creek; which, together with the hurry of Buisness, that has happened since we came to Town, has been a mean's of depriving one of the pleasure of waiting upon your Lordship, as I intended to have done—please to make my Compt. To Colo. Martin.[3]—

I am yr. Lordships most Obedt.

Winchester   &
6th of May 1755   most Humble Servt.

Go. Washington [f. 13]

---

[1] Thomas, Lord Fairfax, Sixth Baron Cameron (1693–1781), was proprietor the of Northern Neck of Virginia consisting of all the land between the Potomac and Rappahannock Rivers (5,282,000 acres). He had inherited it at age sixteen, upon the death of his father in 1710 and moved to Virginia in 1752. His cousin, William Fairfax of Belvoir, managed his affairs. His lands were confiscated during the American War of Independence.

[2] Lord Fairfax resided at Greenway Court, a hunting lodge near Winchester. It was named after his ancestral seat in Kent.

[3] Colonel Thomas Bryan Martin (1731–1798) was the nephew of Lord Fairfax and had accompanied him from England in 1752. He acted as County Lieutenant of the Hampshire County militia on behalf of Lord Fairfax.

George Washington to John Augustine Washington[1]
May 6, 1755

Dear Jack

A very fatiguing Ride, and long Round brought me to the General (the day I parted with you) at Frederick Town; a small Village 15 Miles below the blue Ridge in Mary land from thence we proceeded to this place, where we have halted since Saturday last, and shall depart for Wills Creek to morrow.

I find there is no probability of Marching the Army from Wills Creek till the latter end of this Month, or the first of next, so that you may imagine time will hang heavy upon my hands.

I meet with a familiar complaisance in this Family, especially from the General; who I hope to please without difficulty, for I may say it can scarce be done with as he uses, and requires less ceremony than you can well conceive.—

I have orderd the Horse Gist to Bullskin, and my own here, if serviceable; otherwise you must have them carrd. down when Countess is sent up: I have conceivd a good Opn. of Gist, therefore, I hope you will not let him want for proper usage, if he shd. Be st. instead of ye Greys; which will be the case if they are able to perform the Journey.—

I hope you'll have frequent oppert'tys to expatiate upon ye State of my Affairs, wch. you admr. To such degree of satisfn. To a Person in my situation.— At present I have nothing to add but my Compts. To all friends, particularly the good Family at Belvoir who I hope to hear in good health

I am Dr. Jack yr. Affe. Brother

Winchester
May 6th 1755

Go. Washington [f. 14]

---

[1] John Augustine Washington (1736–1787), Washington's younger brother, was acting as the manager of his estates while Washington was at war.

George Washington to Mary Ball Washington[1]
May 6, 1755

To Mrs. Washington

Near Fredericksbg.

Honourd Madam

I came to this place last Saturday, and shall set out to morrow with the General for Wills Creek; where I fear we shall wait some time for a sufficient number of Waggons to transport us over the Mountains.

I am very happy in the General's Family, and I am treated with a complaisant Freedom which is quite agreeable; so that I have no reason[2] to doubt the satisfaction I proposd in making the Campaigne.

As we have met with nothing yet worth relating I shall only beg my Love to my Brother's and Sister's; and Compliments to Friends.— I am Honour'd Madam Yr most Dutiful & Obedt.

Son

Winchester   Go Washington
May 6th 1755 [f .15]

---

[1] Washington's mother Mary Ball Washington (1706–1789) was then living at Ferry Farm near Fredericksburg, VA.
[2] Fitzpatrick had transcribed "occasion."

153

George Washington to Augustine Washington[1]
May 14, 1755

Dear Brother

I left home the 24th of last month, and overtook the General at Frederick Town in Maryland: from whence we proceeded by slow marches to this place; where, I fear, we shall remain sometime for want of Horses and Carriages to convey our Baggage &c. over the mountains; but more especially for want of Forage; as it cannot be imagin'd that so many Horses as we require, will be subsisted without a great deal.—

We hear nothing particular from the Ohio only that the French are in hourly expectation of being joind by a large body of Indians; but I fancy they will find themselves so warmly attackd in other places, that it will not be convenient for them to spare many.—

I am treated with freedom and Respect by the General and his Family; so that I dont doubt but I shall spend my time very agreeably this Campaign, tho' not advantageously, as I conceive a little experience will be my chief Reward. Please to give my Love to my Sister[2] &c.

I am Dr. Sir

Yr. Most Affecte. Brother

Fort Cumberland
14th of May 1755

Go. Washington

This Letter was not sent[3] [f. 16]

[1] Augustine Washington (1720–1762), Washington's half brother, was in Williamsburg at this time serving as a Burgess for Westmoreland County, *PGW*, 1:272, fn. 1).

[2] Augustine's wife was Anne Aylett Washington (1721–1773). They had married in 1743.

[3] Washington noted in his Letterbook that this letter and several others were never sent. Possibly because he left for Williamsburg on May 15 and was able to talk them personally, *PGW*, 1:273, fn. 7.

George Washington to John Carlyle
May 14, 1755

To Majr. Jno. Carlyle

prest. at Williamsburgh

Sir

I Overtook the General at Frederick Town in Maryld. and proceeded with him by way of Winchester to this place which gave him a good oppertunity to see the absurdity of the Rout, and of Damning it very heartily. Colo. Dunbars Regiment was also obligd to cross over at Connogogee and come down within 6 miles of Winchester to take ye new Road up, which gave me infinite satisfaction.

We are to Halt here till forage can be brought from Philidelphia, which I suppose will introduce the Month of June upon us; and *then* we are to proceed upon our tremendous undertaking of transporting the heavy Artillery over the Mountains, which I believe will compose the greatest difficulty of the Campaigne; for as to any apprehensions of the Enemy I think they need only be provided against, but not regarded, as I fancy the French will be obligd to draw their force *from* the Ohio to repel the Attacks in the North, under the command of Governour Shirley &c, who will make three different attempts imediately.

I coud wish to hear what the Assembly and other's have done, and are doing, together with such occurances as may have happened since my departure.—

I am in very great want of Boots, and have desird my Bror. Jno. To purchase a pair and send them to you, who I hope will contrive them to me, by the first opportunity. I have wrote to my old corrispondant Mrs. Carlyle[1] & must beg my Compliments to my good Friend Dalton,[2] &c.

Fort Cumberland   I am Dr. Sir
14th of May 1755

Yr. Most Hble Servt.

NB. This Letter was never Sent   Go. Washington [f. 17]

155

[1] Sarah Fairfax Carlyle. See below.

[2] Captain John Dalton (d. 1777) of the Fairfax County militia. He was a resident of Alexandria and a business partner of John Carlyle.

George Washington to Sarah Fairfax Carlyle[1]
May 14, 1755

To Mrs. Carlyle
Alexandria

Dear Madam

As I have no higher expectation in view than an intimate corrispondance with my Friends, I hope, in that, I shall not be disappointed; especially by you and Mrs. Fairfax, who was pleasd (tho' seldom) to honour me with yours last time.

We arrrived here the 10th, and for ought I know may Halt till the 10th of next Month, before we receive Waggon's &c. to transport our Baggage and Stores to the Aligany.

We have no news in the Camp to entertain you with at present, but I hope to be furnish'd with something agreeable against my next, when I shall not fail to communicate it. Interim, I am Dr. Madam—

	Yr most Obedt. &
Fort Cumberland	most Hble. Servt.
14th of May 1755	

Go. Washington

This Letter was not sent [f. 18]

[1] Sarah Fairfax Carlyle (1730–1761), daughter of William Fairfax and wife of John Carlyle. She was the sister of Ann Fairfax.

George Washington to John Augustine Washington
May 14, 1755

To Mr. Jno. Auge. Washington
Mount Vernon

Dear Brother

As wearing Boots is quite the Mode, and mine are in a declining State; I must beg the favour of you to procure me a pair that is good, and neat, and send them to Major Carlyle, who I hope will contrive them as quick as my necessity requires.

I see no prospect of moving from this place; as we have neither Horses nor Waggons enough, and no forage for them to subsist upon but what is expected from Philidelphia; Therefore, I am well convinced that the trouble and difficulty we must encounter in passing the Mountain for want of proper conveniences, will equal all other Interruptions of the Campaigne; for I conceive the March of such a Train of Artillery in these Roads to be a tremendous under taking: As to any danger from the Enemy I look upon it as trifling, for I believe they will be obligd to exert their utmost Force to repel the attacks to the Northward, where Governour Shirley and other's with a body of 8,000 Men will annoy their Settlements and attempt their Forts.

The Genl. has appointed me one of his aids de Camps, in which Character I shall serve this Campaigne, agreeably enough, as I am thereby freed from all Commands but his, and give Order's to all, which must be implicitly obey'd.— I have now a good opportunity, and shall not neglect it, of forming an acquaintance which may be serviceable hereafter, if I can find it worth while pushing my Fortune in the Military way.

I have wrote to my two female corrispondants by this opportunity, one of which Letters I have inclos'd you, & beg yr. Deliverance off. I shall expect a Succinct acct. of all that has happen'd since my departure

Fort Cumberland   I am Dear Jack
14th of May 1755   Yr. Most Affecte. Brothr.

                                                   Go. Washington

The above Letter was not sent. [f. 19]

George Washington to Sarah Cary Fairfax
May 14, 1755

To Mrs. Fairfax
Belvoir

Dear Madam.—

I have, at last, with great pain and difficulty, discovered the Reason why Mrs. Wardrope[1] is a greater favourite of Genl. Braddock's than Mrs. Fairfax; and met with more respect at the late review in Alexandria.

The cause I shall communicate, after rallying you for neglecting the means that introduced her to his favour which to say truth was in part (?) a present of dilicious Cake, and potted Wood cocks; that wrought such wonders (?) upon the heart of the General as well[2] as upon those of the gentlemen that they became instant Admirers, not only of the charms, but of the Politeness of this Fair Lady.

We have a *favourable* prospect of halting here three Weeks or a Month longer for Waggons, Horses and Forage; so that it is easy to conceive *my* situation will be very *pleasant* and *agreeable,* when I dreaded this (before I came out) more than every other Incident that might happen in the Campaigne.—

I hope you will favour me with your corrispondance since you see my willing desiresous's[3] to deserve the Honour, and of approving myself

Your most Obedt. &
Fort Cumberland   most Humble Servt.
14th of May 1755

Go. Washington [f. 20]

---

[1] Probably Letitia Lee Wardrop (d. 1776), wife of James Wardrop (d. 1760) of Upper Marlboro, MD. *PGW,* 1:280, fn. 1.

[2] Fitzpatrick noted this phrase as illegible. Abbott and Twohig have transcribed "as well." See *PGW,* "To Sarah Cary Fairfax, May 14, 1755," 1:279–80.

[3] This is Abbott and Twohig's transcription. Fitzpatrick transcribed "desirousness," which is what Washington probably meant to say.

Edward Braddock to George Washington[1]
May 15, 1755

Instructions to George Washington, Esqr.

1. You will repair to Hampton in Virginia with as much expedition as may be; and [?]ately upon your Arrival there you will apply [?] John Hunter Esqr.[2] For the Sum of Four tho[?] Pounds Sterling, for which will receive [?] from Mr. Johnston, Deputy Paymaster,[3] payab[?] to yourself.

2. You will acquaint Mr. Hunter from me that [?] His Majesty's Service under my direction, requires the further Sum of ten thousand Pounds Sterling, to be sent to Fort Cumberland at this place within the space of two Months at farthest from this day, to be entrusted to the Care of such Person as he shall choose for that purpose, who upon his a[?] at the Fort with it, shall have a proper [?] appointed him for the safe Custody of it.

3. You will also acquaint Mr. Hunter that [?] he shall send with the said Money shall [?] reasonable Allowance for his trouble; and that [?] Expence of Insurance and all other Charges th[?] [f. 226] may necessarily attend Sending it shall be allow'd.

4.[4] You will continue at Hampton no longer than two Day's at the farthest, and if you cannot in that time get the whole Sum of four thousand Pounds from Mr. Hunter, you will return to me as speedily as may be with such part of it as you shall be able to receive.

5. You will take care to bring me a positive Answer from Mr. Hunter whether I may depend upon ten thousand Pounds being sent to Fort Cumberland by the time mention'd in these Instructions.

Camp at Fort Cumberland May 15, 1755

E Braddock [f. 227]

[1] These instructions are found in Series 4: General Correspondence, folio 226. Some edges of the manuscript are missing. Those portions that are missing or illegible are marked as a question mark in brackets.

[2] Colonel John Hunter of Hampton Virginia was agent in North America for the money contractors, Thomlinson and Hanbury. John Thomlinson and John Hanbury were contracted by the Government to ship funds to North America to be used by the military. Hunter sold out his interest in the firm and moved to England in 1766.

[3] William Johnston was deputy paymaster in North America. He accompanied Dunbar's column during the march to the Ohio. See Pargellis, *Lord Loudoun in North America* pp. 281–82, for a brief description of the relationship between the paymaster's office and the money contractors.

[4] The number "4" was omitted in the original manuscript.

Memorandum[1]

The 15th of May I was sent to Colo. Hunter for a supply of Money of 4,000 £ Sterling, and arrivd as far as Winchester, on my way thither the day following, from Whence I dispatch'd an express to him (fearing he might be out), to provide that sum, and meet me at Williamsburg with it, and proceeded myself thro Fairfax, where I was detained a Day in getting Horses.—

At Claybourns Ferry[2] the 22d. I met the express I had sent, as he was returning, who brought a Verbal message in the most expressive terms from Governor Dinwiddie, acquainting me that Colo. Hunter was gone to the Northward and that I woud certainly be disappointed in my expectations of this I acquainted Capt. Orme by Letter, and proceeded on the Williamsburg where I arrivd the same Day, and met Mr. Belfour,[3] Partner of Colo. Hunter with near the sum desird, which was completed the next day, time enough to reach Chissels Ordinary[4] in my return.— The 27th. I reached Winchester and expected to have met the troop of Light Horse to Escort me to the Camp, but being disappointed in that I engaged a guard of the Militia with which I set out on the 29th followg. And arrived at the Camp the 30th; from Winchester I wrote the following letter to my Brother Jno. Washington.

*NB The Letter's to Captn. Hunter Orme &c. are inserted hereafter and may be seen in Pages 33, 34, & 35.

Insert them in the order of their dates.[5] [f. 21]

---

[1] Letterbook 2 contains the following memorandum written by Washington, describing his trip to Williamsburg as ordered by General Braddock.

[2] Nathaniel H. Claiborne (1716–1756) operated a ferry over the Pamunkey River on his land at Sweet Hall plantation. It was located near West Point, VA.

[3] James Balfour (d. 1775) of Hampton, VA was a business associate of Hunter.

[4] Chiswell's Ordinary was located about ten miles northwest of Williamsburg in James City County.

[5] Washington wrote this note at the bottom of the page. Letters to John Hunter, James Balfour, and Robert Orme were inserted out of sequence in the Letterbook on the above pages. They have been printed below in chronological order.

George Washington to John Hunter
May 16, 1755

To Jno. Hunter Esqr.

Hampton

Sir

I have Orders from the Genl., and Instructions from Mr. Johnston, to receive 4,000 £ Sterlg. At ye rate of 4.0.7¼ pr. Oz.; which will suffice for the present contingencies.— I have therefore dispatched this express, with order's to make all imaginable haste to you, who I am told will imediately repair to Wmsburg with the money, *and pay it there,* according to contract. I must beg your utmost diligence in this affair as I have Order's not to wait, because the whole Army will halt at Wills Creek till I return, at an immense expence.—

I have Letter's from the Genl. and Paymaster, with Bills and proper Instruction's; all of which I shall deliver when I have the pleasure of meeting you, which I expect will be (in Williamsburg) on Wednesday next, as I am now upon my way down, and shall delay no time on the Journey.—

Winchester   I am &c. GW.
16th May 1755 [f. 33]

George Washington to James Balfour
May 16, 1755

To Mr. Belfour — Partr. To Colo. Hunter
Hampton

Sir

If Colo. Hunter sh be from home, I hope you will open this Lett. to see the Contents, that you may dispatch a messenger to him immediately, to prevent his trouble in getting the 10 or 15 Thd Pounds Mentd in a former Letter but repair immediately to Wmsburg with the 4000 £ which is all I am to receive at prest.

Winchester
16 May 1755

I am Sir your's G.W.— [f. 33]

George Washington to Robert Orme
May 22, 1755

To Robt. Orme Esqr. Aid de Camp

Wills Creek

Dear Sir

In pursuance of His Excellencys Commands, I proceeded to this place with all convenient dispatch; But, as I apprehd, and very justly, that the getting and posting Horses at proper Stages, in order to expedate my return, woud occasion some delay I dispatched an express from Winchester to Hampton advising Colo. Hunter of my business, and desiring him to meet me, in Williamsburg with the money: which sd express This day met on his return from there, with a verbal message from Govr. Dinwiddie informing me that Colo. Hunter set out to the northward last Week for money, and wont be returnd in 14 or 15 Days; & that my journey will prove abortive: however this may happen, I shall continue down till I have information; but thought it first expedient (as I completely believe the Report myself) to give you the earliest intelligence that the Genl. may determine accordingly.—

As I am fatiegued and a good deal disordered by constant Riding (in a droughth that has almost destroyd this part of ye Country) I shall proceed more slowly back, unless I am fortunate enough, contrary to expectation, to receive the money, and in yt case I shall hurry back with the utmost dispatch.—

If His Excellency finds it necessary that the money shoud be had, he has nothing more to do than intimate the same to me; when I shall return back from my place that an express can meet me with his Orders. My Compts. Attds. Morris, Shirley and other Friends of our Party in Camp.

I am Dr. Sir yrs. &c.

Claybourn's Ferry
8 O clock Thursday Mg.

G W_____n [f. 34]

George Washington to Robert Orme
May 23, 1755

To the Same

Dear Sir

Since writg. From Claybourn's Ferry by the Late express, I arrived at this place and met Mr. Belfour, who, I believe, will be able with the assistance of ye Govr. And some other of his Frends, to procure the money by against the morning; which will enable me set out and I hope to get to Winchseter by Tuesday Night next; from whence, I shall proceed to the Camp with all possible dispatch.

As Colo. Hunter is gone to the Northward I coud get no positive answer concerning the further sum of Ten thousand pounds (which he was desird to send to Wills Creek) but Mr. Belfour his partner thinks it may be depended upon. I shall, before I leave Town get his answer in writing, and deliver it on my arrival safe Interim.

I am Sir

Williamsburg
Friday Noon [f. 35]

George Washington to John Augustine Washington
May 28, 1755

[Extract]

To Mr. Jno. Auge. Washington

Mount Vernon

Dear Brother

I came to this place last Night,[1] and was greatly disappointed at not finding the Cavalry according to promise:— I am oblig'd to wait till it does arrive, or till I can procure a guard from the Militia, either of which I suppose will detain me two days; as you may, with almost equal success, attempt to raize the Dead to life again, as the force of this Country; and that from Wills Creek cannot be expected in less than the forementioned time without they are now upon their March.—

The Drougth in this Country, if possible, exceeds what we see below; so that, it is very reasonably conjectur'd, they wont make Corn to suffice the People; and as for Tobacco, they decline all thoughts of making any.

The Inhabitants of this place abound in News, but as I apprehend it is founded upon as much truth as some I heard in my way down, I think it advisable to forego the Recital till a little better authority confirms the report.— & Then you may expect to have a succinct acct.

I shoud be glad to hear you live in Harmony and good fellowship with the family at Belvoir,[2] as it is in their power to be very serviceable upon many occasion's to us as young beginner's: I would advise you visiting often as one step towards the rest, if any more is necessary, your own good sense will sufficient [f. 22] dictate; for to that Family I am under many obligations particularly to the old Gentleman.—[3]

Mrs. Fairfax[4] and Mrs. Spearing[5] expressd an inclination to hear whether I like [?] reaching this place (with my charge safe) you may therefore acquaint them that, I met with no other Interruption than the difficulty of gettg. Horses after I found her's for want of Shoes grew lame,

167

I was oblig'd to get a fresh horse every 15 or 20 Miles, which renderd the journey tiresome. I shou'd have receiv'd greater relief from the fatigues of my journey, and my time woud have been spent much more agreeably had I halted below, rather than at this vile post[6] but I little imagin'd I shoud have occasion to wait for a Guard who ought to have waited for me; If either must have waited at all....[7] [f. 23]

[1] This letter was written from Winchester, VA, where Washington arrived on May 27.

[2] Belvoir was the estate of the Fairfax family.

[3] William Fairfax.

[4] William Fairfax's second wife, Deborah Clarke Fairfax, had died in 1747. This refers to Sarah Cary Fairfax.

[5] Ann Spearing was the wife of Lieutenant Thomas Spearing of Captain Gates's New York Independent Company. She lived at Belvoir, 1754–1755, while Lieutenant Spearing was stationed in garrison at Fort Cumberland and during his service under Braddock.

[6] Abbott and Twohig transcribed "vile hole." The original was crossed out and difficult to read.

[7] The remainder of the letter consists of a discussion of money owed to William Fairfax for horses purchased "sometime ago," and a long postscript in which he considers running for a seat in the House of Burgesses.

Memorandum

May 30th. Upon my return from Williamsburg I found that Sir Jno. St. Clair, with Majr. Chapman & a Detachmt. of 500 Men were gone to the Little Meadows in ordr. To prepare the Roads, erect a small Fort, and to lay a Deposit of Provision's there. The 2d. of June Mr. Spendelowe discovered a communication from Fort Cumberland to the Old Road leadg. To the Aligany witht xing those Enormous Mountains which had provd so prejudicial to our Waggon Horses. This intercourse was opend by the branch of Wills Creek by the 7th., When Sir Peter Halkett with the first Brigade of the Line began its March, and Incampd within a Mile of Ye old Road; which is abt. 5 Miles from ye Fort ye same day. This Encampt. Was first called by the Name of ye Grove but afterwards altered to that of Spendeloe's Camp.

This Day also Captn. Gates's Independant Compy., The remaining Companies of ye Provencial Troops, and the whole Park of Artillery were orderd to hold themselves in readiness to March at an hour's warng. Under the Comd. Of Lieutt. Colo. Burton; which they accordingly did ye 9th followg: and with gt. difficulty, got up to Sir Peter Halketts Brigade. The difficulty arriving in this March by too gt. a number of Waggon's was the Occasion of a Council being calld so soon as the General arrivd (with Colo. Dunbar's Regimt.) the same day; In which Council it was determind to retrench the number of Waggon's and increase the pack Loads for Horses; in order Thereto, the Officer's were calld together, and the Genl. represented to them the necessity There was to procure all the horses it was possible for his Majesty's Service; advisd Them to send back such of their Baggage as they coud do witht. and apply the Horses (which by that mean's woud be become spar'd to [f. 36] carry provision's for the Army, which was accordingly done with great cheerfulness and zeal. [f. 37]

George Washington to William Fairfax
June 7, 1755

To the Honble. Mr. Wm. Fairfax Esqr.

Honble. Sir

I arriv'd with my charge safe in Camp the 30th. Of last Month, after waiting a Day and piece in Winchester expecting ye Cavalry to Escort me up; in which I was disappointed, and obligd to make use of a small Guard of the Militia of Frederick.

The General, by frequent breaches of Contracts, has lost all degree of patience; and for want of that consideration & moderation which shoud be used by a man of Sense upon these occasion's, will, I fear, represent us [?][1] in a light we little deserve; for instead of blaming the Individuals as he ought, he charges all his Disappointments to a publick Supineness; and looks upon the Country, I believe, as void of both Honour and Honesty; we have frequent disputes on this head, which are maintaind with warmth on both sides especially on his, who is incapable of Arguing witht; or giving up any point he asserts, let it be ever so incompatable with Reason. There is a Line of Communication to be open from Pennsylvania to the French Fort Duquisne,[2] along wch we are to receive, after a little time, all our Convoys of Provisions &c.; and to give all manner of encouragement to a People who ought rather to be chastis'd for their insensibility of their own danger, and disobedience of their Sovereigns expectation. They are to be the chosen people, because they have furnishd what their absolute Interest alone induced them to do, that is 150 Waggons, and an Equivalent number of horses.—[3]

Majr. Chapman with a Detachment of 500 Men & the Quarter Master General,[4] marched two or three Days before I arrived [f. 25] here, to prepare the roads and lay a deposit of Provisions in a small Fort which they are to Erect at the Little meadows.

To morrow Sir Peter Halkett with the first Brigade begin their march; and on Monday the General with 2d. follows.

Our Hospital is fill'd with the Sick, and the number's increase daily, with the bloody Flux, which has not yet provd Mortal to many.— General Innis has accepted of a Commission to be Governor of Cumberland Fort, where he is to reside, and will shortly receive another to be hang man, or something of that kind.— By a Letter from Governor Morris we have advice that a Party of three hundd. Men pass'd Oswego on their way to Fort Duquinse, and that another, and larger Detachment was expected to pass that place every moment.— By the Publick accts. From Pennylvania we are assur'd that 900 Men has certainly passd Oswego, to reinforce the French on Ohio, so that from the accts., we have Reason to believe we shall have more to do than go up the Hills to come Down again.—[5]

We are impatient to hear what the power's at home are doing; whether Peace or war is like to be the event of all these Preparations.

I am Honble. Sir

Camp at Wills Creek   Yr. Most Obedt. Servt.
7th of June 1755

Go. W_____n [f. 26]

[1] This word is crossed out and illegible.
[2] Pennsylvanian workers under the command of Colonel James Burd (1726–1793) were constructing a wagon road from Shippensburg, PA intending to join up with Braddock's Road on the Youghiogheny River. This would provide a direct route of supply for the army from the grain-producing counties in Eastern Pennsylvania to the Ohio. See Lily Lee Nixon, "Colonel James Burd in the Braddock Campaign," *The Western Pennsylvania Historical Magazine,* Vol. 17, No. 4, December 1934, pp. 235–46.
[3] This is a reference to the agreement made on April 19 between General Braddock and Benjamin Franklin in which the latter promised to produce 150 wagons, Benjamin Franklin, *Autobiography*, pp. 146–49.
[4] Lieutenant Colonel Sir John St. Clair.
[5] William Johnson had received the above information at his home at Mount Johnson in New York from Jean Silvestre, a French deserter, see "Examination of Jean Silvestre and Wife, May 16, 1755," in *PWJ,* 1:508–10. It is possible that the couriers who were dispatched on May 20 carried the news to Governor Morris who forwarded it to General Braddock, "Indian Proceedings, May 15 to June 21, 1755," *PWJ,* 1:633.

George Washington to George William Fairfax
June 7, 1755

To George Wm. Fairfax Esqr.

Belvoir

Sir

I had not the pleasure of receiving your favour till after my return from Williamsburg, when it was not in my power to be so serviceable in the affair of your Horses as I coud wish; for they were sent out with a Detachment of 500 Men a few days before. I made immediate enquiry, and application for them; and believe I shall be able, notwithstanding our gt. want of Horses, to procure their liberty when we come up with the Detachment; but when that will be, or in what order you may receive them, I cant absolutely say; for we are informd they have killd some of their Horses outright and disabled others for which Reason I think it wou'd be too great to expect yours will escape the Calamitys that befall those of other's: They are appraisd (as I saw by one of the Waggon Master's Books')[1] to £16 the two; which with your Servant Simpson is all that I can understand is here, belonging to you.—

As I have taken this opportunity of writing to Colo. Fairfax, and being just at this time a good deal hurried, which prevents me from enlargeing so fully as I otherwise wou'd, I shall beg to refer you to him for what little news is stirring in the Camp.— Please to make my Compliments to all Friends who think me worthy of their enquireys.

I am Sir

Camp at Wills Creek
    7th. June 1755

Yr. Most Obedt. & most Hble.

Go. W_____n [f. 27]

[1] The Wagon master was John Scott.

George Washington to Mary Ball Washington
June 7, 1755

Near Fredericksg

Honourd Madam

I was favourd with yours by Mr. Dick,[1] and am sorry it is not in my power to provide you with either a Dutch man, or the Butter as you desire, for we are quite out of that part of the Country where either are to be had, as there are few or no Inhabitants where we now lie Encampd, & butter cannot be had here to supply the wants of the Camp.

I was sorry it was not in my power to call upon you as I went to, or came from Williamsburg to'ther Day, which I shou'd have done if the business I went upon, which was for money, woud have sufferd me to have made an hour's delay.—

I hope you will spend the chief part of your time at Mount Vernon as you say, where I am certain everything will be orderd as much for your satisfaction as possible, in the Situation we are in.

There is a Detachment of 500 Men Marchd from this towards the Aligany, to prepare the Roads &c. and it is imagin'd the main body will move now in abt. 5 days time. As nothing else that is remarkable, occur's to me, I shall conclude, after begging my love and Compliments to all Friends Dear Madam yr. Most Affecte.

And Dutiful son

Camp at Wills
Creek 7th. June 1755

Go. Washington [f. 28]

---

[1] Charles Dick (1715–1782) had served as a commissary for Virginia forces in 1754.

George Washington to John Carlyle
June 7, 1755

To Major Carlyle

Alexanda.

Dear Sir

I take this opportunity, as it is the last I can expect before we leave this place, of enquiring after your health, which hope is greatly amended since I saw you in Williamsburg. I have not time, as we are now very much hurried, to communicate Very particularly the little News that is stirring in the Camp; from whence, before I arrivd, was Detch'd a body of 500 Men under the Command of Major Chapman & the Quarter Master General, who are to prepare the Roads and lay a Deposit of Provision's at the Little Meadows; where they are to Erect some kind of Defensive Works to secure our convoys. Tomorrow Sir Peter Halkett with the first Brigade March off and abt. The Monday following the Genl. and the 2d. will move from hence. We have no certain accts. of the French on Ohio; but have advises by Letter from Governor Morris that a body of three hundd. past Oswego, and that a still larger body was hourly expected, so that I apprehend we shall not take possession of Fort Duquisne so quickly as was imagind.

The Inclosd is to my good Friend Mrs. Carlyle, who I hope will not suffer our former corrispondance to drop; my sincere wishes and Compliments attends all enquiring Friends; and I am Dr. Sir yr. Most Obedt. Servt.

Fort Cumberland   G W_____n.
June 7th. 1755 [f. 29]

George Washington to Sarah Fairfax Carlyle
June 7, 1755

To Mrs. Carlyle

Alexandria

Dear Madam

As I have no higher expectation in view than an intimate Correspondance with my Friends, I hope in that I shall not be disappointed; especially by you and Mrs. Fairfax, who was pleasd (tho seldom) to honour me with your's last time a year.

I arrivd here in tolerable health tho something fatigued with the Journey; and found Sir Jno. St. Clair was Detachd with 500 Men to amend the Roads, the main body might pass with the greater ease, who I suppose will be all in motion by Tuesday next.—

Please to make my Compliments agreeable to Mrs. Spearing who has my most sincere and hearty wishes for every thing her Heart can desire. I am Dear Madam yr. Most Obedt. & most

Camp at Wills Creek   Hble. Servt.
7th. of June 1755

Go. Washington [f. 30]

175

George Washington to John Augustine Washington
June 7, 1755

To Mr. Jno. Auge. Washington

Mount Vernon

Dear Brother

As much hurried as I am at present, I cant think of leaving this place without writing to you; tho I have no time to be particular. I was Escorted by 8 Men of the Militia from Winchester to this place; which 8 Men were 2 Days assembling; but I believe they woud not have been more than as many seconds dispersing if I had been attackd. Upon my arrival here, I found Sir Jno. St. Clair with a body of 500 Men had Marchd to prepare the Roads, lay a deposit of Provisions at the Little Meadows and to erect some kind of defensive work there.—

Tomorrow Sir Peter with the first Brigade begin their March, and on Monday the General and the 2d will follow. We have no certain acct. from the Ohio: but have advices from Philidelphia that a body of 300 F. passd Oswego on their way to Fort Duquisne, and that a larger Detachment was hourly expected. A Captn. Of Sir Peter's Regimt.[1] With several of the common Soldiers of the different Corps has died since our Incampmt. Here, and many others are now sick with a kind of bloody Flux. I wrote from Winchester a Letter which I hope you have receivd and shoud be glad of an answer as soon as possible; any Letter's to me, directed to the care of Mr. Cox,[2] at Winchester, will be certain of a conveyance I am Dr. Jack yr. Most Affe. Brother.

GW

Camp at Wills Creek
7th. of June 1755 [f. 32]

[1] Captain Bromley of the 44th Regiment.
[2] William Cocks (d. 1769) of Winchester was serving as a commissary in 1755. He was responsible for forwarding supplies from Winchester to Wills Creek. He later commanded the 1st Company of Virginia Rangers, 1755–1756.

George Washington to John Augustine Washington
June 14, 1755

[Extract]

To Mr. Jno. Auge. Washington

Mount Vernon

Dear Brother

...As I have wrote to you twice since the first Inst., I shall only add that ye difficulty's arising in our March from havg. a number of Waggons, will, I fear, prove insurmountable unless some scheme can be fallen upon to Retrench the Waggons, & in crease the back Loads which is what I recommended at first, & I believe is now found to be the most salutary means of transporting our Provision's & stores to Ohio.—

Camp at George's Creek   I am Dr. Jack yr &c.
14ᵗʰ June 1755

P.S.: I have been able to procure Townshend Washington a Comn. To be assistant Comy. with pay at 5/: Sterg. pr. Day[1] and Anthony Strother a pair of Colour's in Colo. Dunbars Regiment.[2] [f. 38]

---

[1] Townshend Washington, Jr. (1736–1761) of Chotank was a distant cousin of Washington's. Washington had presumably procured him a position as an assistant to commissary Robert Leake.
[2] Anthony Strother, Jr. (1736–1790) of Fredericksburg. The term "a pair of Colour's" referred to a commission as ensign.

Roger Morris to George Washington[1]
June 19, 1755

Dear Washington,

I am desird by the General, to let you know that he marches to morrow, & next day, but that he shall halt, at the Meadows Two or three days. It is the desire of every particular in this family, & the Generals positive Commands to you, not to stir, but by the Advice of the Person under whose Care you are, till your are better, which we all hope will be very soon.— This I can personally assure you, that you may follow the Advice of Do. Murdoch,[2] Surgeon to Colo. Dunbar, to whom I know you were recommended as a proper Man by Dr. Stephen.[3]

Yours &c.

Roger Morris

Camp at this side of
the Youghangany— Monday
five o'clock in the Afternoon. [f. 233]

---

[1] This letter is found in Series 4. General Correspondence, folio 233.

[2] Dr. Robert Murdoch, surgeon of the 48th Regiment. He was from Ireland but received his medical degree from the University of Edinbourgh in 1754.

[3] Captain Adam Stephen had received a medical degree from the University of Edinbourgh.

George Washington to John Augustine Washington
June 28, 1755

To Mr. Jno. Auge. Washington

Mount Vernon

Dear Brother,

Immediately upon our leavg. ye. C at Georg. Ck. Ye 9th Inst. (from whe. I wrote to yo.) I was siezd w violt. Fevers & Pns. In my hd. wch. cond. w'out Intermisn. Til ye 23 follg. when I was reliev'd by ye Genls. absol'y. ordering the Phyns. to give me Doctr. Jas. Powder, (one of ye most exclt. mede. in ye W). For it gave me immet. ease, and removed my Fevrs. & othr. Compts. In 4 Days Time. My illness was too violent to suffer me to ride, therefore I was indebted to a coverd waggon for some part of my Tranpn.; but even in this I cd. not conte. For ye Joltg. was so gt. that I was left upon ye Road with a Guard and necessys; to wait the Arrl. of Colo. Dunbars Detacht, whh. was 2 days M. behind. The Genl. giving me his wd. of honr. That I shd. be brought up before he reachd the French Fort. This promise, and ye Doctr. Threats that if I perseverd it woud endanger my Life, determind me to halt for ye above Detacht.—

As I expect the Comn. Betn. This & Wills's Ck. Must soon be too dangerous for single persons to pass, it will possibly stop ye Interce. of Lettrs. in any measure; Therefore I shall attempt (and will go through if I have strength) to give you an acct of our proceedings, of our Situation, & of our prospects at present; which I desire yo. May come. To Colo. Fairfax & any of my Corrispts.; for I am too weak to write more than this Lettr.— In ye Lr. wch. I wrote fm. Georges Ck. I acqd. You that unless ye numer. of wagns. were Retrenchd & ye carryg. Hs. incrd. yt we never shd. be able to see Duquinse: This in 2 Days afterwards, wch. was abt. ye time they got to ye little Meadows with some of yr. Waggon's and strongest Teams, they themselves were convinced off, for [f. 40] they found that beside ye almost imposy. of gettg. ye wagns. along at all; that they had often a Rear of 3 or 4 Miles of Waggons, & tht. ye Soldrs.

Guarding them were so dispersd that if we had been attackd either in Front, Center or Rear that part so attackd, must have been cut off and totally dispersd before they coud be properly sustaind by any other Corps.

At the little Meadws. There was a 2d. Council calld, for there had been one wherein it was represented to all the Offrs. of the difft. Corps ye gt. necessity there was for Hs. And how laudable it wd. be to retrench their Baggage and offer the spare Hs. For ye Publick Service. In order to encourage this I gave up my best Horse (whc. I have nevr. hd. of since) & took no more baggage than half my Portmanteau wd. easily contn. It was also sd ye numbrs. Were to be lessend but this was only from 210 to 12, to 100 wch. had no perceivable difference.

The Genl. before they met in Council askd my prive. Opinn. Concerng. Ye Expn;— I urged it in the warmest Terms I was Master off, to push on, if we even did it with a chosn Detacht for tht. Purpose, with the Artillery and such other things as were absolutely necessary; leavg. Ye heavy artilly. Other Convoys with the Remainder of ye Army, to follw by slow and regular Marches, which they might do safely while we were advanced in Front. As one Reason to support this Opinion, I inform'd tht. if we cd. credt. our Intelligence, the French were weak at ye Forks but hourly expectd. Reinfts. wch. to my certain knowledge coud not arrive with Provns. or any supplies durg. ye continuance of ye Drought as the Buffalo River[1] down wch is their only commn. to Venango,[2] must be as Dry as we now fd. ye gt. xing of ye Youghe. Wch may be passd dry shod. This was a Scheme that took, & it was decd. that ye Genl. with 1200 chosen Men and Officers of all ye differt. Corps, with the following Field Officer's (vizt[3] Sr. Petr. Halkett who acts as Brigadier, Lt. Colo. Gage Lt. C. Burton, and Majr. Sparke, with such a certain number of Waggons as ye [f. 41] Train wd. absolutely require, shoud March as soon as things woud be got in readiness for them; which was completed, and we on our March by ye 19th., leavg. Colo. Dunbar & Majr. Chapman with ye residue of ye Regts., Companys most of ye Women and in short every thing behind except such Provision's & other necessarys as we took, and carried upon Horses.—

We set our with less than 30 Carriages (Incldg. all those that transported the Howitzers, 12 prs., 6 prs., &c. & all of those strongly Horsed; which was a prospect yt. Conveyd ye most infinite delight to see, tho' I was excessively ill at ye time.— But this prospect was soon over turned, & all my Sanguine hopes brought very low when I found, that instead of pushing on with vigour, without regarding a little rough Road, they were halting to Level every Mold Hill, & to erect Bridges over every brook; by which means we were 4 Days gettg. 12 Miles; where I was left by the Doctrs. Advice and ye Genls. absolute Orders, otherwise I woud not have been prevaild upon to remain behind my own Detacht. As I then imagin'd and believ'd I shall now find it not very easy to Join my own Corps again, which is 25 Miles advanced before us; tho I had the Genls. word of Honr. Pledg'd in ye most Solemn manner, that I shd bt. up before he arrivd at Duquisne. They have had frequent Alarms and several Men Scalp'd, but this is only done to Retard the March, and harass the Men if they are to be turnd out every time a small party of them attack the Guards at Night; for I am certain they have not sufficient strength to make head against the whole.

I have been now 6 Days with Colo. Dunbars Corps, who are in a miserable Condition for want of Horses; not havg. more one half enough for their Wagns. so that ye only method he has of proceeding is to March [f. 42] on himself with as many Waggon's as those will draw, and then Halt till ye Remainder are brought up which requires two Days more; and I believe shortly he will not be able to stir at all; but there has been vile management in regard to Horses; and while I am mentiong. This, I must not forget to desire, that you'll acqt. Colo. G. Fx. That I have made the most diligent enquiry after his Man & Horses, but can hear nothing of either; at least nothing that can be credited. I was told that the Fellow was taken ill upon the Road while he was with Sr. Jno. St. Clairs Detacht. the certainty of this I cannot answer for, but believe there is nothing more certn. than that he is not with any part of ye Army. And unless the Horses stray and make home Themselves I believe there is 1000 to 1 against his ever seeing them again: for I gave up a horse only one Day, & never coud see or hear of him afterwards: My Strength wont admit me to say more; tho I have not said half what I intended cong. our Affrs. here— Business, I shall not think of but depd solely upon yr. mant. of all my affrs, & doubt not, but they will be well conducted.— You may thank my Fds. for ye Lettrs. I have recd wch has not been *one* from *any Mortal* since I left

Fairfax, except yourself and Mr. Dalton. It is a piece of regard & kindness which I shd endr. to acknowe. Was I able and sufferd to write. All your Letters to me I wd. have you send to Mr. Cocks of Winchester or to Govr. Innis at Fort Cumberd, & then you may be certn of their comg. safe to hand otherwise I cant say as much. Make my Complimts. to all who think me worthy of yr. Inquirys.

I am

Gt. xing of ye Youge.[4]
June 28th. 1755 [f. 43]

P.S. Added afterwards, to the foregoing Letter as follows

A Great Misfortune that attended me in my Sickness was, looseing the use of my Servant, for poor Jno.[5] was taken abt. the same time that I was, & with nearly the same disorder; and was confind as long; so that we did not see each other for several Days.— He is also tolerably well recoverd.— we are now advand almost as far as ye. gt. Meadows; and I shall set out tomorrow morning for my own Corps, with an Escort of 100 Men[6] which is to guard some Provision's up; so that my Fears and doubts on that head are quite removd. I had a Letter Yesterday from Orme, who writes me word that they have passd ye Youghyangane for ye last time,[7] that they have sent out Partys to scour the Country thereabouts,[8] and have Reason to believe that the French are greatly alarmd at their approach.—

2d. July 1755 [f. 44]

[1] Rivière au Boeuf, or present-day French Creek, was the main French line of communication between Lake Erie and the Ohio River. It was very shallow and the French often had difficulties transporting supplies to Fort Duquesne.

[2] Venango was on the Allegheny River at the mouth of French Creek where the French constructed Fort Machault. It is presently the site of Franklin, PA.

[3] There is no closing parenthesis.

[4] The "Great Crossing" of the Youghiogheny River was at present-day Smithfield, PA.

[5] John Alton was Washington's manservant.

[6] This detachment, commanded by Captain Adam Stephen, moved forward from Dunbar's column on July 1 and joined up with Braddock on July 5.

[7] Braddock's army crossed the Youghiogheny River a second time at "Stewart's Crossing," near present-day Connellsville, PA.

[8] On June 26 Braddock's army arrived at the Rock Fort, near Jumonville Glen, where they found a recently abandoned Indian Camp with the fires still smoldering. A detachment of 90 volunteers under the command of Captain Richard Dobson of the 48th Regiment was sent along the path to Redstone Creek in search of the enemy. They did not meet the enemy but found and destroyed a large bateau and cache of provisions and rejoined Braddock on June 27 at Gist's Plantation. Sargent, "Robert Orme's Journal," 343–44.

William Fairfax to George Washington[1]
June 28, 1755

Dear Sir

I rec'd your Favor of the 7th. inst. Which I show'd to our particular Friends. We rejoyce at your safe Return with the necessary Cash wanted to begin your Progress and are concern'd at the G___'s unreasonable Impatience [?][2] the unmerited Censure of our Want of public Zeal to answer all his Demands. We allow He may know his Wants, and We are the Judges to know our Ability in the Supply. If We are misrepresented home, our Correspondents will acquaint Us therewith and give Us an Opportunity to acquit our Selves of any unjust Complaints— G':Fx[3] writes to Me, that He thinks himself obligd to go as far as Will's Creek in quest of and to get Enquiry of his Plowman and Horses, unduly taken from the Plow and carried away without a Valuation and perhaps without Remedy. Will any military Officer take Such a violent Method in Great Britain with Impunity! If so, I do not understand what I read in the Articles of War. We shall be a little impatient till We can know You have passed the rugged and Sometimes thought, [f. 235] impassable Mountains calld the Allegany and have descended into the fertile Plains of the Ohio, driving back the French to their narrow Limits in Canada— The Ho of Burgesses are now in Debate and forming a Lottery Bill as the most probable Means of raising Money to defray the public Contingencys, Others imagine a Land-Tax would be more Effectual. Our latest advices inform, that the King embarqu'd for Hanover the 29th of April— The Duke[4] at the Head of the Regency. A French Squadron from Brest sayld to the wtern Parts of Ireland, Sr. Edwd Hawke & Adml. Boscawen gone after them—[5] The Bearer Capt Shaw lately from England, last from So. Carolina[6] is recommended by the Duke as an Officer worthy of General Braddock's Regards and goes to receive his Commands. I can doubt but your Merit prevents You from being Maltreated on Acct. of your endeavoring to vindicate your Countrymen wherein They may be fairly vindicated. Please to make my kind Complts. To Capt. Cholmondley, Lt. Locke[7] and Such other Officers as appear to think Me worthy of their Remembrance. Yr. Mother & Family are well and Send their Several Greetings, desiring often to know of yr Welfare & Progress. I am dear Sr. Your faithful & affcte Friend &c.

W. Fairfax [f. 236]

[1] This letter is found in Series 4. General Correspondence, folio 235.

[2] The manuscript is torn here, but the missing word is probably "and."

[3] George William Fairfax.

[4] King George II (1683–1760) left London for Hanover on April 28 and returned on September 16. William Augustus, Duke of Cumberland (1721–1765) headed the council of advisers that governed the country in his absence.

[5] This was a false rumor. No French fleet had sailed to Ireland and neither Vice-Admiral Edward Boscawen (1711–1761) nor Admiral Edward Hawke (1705–1781) had sailed against them.

[6] Lachlan Shaw had resigned his commission in the 25th Regiment in 1753 and moved to South Carolina where he served as a lieutenant in Captain Raymond Demeré's South Carolina Independent Company from 1754 until at least 1760. He was delivering £2,000 appropriated by the South Carolina Assembly for the Ohio Expedition. *PGW,* 1:318, fn. 9.

[7] Captain Robert Cholmondeley (1726–1755), or Cholmley, of the 48th Regiment, was killed at the Battle of Monongahela. Lieutenant Robert Locke of the 44th Regiment was wounded at Monongahela.

George Washington to Robert Orme
June 30, 1755

To Robt. Orme Esqr. Aid de Camp

Wills Creek[1]

Dear Orme

I came to this Camp on thursday last, with the Rear of Colo. Dunbar's Detacht. and shou'd have continued on with his Front, to day, but was prevented by Rain.—

My Fevers are very moderate, and I hope all near a Crisis, when I shall have nothing to encounter but excessive weakness and the difficulty of getting to you; which I woud not fail in doing ere you reach Duqusine, for 500 £; but I have no doubt of doing this, as the General has given me his word of honour, in the most solemn manner.

As the Doctr. Thinks it imprudent for me to use much exercise for 2 or 3 days, it will prevent my coming up; therefore I shoud be glad to be advisd of your Marches from Gists, and how you are likely to get on; for you may rest assurd, that Colo. Dunbar cannot get from this present Incampment in less than Two or three Days; and I believe really, it will be as much as he possibly can do to reach the Meadows at all, so that you will be greatly advancd before us. I am too weak to add more than my Compts. To the Genl Family, &c. & again to desire that you will oblige me on the above Request, and advise the most effectual means to join you. I am Dr. Orme

Your most Obt. Servt.

Great Crossing
June 30th 1755   Go. Washington [f. 45]

[1] Washington was actually at the Great Crossing of the Youghiogheny on June 30.

George Washington to James Innes
July 2, 1755

To Govr. Innis of Fort Cumberland

Dear Sir

I shoud take in infinitely kind, if you wd. be good enough to dispatch, by the first safe opportunity any Letters that you may receive either to, or from me; for I have been greatly surprised at not receiving any Letter's from my Friends since I came out; and must impute it to miscarriage, some where, for I am certain it cannot be owing to their not writing.

I have been excessively ill, but am now recovering from violent Fevers & Pains, of wch. my disorder consisted.—

The Doctors forbid my writing, as very injurious to my health, therefore I cannot have the pleasure of giving you a particular acct. of our situation &c. but I shall refer you to Mr. Caton,[1] who has had an opportunity of seeing the whole.

I am Yr. most Obt. Servt.

Camp between ye gt. xing
and Meadows July 2d 1755

Go. Washington [f. 46]

[1] Captain Thomas Caton of the Frederick County, VA militia resided near Maidstone, VA across the Potomac from the mouth of the Conococheague River.

Memorandum

NB:

The 8th of July I rejoined (in a covered waggon) the advanced division of the Army under the immediate Comd. Of the General.— On the 9th I attended him on horse back tho. very weak and low. On this day he was attacked and defeated by a party of French & Inds. Adjudged not to exceed 300.— When all hope of rallying the dismayed troops & recovering the ground, our provisions & stores were given up I was ordered to Dunbar's Camp. [f. 46]

Anthony Strother, Sr to George Washington[1]
July 9, 1755

Fredr. July 9th 1755

Sir

The extraordinary favour you have conferd on me and my Son, in procureing him a Comission on the establishment calls for our most gratefull Acknowledgments, which give me leave to assure you I shall ever retain a sense of. When I was at Alexandria I could not be informd for certain whether you were to go out, and indeed must own my Attention was so taken up with so unusuall a sight that I never once thought of applying to you for your interest which neglect you have been too generous to resent.

Our friends here are all well, your Sister Lewis has got another son[2]— I wish you health and prosperity I am

Sir

Yr most obliged
Humble servt.

Anthony Strother [f. 238]

[1] This letter is found in Series 4. General Correspondence, folio 238. Anthony Strother was a merchant in Fredericksburg and old friend of the Washington family.

[2] Washington's sister, Betty Washington (1733–1797) was the married to Fielding Lewis (1725–1782). Their son Warner Lewis was born on June 24 but died in 1756.

George Washington to James Innes
July 15, 1755[1]

To Governor Innis — Fort Cumberland

Sir

Captn. Orme being confind to his Litter & not well able to write, has desir'd me to acknowledge the receipt of yours; He begs the favour of you to have the room that the Genl. lodgd in prepard for Colo. Burton, himself, and Captn. Morris; who are all wounded;[2] also, that some small place may be had where convenient for Cooking; and that, if any fresh Provn and other suitable necessarys for persons in their infirm condition can be had, that you will be kind enough to engage it. He also begs, that, you will order the present wch. was sent by Governor Morris to the Genl. and his Family, into the care of Mr. A le Roy the Steward,[3] who is sent on for that, and other purposes.— The Horses that carry the wounded Genl. in Litters are so much fatiegued that we dread their performance, therefore it is desird, that you will be kind enough to send out 8 or 10 fresh horses for their relief, which will enable us to reach the Fort this Evening. I doubt not but you have had an acct. of the poor Genls. death by some of the affrighted Waggoners, who came off without leave.—

Little Meadows   I am Sir
15th July 1755   Yr. most Obt. Servt.
                                        Go. W_____n [f. 47]

[1] It is probable that this letter was actually written on July 17. Washington and the small group of officers he was with arrived at Little Meadows on July 17. They had spent the night of July 15 camped a few miles east of the Youghiogheny River. They arrived at Fort Cumberland later on July 17, *PGW,* 1:334.

[2] Captain Robert Orme had been wounded in the thigh, Lieutenant Colonel Ralph Burton had been shot in the hip, and Captain Roger Morris was shot through the nose, *PGW,* 1:33435, fn. 1.

[3] The Steward was probably Abraham le Roy (died c. 1765), a Huguenot clockmaker who had settled in Pennsylvania in 1754, *PGW,* 1:335, fn. 2.

George **Washington to Mary Ball Washington**
July 18, 1755.

To Mrs. Washington
near Fredg.

Honour'd Madm.

As I doubt not but you have heard of our defeat and perhaps have had it represented in a worse light (if possible) than it deserves; I have taken this earliest opportunity to give you some acct. of the Engagement, as it happen'd within 7 miles of the French Fort on Wednesday the 9th. Inst.—
We Marchd on to that place witht. any considerable loss, havg only now and then a stragler pickd up by the French Scoutg Indns. When we came there, we were attackd By a body of French and Indns. whose number (I am certain) did not exceed 300 Men;[1] our's consistig of abt. 1,300 well armd Troops; chiefly of the English Soldiers, who were struck with such a panick, that they behavd with more cowardice than it is possible to conceive; The Officers behav'd Gallantly in order to encourage their Men, for which they sufferd greatly; There being near 60 killd and wounded; a large proportion out ye number we had! The Virginia Troops shewd a good deal of Bravery, & were near all killd, for I believe out of 3 Companys that were there, there is scarce 30 men left alive; Captn. Peyrouny & all his Officers down to a Corporal was killd;[2] Capt. Polson shard near as hard a Fate, for only one of his was left:[3] In short the dastardly Behaviour of those they call regular's, exposd all other's that were inclind to do their duty to almost certain death; and at last, in dispight of all the efforts of the Officer's to the Contrary, they broke, and run as Sheep pursued by dogs; and it was impossible to Rally them. The Genl. was wounded; of wch he died 3 Days after; Sir Peter Halket was killd in the Field where died many other brave Officer's; I luckily escapd [f. 48] witht. a wound, tho' I had four Bullets through my Coat, and two Horses shot under me; Captns. Orme & Morris two of the Genls Aids de Camps, were wounded early in the Engagemt. Which renderd the duty hard upon me, as I was the only person then left to distribute the Genls. Orders, which I was scarcely able to do, as I was not half recoverd from a violent illness that confin'd

me to my Bed, and a waggon, for above 10 Days; I am still in a weak and Feeble condn. which induces me to halt here 2 or 3 Days in hopes of recovg. a little Strength, to enable me to proceed homewards; from whence, I fear I shall not be able to stir till towards Sepr., so that I shall not have the pleasure of seeing you till then, unless it be in Fairfax; please give my love to Mr. Lewis and my Sister, and Compts. to Mr. Jackson[4] and all other Fds that enquire after me.

I am Hond Madm. Yr
Most Dutiful Son

GW__n

P.S.

You may acqt. Priscilla Mullican that her Son Charles is very well, havg. only recd. a slight wd. in his Foot wch will be curd witht. detrimt. To him in a very small time.—[5] We had abt. 300 Men Killd and as many, or more wounded, and this chiefly done by our own Men. [f. 49]

[1] The French and Indian forces numbered 72 *Troupes de la marine,* 146 Canadian militia, and 637 Native Americans.

[2] Captain William la Péronie, Lieutenant John Wright, and Ensign Edmund Waggoner of la Péronie's company of rangers were all killed at the Battle of Monongahela.

[3] Captain William Poulson and his lieutenant, John Hamilton were both killed. The surviving officer was Ensign Hector McNeill.

[4] Robert Jackson (d. 1764) was a merchant from Fredericksburg and close friend of the Washington family.

[5] Neither Priscilla Mullican, or her son Charles have been positively identified.

George Washington to Robert Dinwiddie
July 18, 1755

To the Honble. Robt. Dinwiddie Esqr.

Williamsburgh

Honble. Sir

As I am favourd with an opportunity, I shoud think myself inexcusable, was I to omit givg. You some acct. of our late Engagemt. with the French on ye Monongahela the 9th. Inst.

We continued our March from Fort Cumberland to Frazer's[1] (which is within 7 Miles of Duquinse) witht. meetg. With any extraordinary event, havg. only a stragler or two picked Up by the French Indians. When we came to this place, we were attackd, (very unexpectedly I must own) by abt. 300 French and Indns.; Our numbers consisted of abt. 1300 men well armd Men, chiefly Regular's, who were immediately struck with such a deadly Panick, that nothing but confusion and disobedience of order's prevaild amongst them: The Officer's in Genl. behavd with incomparable bravery, for which they greatly sufferd, there being near 60 killd and woundd. A large Porportion out of the number we had!— The Virginian Companies behavd like Men, and died like Soldier's; for I believe out of 3 Companys that were there that Day, scarce 30 were left alive: Captn. Peyrouny and all his Officer's down to a Corporal, were killd; Captn. Polson shar'd almost as hard a Fate, for only one of his Escap'd: In short the dastardly behaviour of the English Solider's expos'd all those who were inclin'd to do their duty, to almost certain Death; and at length, in despight of every effort to the contrary, broke & run as Sheep before the Hounds, leavg. The Artillery, Ammunition, Provisions, and, every individual thing we had with us as a prey to the Enemy; and when we endeavourd to Rally them in hopes of regaining our invaluable loss, it was with as much success as if we had attempted to have stopd the wild Bears of the Mountains. [f. 50]

The Genl. was wounded behind in the Shoulder, & into the Breast, of wch. he died three days after; his two Aids de Camp were both wounded, but are in a fair way of Recovering; Colo. Burton & Sir Jno. St. Clair are also wounded, and I hope will get over it; Sir Peter Halket, with many other brave Officers were killd in the Field: I luckily escaped witht a wound tho' I had four Bullets through my Coat and two Horses shot under me. It is supposed that we had 300 or more dead in the Field; abt that number we brought off wounded; and it is imagin'd (I believe with great justice too) that two thirds of both those number's receiv'd their shott from our own cowardly dogs of Soldier's, who gatherd themselves into a body contrary to orders 10 or 12 deep, woud then level, Fire, & shoot down ye Men before them.

I Tremble at ye consequences that this defeat may have upon our back settlers, who I suppose will all leave their habitation's unless there are proper measures taken for their security.

Colo. Dunbar, who commands at present, intends as soon as his Men are recruited at this place to continue his March to Philia. into *Winter* Quarter's;[2] so that there will be no Men left here unless it is the poor remains of ye Virginia Troops; who survive and will be too small to guard our Frontiers. As Captn. Orme is writg. To yr. honour I doubt not but he will give you a circumstantial acct. of all things, which will make it needless for me to add more than that I am

Honble. Sir Yr. most Obt.
& most Hble. Servt.

Fort Cumberland
July 18ᵗʰ. 1755   G W_____n [f. 51]

---

[1] John Frazier (or Fraser), Indian trader and gunsmith maintained a trading house at the mouth of Turtle Creek on the Monongahela in 1753–1754.

[2] Colonel Dunbar marched from Fort Cumberland to Philadelphia with all the able-bodied regulars on August 2 for winter quarters. He was heavily criticized for this action.

George Washington to John Augustine Washington
July 18, 1755

To Mr. Jno. Auge. Washington

Mount Vernon

Dear Brother

As I have heard since my arrivl. at this place, a circumstantial acct. of my death and dying Speech, I take this early opportunity of contradicting both and of assuring you that I now exist and appear in the land of the living by the miraculous care of Providence, that protected me beyond all human expectation; I had 4 Bullets through my Coat, and two Horses shot under me, and yet escapd unhurt.

We have been most scandalously beaten by a trifling body of men; but fatigue, and the want of time prevents me from giving any of the details up till I have the happiness of seeing you at home; which I now most ardently wish for, since we are drove in thus far. A Weak, and Feeble State of Health, obliges me to halt here for 2 or 3 days, to recover a little strength, that I may thereby be enabled to proceed homewards with more ease; You may expect to see me there on Saturday or Sunday Se'night, which is as soon as I can well be down *as* I shall take my Bullskin Plantation's in my way. Pray give my Compts. to all my Fds.

I am Dr. Jack yr. most Affecte. Brothr.

Fort Cumberld.
18ᵗʰ. July 1755.   G W_____n [f. 52]

195

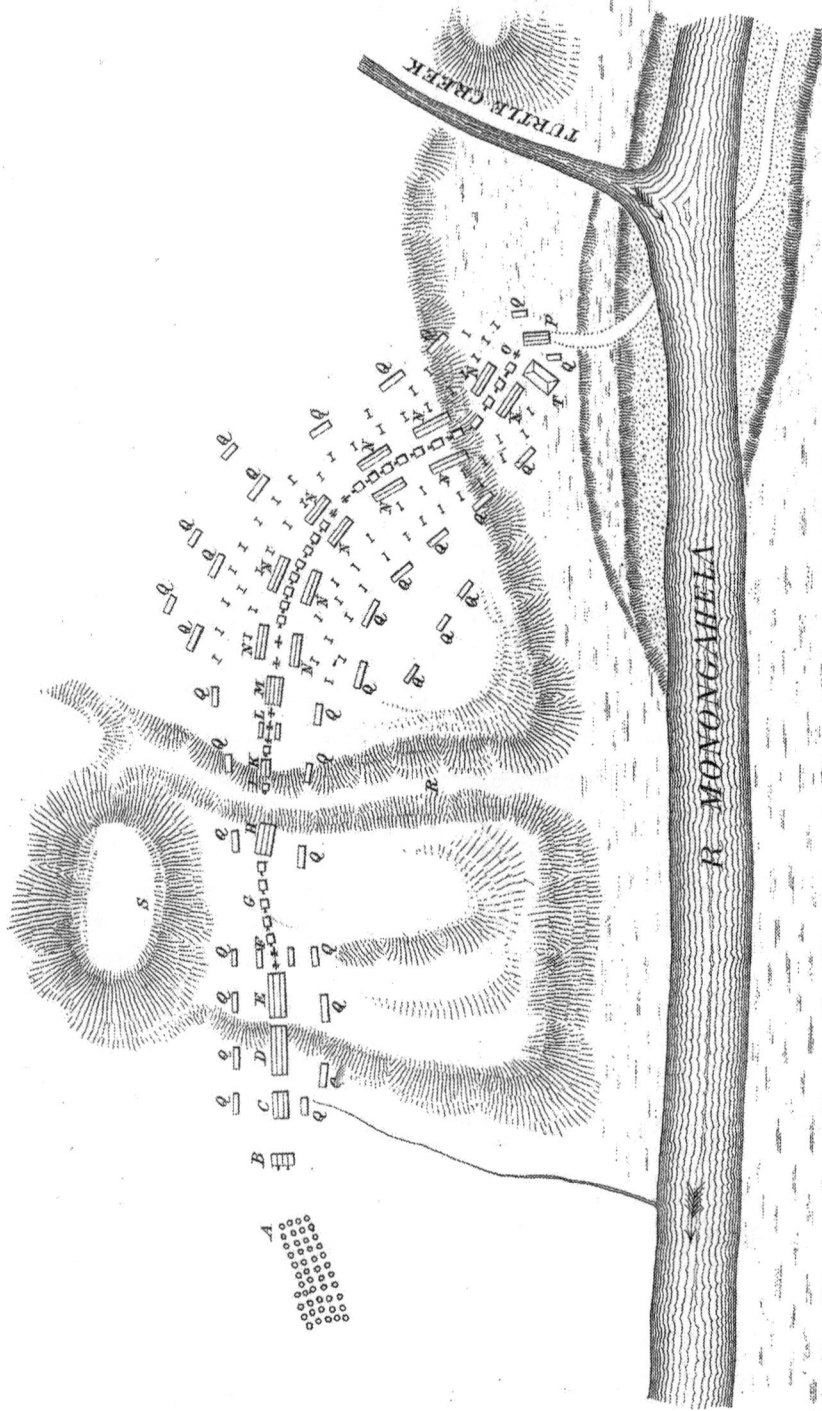

TURTLE CREEK

R. MONONGAHELA

No. I.

A Sketch of the Field of Battle of the 9th of July, upon the Monongahela, seven miles from Fort du Quesne, shewing the Disposition of the Troops when the Action began.

EXPLANATION.

⫿ British Troops; the long lines express the number of Files. O French and Indians. ✝ Cannon and Howitzers. ⧠ Waggons, Carts, and Tumbrils. I Cattle and Packhorses.

A, French and Indians when first discovered by the Guides.

B, Guides and six light Horse.

C, Vanguard of the advanced Party.

D, Advanced Party, commanded by Lt. Col. Gage.

E, Working Party, commanded by Sir Jn. St. Clair, D.Q.M.G.

F, Two Field Pieces.

G, Waggons with Powder and Tools.

H, Rear Guard of the advanced Party.

I, Light Horse leading the Convoy. *K*, Sailors and Pioneers, with a Tumbril of Tools, etc. *L*, Three Field Pieces. *M*, General's Guard. *N*, Main Body upon the Flanks of the Convoy, with the Cattle and Packhorses between them and the Flank Guards. *O*, Field Piece in y^e rear of y^e Convoy. *P*, Rear Guards. *Q*, Flank Guards. *R*, A Hollow Way. *S*, a Hill which the Indians did most of the Execution from. *T*, Frazer's House.

(Signed) Pat. Mackellar, Eng^r.

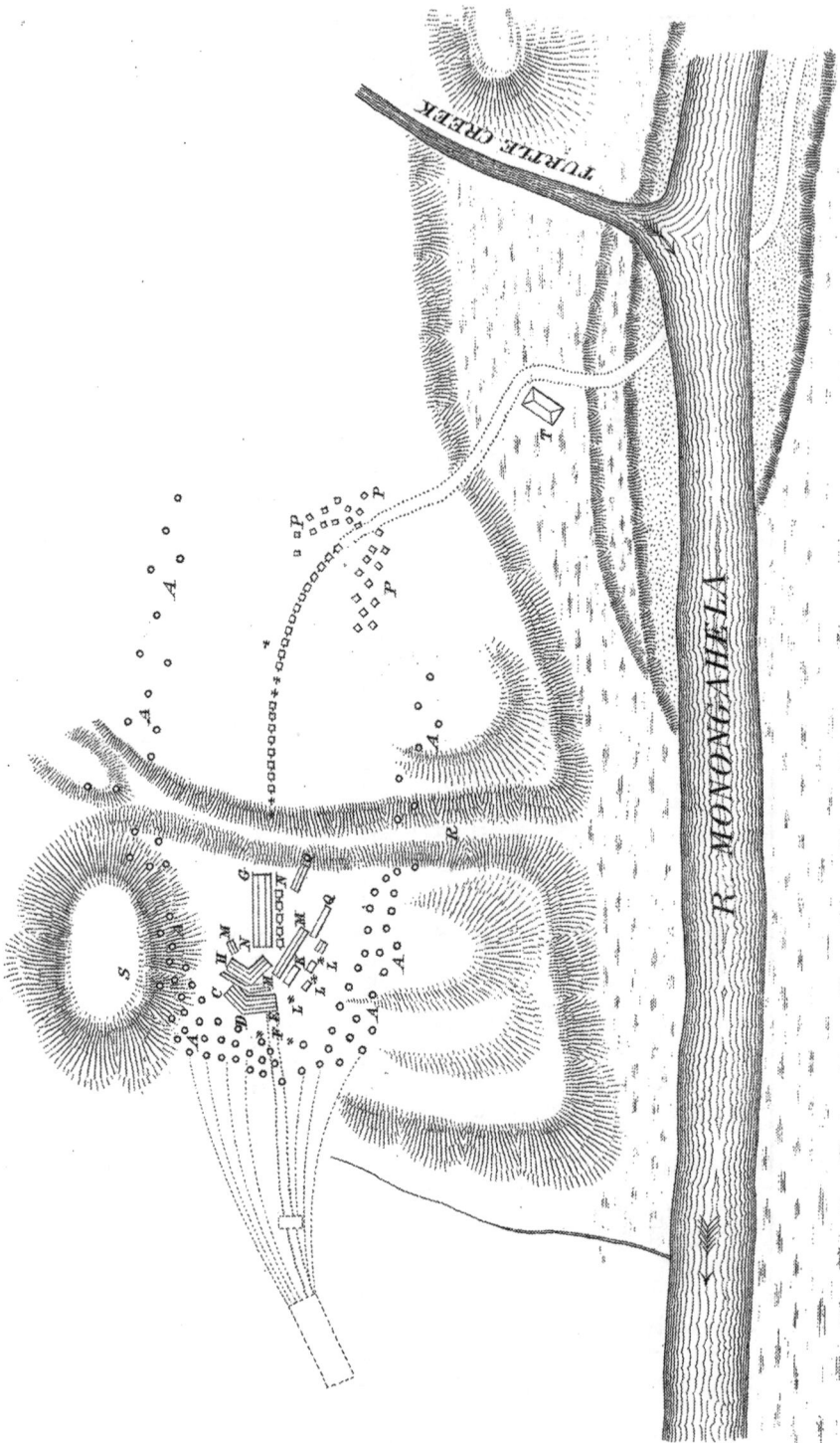

TURTLE CREEK

R. MONONGAHELA

T

P
P
P

A
A
A
A

A
A

R

S
G
N
C
H
M
L
L
A
L
A
M
O

No. 2.

A SKETCH OF THE FIELD OF BATTLE, SHEWING THE DISPOSITION OF THE TROOPS ABOUT 2 O'CLOCK, WHEN THE WHOLE OF THE MAIN BODY HAD JOINED THE ADVANCED AND WORKING PARTYS, THEN BEAT BACK FROM THE GROUND THEY OCCUPIED AS IN PLAN No. I.

EXPLANATION.

A, The French and Indians skulking behind Trees, round the British.

F, The two Field Pieces of the advanced Party abandoned.

C, D, E, H, K, M, N, Q, The whole Body of the British joined with little or no Order, but endeavouring to make Fronts towards yᵉ Enemies Fire. *L,* The three Field Pieces of the main Body. *P,* The rear Guard divided (round the rear of the Convoy now closed up) behind Trees having been attack'd by a few Indians.

N.B. The Disposition on both Sides continued about two hours nearly as here represented, the British endeavouring to recover the Guns (*F*) and to gain the Hill (*S*) to no purpose. The British were at length beat from the Guns (*L*). The General was wounded soon after. They were at last beat across the Hollow Way (*R*) and made no further Stand. The Retreat was full of Confusion and Hurry, but after a few Miles there was a Body got to rally.

(Signed)   PAT. MACKELLAR, Engʳ.

George Washington to Robert Orme
July 28, 1755

To Robert Orme Esqr.—

Philadelphia[1]

To Robert Orme

I arrived at Home the day before yesterday, without meeting with an Egachee,[2] or any other remarkable event. I calld at Belhaven[3] purposely to acquaint Majr. Carlyle with your desire, who will use all possible means to procure a Vessel though I fear it will be some what difficult at present, as the Shipping have most of them employ'd, in Transporting the Tobo. from the difft. Warehouses to Europe.[4]

It is impossible to relate the difft. Accts. that was given of our late unhappy Engagemt.; but all tendd, greatly to the disadvantage of the poor deceasd Genl, who is censur'd on all hands.— As I have no certn. conveyance for this Letter I shall only add my sincere compts. to Morris, Burton, Gage & Dobson and shall taken an opportunity of writg. to you at Philidelphia, and of being more particular, I am my Dear Orme Your Truly

Affe. G____ W____n

Mount Vernon
July 28th. 1755

I Shoud take it particularly kind if Morris woud get the Order's copied from the 16th. of June to the 9th. of July, and send them to me by the first safe conveyance.—[5] [f. 54]

[1] Orme was still at Fort Cumberland. He remained there recovering from his wounds and left for Philadelphia sometime in August.

[2] Fitzpatrick believed "Egachee" was a corruption of "aegis," Fitzpatrick, 2:153. Others have stated it may be derived from an Indian word, *PGW,* 1:347.

[3] Now Alexandria, VA.

[4] Orme returned to England, resigned his commission, and married Audrey Townshend (d. 1781), daughter of Charles Townshend, 3rd Viscount Townshend.

[5] This is a request for copies of General Braddock's orders so that Washington could complete the orderly books. Roger Morris's reply is below.

Roger Morris to George Washington
November 3, 1755[1]

Dear Washington.

Yours of the 17th. 8ctr. from Winchester I recievd from Gist,[2] when I was at Newcastle[3] with Governor Morris.

I own, I am at a loss what to say in answer to some particulars in your Letter; & shall only appeal to your own judgment, from what I say.

I have not since we parted at Fort Cumberland, recievd a single Line from you; Orme indeed had a Letter wherein you desird I woud send you a Copy of the Orders given from the time gen. Braddock left the little Meadows to the Time of the Battle on the Monongahela.

Major Halkets & my Orderly Books, being lost I could not gett an authentick one, that twas proper, & therefore was oblig'd from Necessity, to omit what I woud have comply'd with, with Pleasure, if I had had [416] it in my Power.

We are here greatly alarm'd, the Particulars of which you will receive a better Information of from Gist.

I am left here recruiting, but I am told Application is made, to Genl. Shirley to order back, the two Regts. that are now at Albany,[4] or such part of them as he thinks can be spared.— I own I dont imagine they can come, or if they do, that they will come time enough to prevent the Mischief, that will be done by the Indians.

I must now conclude, as Gist is waiting, to desire you to forbear your Judgment, till I am convicted by Proof, or very strong Presumption, of [?][5] am sure at present. I am innocent of.

I am as I always was
your very well Wisher,
& obedt. Sert.

Philadelphia
Nov. 3d. 1755

Roger Morris [f. 417]

ROGER MORRIS TO GEORGE WASHINGTON

[1] Found in Series 4. General Correspondence.

[2] Gist, Christopher (1706–1759) had acted as an Indian trader prior to the war. He served as a guide for Washington on his trip to the French forts in the winter of 1753–1754, and then as a scout for Braddock in 1755. Gist was captain of the Virginia Company of Scouts from October, 1755 to May, 1757, when they were disbanded. He then served for a short period as a lieutenant in the Virginia Regiment until July, 1757, when he was appointed a Deputy Superintendent of Indian Affairs serving under Edmund Atkin in the Southern Department.

[3] Newcastle, DE.

[4] After returning to Fort Cumberland, Colonel Dunbar marched with the 44th and 48th Regiments to Philadelphia, where he stayed until October 1, when he marched the regiments to Albany.

[5] The document is torn.

Appendix I
British Casualties

The following is a list of the officers who were present at the Battle of Monongahela that appeared in the *Gentlemen's Magazine*, August, 1755, and was reprinted by Lowdermilk. There are two other known rosters of the participants, one was included in the "Seaman's Journal" in Sargent's *History of the Braddock Expedition*, and the other with "The Journal of a British Officer," in Hamilton, *Braddock's Defeat*. This list is not entirely accurate.

STAFF

OFFICERS' NAMES.	RANK	KILLED OR WOUNDED
Edward Braddock, Esq.	Genl. and com. in chief	Mortally wounded.
Robert Orme, Esq.		Wounded.
Roger Morris, Esq.	Aids de Camp.	"
George Washington, Esq.		
William Shirley, Esq.	Secretary	Killed.
Sir John St. Clair	Dep'y Quar. Mas'r Gn'l	Wounded.
Matthew Leslie, Gent.	Gen'l Assist. do.	"
Francis Halkett, Esq.	Major Brigade.	

FORTY-FOURTH REGIMENT

OFFICERS' NAMES.	RANK	KILLED OR WOUNDED
Sir Peter Halkett	Colonel	Killed.
Gage, Esq.	Lieut. Colonel.	Wounded.
Tatton	Captain.	Killed.
Hobson	"	
Beckworth	"	
Githius[1]	"	KIlled.
Falconer	Lieutenant	
Sittler	"	Wounded.
Bailey	Lieutenant	
Dunbar	"	Wounded.

FORTY-FOURTH REGIMENT

OFFICERS' NAMES.	RANK	KILLED OR WOUNDED
Pottenger	"	
Halkett	"	Killed.
Treby	"	Wounded.
Allen	"	Died of wounds.
Simpson	"	Wounded.
Lock[2]	"	Wounded.
Disney	Ensign	"
Kennedy	"	"
Townshend	"	Killed.
Preston	"	
Clarke	"	
Nortlow	"	Killed.
Pennington[3]	"	

FORTY-EIGHTH REGIMENT

OFFICERS' NAMES.	RANK	KILLED OR WOUNDED
Burton, Esq.	Lieut. Colonel.	Slightly wounded.
Sparks, Esq.	Major.	
Dobson, Esq.	Captain.	
Cholmondeley	"	Killed.
Bowyer, Esq.	"	Wounded.
Ross, Esq.[4]	"	"
Barbutt, Esq.	Lieutenant.	
Walsham, Esq.	"	
Crymble, Esq.	"	Killed.
Widman, Esq.	"	"
Hansard, Esq.	"	"
Gladwin, Esq.	"	Wounded.
Hotham, Esq.	"	
Edmonstone, Esq.	"	Wounded.
Cope, Esq.	"	
Brereton, Esq.	"	Killed.
Stuart, Esq.[5]	"	"
Montresore	Ensign	Wounded.
Dunbar	"	
Harrison	"	
Coleblatt	"	
Macmullen	"	Wounded.
Crowe	"	"
Stirling[6]	"	"

VIRGINIA OFFICERS

OFFICERS' NAMES.	RANK	KILLED OR WOUNDED
Stevens	Captain	Wounded.
Waggoner	"	
Polson	"	Killed.
Peyronie	"	
Stewart	"	
Hamilton	Lieutenant	Killed.
Woodward	"	
Wright	"	Killed.
Splitdorph	"	"
Stewart	"	Wounded.
Waggener	"	Killed.
M'Neill[7]	"	

INDEPENDENTS

Gates	Captain.	Wounded.
Sumain	Lieutenant.	Killed.
Miller	"	
Haworth	"	Wounded.
Grey[8]	"	"

ARTILLERY

Orde	Captain.	
Smith	Capt. Lieut.	Killed.
Buchanan	Lieutenant	Wounded.
M'Cloud	"	
McCuller[9]	"	"

ENGINEERS

McKeller, Esq.	Major.	Wounded.
Gordon, Esq.	Captain.	"
Williamson, Esq.	Capt. Lieutenant.	"

NAVAL OFFICERS

Spendelowe	Lieutenant	Killed.
Haynes	Midshipman.	
Talbot[11]	"	Killed.

	VOLUNTEERS	
OFFICERS' NAMES.	RANK	KILLED OR WOUNDED
Stone	Captain.	Killed.
Hayer	"	Wounded.

[1] The captains of the 44th present at the Battle of Monongahela were Charles Tatton, Samuel Hobson, Richard Gethins, and John Beckwith.

[2] The lieutenants of the 44th were Thomas Falconer, William Littler, Richard Bailey, William Dunbar, James Pottinger, James Halkett, John Treby, James Allen, Andrew Simpson, and Robert Lock.

[3] The ensigns of the 44th present were Daniel Disney, Quintan Kennedy, Robert Townshend, William Preston, George Clarke, William Nortlow, and George Pennington.

[4] The captains of the 48th Regiment listed as participants in the Battle of the Monongahela were Robert Dobson, Robert Cholmley, Richard Bowyer, and Robert Ross.

[5] The lieutenants of the 48th were Theodore Barbutt, John Walsham, Walter Crymble, William Widman, Jonathan Hansard, Henry Gladwin, William Edmeston, Jonathan Cope, and Percival Brierton. Hotham was probably Lieutenant Jonathan Hawthorn. Stuart has not been identified but is probably Lieutenant John Hart, who was included in the detachment per Braddock's orders of June 17, 1755, see p. 122. Hart was listed as killed in the list found in Hamilton, *Braddock's Defeat,* p. 56.

[6] The ensigns of the 48th were John Montresor, Jonathan Dunbar, Henry Harrison, Alexander McMullen, Richard Crowe, and Robert Stirling. Ensign Coleblatt probably refers to Joseph Cowart.

[7] The Virginia officers listed are Captains Adam Stephens, Thomas Waggoner, William Polson, William la Péronie, and Robert Stewart. The Lieutenants were John Hamilton, Henry Woodward, Jonathan Wright, Gustavus Splitdorph, Walter Steuart, Edmund Waggoner, and Hector McNeill.

[8] The officers of the independent companies listed are Captain Horatio Gates, and Lieutenants Simon Sumain, Richard Miller, Probart (Robert) Howarth, and John Grey. Gates, Sumain, and Miller all served in the New York Independent Companies while Howarth and Grey both served in the South Carolina Company. It is not clear why the South Carolina officers were with Braddock as the South Carolina Company served in Dunbar's Division. It is possible that Gates's command was actually an ad hoc company drawn from the three independent companies serving under Braddock. Another possibility, is that the detachment brought forward under Captain Adam Stephen, that joined Braddock's Army on July 8, included a portion of the South Carolina Company.

[9] The artillery officers are Captain Thomas Orde, Captain Lieutenant Robert Smith, and Lieutenants William McCloud, James Buchanan, and John McCuller.

[10] The engineers were Major Patrick Mackellar, Captain Henry Gordon, and Captain Lieutenant Adam Williamson.

[11] The naval detachment was commanded by Lieutenant Charles Spendelowe. Midshipmen Haynes and Talbot have not been identified.

[12] Captain Stone of the 47th Regiment and Captain Matthew Floyer of the 40th Regiment had both arrived in Virginia from London in June with dispatches for General Braddock. Lieutenant Governor Dinwiddie wrote on June 18 that he had provided them with horses. They must have joined Braddock's Army shortly before the battle of Monongahela. See "Robert Dinwiddie to Edward Braddock, June 16, 1755," and "Robert Dinwiddie to Horatio Sharpe, June 18, 1755," in Brock, *Official Records of Robert Dinwiddie,* 2:64–65, and 2:67–68.

Appendix II:
Biographical Remarks

Allen, James (d. 1755)
Allen was a lieutenant in the 44th Regiment. He was ordered to train the provincial troops, April 2, 1755. Allen died from wounds received at the Battle of Monongahela.

Alton, John
A white manservant to George Washington who accompanied him on the Braddock expedition.

Anderson, James
A private in the 48th Regiment of Foot court-martialed and convicted to receive 1,000 lashes on March 29, 1755.

Augustus, William, Duke of Cumberland (1721-1765)
He was the third son of King George II and Captain General of the British Army, 1745–1757. He handpicked Braddock to command in North America and four-pronged British offensive of 1755 was based on his plan of operation. Cumberland commanded the British Army in Germany in 1757 and was forced to surrender at Kloster-Zeven on September 8, 1757. He resigned in disgrace on October 15, 1757. Prior to his death in 1765, he briefly served as Prime Minister without portfolio.

Bailey, Richard
A lieutenant in the 44th Regiment. He fought at the Battle of Monongahela.

Balfour, James (d. 1775)
A merchant from Hampton, Virginia. He was a partner of John Hunter and assumed the management of his business affairs in 1752.

Ballinger (Barringer), Mary Wright (1708-1800)
The widow of Josiah Ballinger (d. 1748). She was a Quaker who resided

near the present intersection of Virginia Routes 672 and 739. She abandoned her residence shortly after Braddock's defeat when Indians began to raid the area.

Barbutt, Theodore
Barbutt was a lieutenant in the 48th Regiment. He fought and was wounded at the Battle of Monongahela.

Beckwith, John
A captain in the 44th Regiment. He fought at the Battle of Monongahela. Beckwith was promoted to major of the 44th Regiment on July 18, 1758 shortly after the Battle of Ticonderoga and lieutenant colonel of the 44th Regiment on January 13, 1762. He resigned his commission in 1764.

Bowyer, Richard
Bowyer was a captain in the 48th Regiment. He was wounded at the Battle of the Monongahela.

Braddock, Edward (1694–1755)
Braddock joined the Coldstream Guards as an ensign in 1710. He was promoted to lieutenant 1716, lieutenant of grenadiers in 1727, captain lieutenant in 1734, captain in 1736, lieutenant colonel and 2nd major in 1743, and 1st major May 1745. He commanded two battalions of the Coldstream Guards during the Scottish Revolt of 1745 but saw no action. Braddock was then promoted to lieutenant colonel in November 1745 and served in Flanders at Flushing in 1746–1747. He was named colonel of the 14th Foot in 1753 and acted as governor of Gibraltar, 1753–1754. Braddock was commissioned Major General on March 29, 1754. Cumberland pronounced commander in chief of British forces in North America in November 1754. He was mortally wounded at the Battle of Monongahela and died on July 12, 1755.

Brierton (Bereton), Percival (d. 1755)
A lieutenant in the 48th Regiment. He was killed at the Battle of Monongahela.

212

Bromley, Captain (d. 1755)

A captain in the 44th Regiment. He died from dysentery at Fort Cumberland in May 1755.

Buchanan, Francis James

Buchanan was a lieutenant in the Royal Artillery. He was wounded at the Battle of the Monongahela. Buchanan was promoted to captain in 1759.

Burton, Ralph (d. 1768)

Burton exchanged his commission as Major in the Second troop of Horse Grenadiers for a commission as lieutenant Colonel in the 48th Regiment in 1754. He was wounded in the hip at the Battle of Monongahela while leading a charge up the hill to the enemy's main position. Burton served in North America for the remainder of the French and Indian War, in New York from late 1755–1757, at Louisbourg, in 1758, at the Siege of Quebec in 1759. There he was slightly wounded in the assault at Montmorency Falls on July 31, and then commanded the 48th in reserve at Battle of Quebec on September 13. Burton remained in Quebec during the winter of 1759–1760 and commanded the right wing of the British line at the Battle of Sainte-Foy on April 28, 1760. He then served in the West Indies in 1762 and was promoted to major general on July 10, 1762. Burton returned to Canada in 1763 and was named governor of Montreal. In October 1764 General Thomas Gage appointed Burton Brigadier (commander in chief) of the Northern Department of Quebec and the Upper Great Lakes. He then became colonel of the 3rd Regiment of Foot in November 1764. Shortly thereafter, Burton became embroiled in a series of disputes with Governor James Murray. By 1766, the two were no longer on speaking terms and both were recalled to England. Burton returned to Yorkshire and died at Scarborough in 1768.

Burwell, Carter (1716–1756)

Burwell was a leading member of the Virginia House of Burgesses and chairman of the committee of military expenditures.

Byrd, III, William (1729–1777)

He served as a commissioner for Virginia to the Cherokee and Catawba in 1755–1756. He then served as a volunteer under Lord Loudoun during the aborted expedition against Louisbourg in 1757. Loudoun then commissioned him to recruit Cherokee to fight with the Forbes Expedition against Fort Duquesne in 1758. Byrd was commissioned colonel of 2nd Virginia Regiment in April 1758. He then succeeded Washington as colonel of the 1st Virginia Regiment in 1759 and commanded Virginia operations against the Cherokee in 1760–1761. Byrd resigned his commission in August 1761.

Carlyle, John (1720–1780)
Carlyle was a major of Fairfax County militia. Carlyle was a Scot merchant from Dumfrieshire and an early resident of Alexandria, Virginia. He was married to Sarah, daughter of William Fairfax, one of the most powerful men in Virginia and was the brother-in-law of Lawrence Washington. Carlyle had served as commissary to the Virginia Regiment in 1754. Braddock used his home in Alexandria as his headquarters. Carlyle became county lieutenant and colonel of the Fairfax County militia in 1758.

Carlyle, Sarah Fairfax (1730–1761)
The wife of Major John Carlyle and daughter of Colonel William Fairfax. She was a friend and correspondent of George Washington.

Caton, Thomas
Caton was a captain in the Frederick County Virginia militia and a justice of the peace who lived along the Potomac across from the mouth of the Conococheague River. He commanded scouting parties along that portion of the Virginia frontier in 1755 and 1756.

Chapman, Russell
Chapman was commissioned captain in the 44th Regiment in 1741 and promoted to major in 1751. Chapman commanded the advance detachment sent to Little Meadows in June 1755. He served as second-in-command of Dunbar's Division. Chapman was commissioned lieutenant colonel of the 60th Regiment on January 5, 1756. He resigned his commission in 1757.

Cholmley (Cholmondeley), Robert (1726–1755)

Cholmley was commissioned captain in the 48ᵗʰ Regiment. He fought in the vanguard at the Battle of the Monongahela and was killed in the early phase of the battle.

Claibourne, Nathaniel (d. 1756)

Claibourne operated a ferry on the Pamunkey River on the road between Williamsburg and Winchester, Virginia.

Clarke, George

An ensign in the 44ᵗʰ Regiment. He fought at the Battle of the Monongahela and was promoted to Lieutenant later in 1755.

Cocke, Thomas

Cocke was commissioned captain of a company of Virginia rangers in December 1754. He served in Dunbar's Division during the Braddock expedition. Cocke served as a captain in the Virginia Regiment from October 1755 until June 1757. He then served as a captain in the 2ⁿᵈ Virginia Regiment and participated in the Forbes Expedition, 1758.

Cocks, William (d. 1769)

Cocks was a resident of Winchester, Virginia who served as a deputy commissary transporting supplies and ordnance from Winchester to Wills Creek in 1755. He was later commissioned to command the 1ˢᵗ Company of Virginia Rangers and was assigned to protect the frontier along Patterson Creek in late 1755–1756, and oversaw the construction of Cock's Fort. Cocks was given leave to return to Winchester in July 1756 and his company was disbanded shortly thereafter. He served as a volunteer with the 1ˢᵗ Virginia Regiment during the Forbes Expedition in 1758 and was commissioned an ensign in November 1758. He was serving as a lieutenant in the Virginia Regiment in 1762. Washington resided at his home during his stays in Winchester throughout the war.

Coleman, Richard (d. 1763)

Born in England, Coleman immigrated to Virginia around 1720. He settled on Sugarland Run about one mile northwest of present day Dranesville, where he operated an ordinary and a mill until his death in 1763.

215

Connelly, Thomas

Connelly was a private in the 48th Regiment. Court-martialed on May 14, 1755 for theft and sentenced to receive 1,000 lashes.

Cope, Jonathan

A lieutenant in the 48th Regiment. He fought at the Battle of Monongahela.

Coulon de Villiers de Jumonville, Joseph (1718–1754)

Jumonville entered the *Troupes de la marine* as a cadet in 1733 serving under his father at Green Bay. He served in the campaign against the Chickasaw in 1739. Jumonville was commissioned an ensign in 1743 and served in Acadia in 1745–1746. In May 1754, He was given command of a small detachment sent to summon the English to depart from the Ohio Country. He was killed in Washington's surprise attack at what is now called Jumonville Glen on May 28, 1754. This skirmish led to the outbreak of the French and Indian War.

Coulon de Villiers, Louis (1710–1757)

The older brother of Jumonville, Louis Coulon de Villiers had also served under his father as a cadet at Fort St. Joseph and Green Bay. He was wounded in the skirmish against Sac and Fox at Little Lake Butte des Morts, in September 1733. Coulon was promoted to second ensign in 1734 and served in the campaign against the Chickasaw in 1739. He was at Crown Point for a time in the early 1740s and then served in Acadia, where he participated in the raid on Grand Pré in February 1747. Coulon de Villiers was appointed commander of Fort des Miamis in 1748 and served under Pierre-Joseph Céleron de Blainville as second in command on his mission to the Ohio in 1749. Promoted to captain in 1753, Coulon de Villiers commanded the French forces at the Battle of Great Meadows on July 3, 1754. In 1756 he commanded a large detachment of Indians and militia charged with harassing the British convoys delivering supplies to Fort Oswego. He served at the siege of Fort Oswego in August 1756 and in the siege of Fort William Henry in 1757. He contracted small pox and died in Quebec on November 2, 1757.

Cowart, Joseph

An ensign in the 48th Regiment who fought at the Battle of Monongahela.

Cox, Friend

Cox settled at the mouth of the Little Cacapon River at the site where the road from Winchester to Fort Cumberland crossed the Potomac. Cox's Fort was later built on his land in May 1756.

Cresap, Thomas (1694–1790)

Cresap was an Indian trader who settled at Shawnee Old Town, now Oldtown, Maryland, in 1736. He was called "Big Spoon" by the natives for the large ladle he used to pour the soup that was available to all those who came to his home. In 1751 he aided Nemacolin, a Delaware chief, blaze the trail to the forks of the Ohio that Braddock followed. He owned the storehouse at the mouth of the Conococheague River that Braddock used as a supply depot.

Crowe, Richard

An ensign in the 48th Regiment who fought and was wounded at the Battle of Monongahela.

Crymble, Walter (d. 1755)

A lieutenant in the 48th Regiment who was killed at the Battle of Monongahela.

Dagworthy, John (d. 1784)

Dagworthy was serving as a storekeeper in Trenton, New Jersey in 1746 when he received a royal commission as Captain to raise a company for the proposed expedition against Canada. He moved to Maryland in 1754 and was given command of Maryland troops, commanding the company of Maryland Rangers in Braddock's army. Attached to Dunbar's Division, he did not participate in the Battle of Monongahela. He then served in command of the Maryland troops in garrison at Fort Cumberland and was involved in a series of disputes over command with the Virginians. He was placed in command at Fort Frederick in 1756 and was promoted to lieutenant colonel. Dagworthy commanded the Maryland Regiment serving on the Forbes Expedition in 1758. He served in the War of American Independence as brigadier general of the Sussex County Delaware militia.

Dalton, Henry

A private in the 48th Regiment who was court-martialed on May 26, 1755 for the shooting death of fellow soldier, Henry Pelkington. The shooting was rule an accident and he was acquitted.

Dalton, John (d. 1777)

Dalton was a resident of Alexandria, Virginia and a business partner of John Carlyle. He also served as a captain in the Fairfax County militia. He commanded a group of volunteer militia on the frontier in Spring, 1756.

Darty, George

Darty was an enlisted soldier in the South Carolina Independent Company who was court-martialed for desertion on May 16, 1755 and sentenced to receive 200 lashes.

de Lancey, James (1703–1760)

Born in New York, de Lancey was a graduate of Cambridge and leader of a powerful faction of Albany merchants. He had presided over the Albany Congress in June, 1754. He served as chief justice of the New York Superior Court and acted as lieutenant governor from 1753–1755 and again from 1757 until his death in 1760.

Demeré, Paul (d. 1760)

Demeré was promoted to captain and took command of the South Carolina Independent Company in garrison at Fort Cumberland sometime in late 1754. He was serving in Dunbar's Division and therefore was not present at the Battle of Monongahela. Demeré took command at Fort Loudoun in the Cherokee Country in August, 1757. Fort Loudoun was besieged during the Cherokee Uprising of 1760 from June until Demeré was forced to surrender on August 7. While leading the garrison back to South Carolina, Demeré was wounded and taken prisoner by the Cherokee at Ball Play Creek on August 10. There he was scalped alive and forced to dance until dead.

Dent, Elizabeth (1727-1796)
Elizabeth Dent was a resident of Maryland and a friend of the Fairfax family. She appears to have been visiting the Fairfax Estate at Belvoir in 1755.

Dick, Charles (1715-1782)
Charles Dick was appointed a commissary for Virginia troops by Lieutenant Governor Robert Dinwiddie in December, 1754.

Dinwiddie, Robert (1692-1770)
Dinwiddie was born in Glasgow in 1692 and attended Glasgow University. He began his career as a clerk in the customs office in Bermuda in 1721 and was named to the council of Bermuda in 1730. In 1738 he become collector of customs for Bermuda and was appointed surveyor general of customs for southern colonies. He lived in Virginia for a short time in the early 1740s and was admitted to the Virginia Council in 1741. In December, 1743, Dinwiddie was serving in Barbados as inspector general. He returned to England in 1746 and was appointed lieutenant governor of Virginia in 1751. He quickly became interested in western settlement and was a leader in urging British occupation of the Ohio River Valley. Dinwiddie was recalled and returned to England in January, 1758. He died at Bath on July 16, 1770.

Disney, Daniel
Disney was an ensign in the 44th Regiment and was wounded at that Battle of the Monongahela, July 9, 1755. He served as the regimental adjutant and kept a copy of Halkett's Orderly Book that he saved during the battle. He was promoted to captain in 1760. Disney was promoted to major in 1776 and served in North America during the American War of Independence in the 38th Regiment.

Dobbs, Edward Brice (1729-1803)
The son of Governor Arthur Dobbs of North Carolina, he accompanied his father to North America in 1754. He commanded company of North Carolina Rangers serving in Dunbar's Division in 1755. Dobbs contracted an ailment that impaired his eyesight and he remained in Fort Cumberland when Braddock marched in June, 1755. He was appointed to the Council

of North Carolina in 1756. In June 1756 Dobbs was appointed major in command of four companies of North Carolina troops serving in New York.

Dobson, Robert
Dobson was serving as the senior captain of the 48th Regiment in 1755. He commanded the scouting party sent out from Stewart's Crossing. He fought at the Battle of Monongahela and Braddock appointed him an aide-de-camp during the battle. Dobson sold his commission and returned to England shortly after the Battle of Monongahela.

Dowden, Michael
Dowden operated an ordinary at present-day Clarksburg, Maryland. Dunbar's Division camped there on its way to Fort Frederick.

Draumer, Samuel
Draumer was an enlisted soldier in the 44th Regiment who was court-martialed for desertion on May 16, 1755 and sentenced to receive 200 lashes.

Dumas, Jean-Daniel (1712-1792)
Dumas had served in the Agnais Regiment during the War of Austrian Succession and rose to the rank of captain. He joined the *Troupes de la marine* with the rank of captain in 1750 and was sent to Canada. He was sent to Fort Duquesne in July, 1754. He took command of French forces at the Battle of Monongahela after the death of Captain Daniel-Hyacinthe Liénard de Beaujeu. Dumas served as commander of French forces in Ohio from August, 1755 to November, 1756. He served at the Siege of Fort William Henry in 1757. In January, 1759 Dumas was appointed major general inspector of Canadian troops. He served at the Siege of Quebec and commanded the militia on the French right flank at the Battle of Quebec, September 13, 1759. After the war he was promoted to colonel in 1761, served as governor Isle de France and Isle Bourbon in 1767–1768, eventually rose to the rank of major general in 1780.

Dunbar, Jonathan
Dunbar was an ensign in the 48th Regiment who fought at the Battle of Monongahela.

Dunbar, Thomas (d. 1767)
Dunbar had served in the 18th Regiment for some twenty-five years. He was promoted to lieutenant colonel in 1745 and fought at the Battle of Culloden, 1745. He was named colonel of the 48th Regiment, in April, 1752. He commanded the second division in Braddock's army, charged with bringing up the army's supplies. He took command of British forces after the Battle of Monongahela and was heavily criticized for retreating to Philadelphia in August, 1755. Dunbar resigned his commission in November, 1755 and returned to England. He was next appointed lieutenant governor of Gibraltar in 1758. He rejoined the military about this time and was promoted to major general in 1758 and lieutenant general in 1760.

Dunbar, William (d. 1788)
William Dunbar was a lieutenant in the 44th Regiment in 1755. He was apparently serving with the Grenadier Company and fought in the advance party at the Battle of the Monongahela. He was employed in delivering provisions to the garrison at Fort Oswego in March, 1756.

Edmeston, William
Edmeston was serving as a lieutenant in the 48th Regiment. He fought and was wounded at the Battle of the Monongahela. He was promoted captain in the 48th Regiment in March 1758. Edmeston and his brother Robert were granted 10,000 acres in New York in 1770 at the present site of Edmeston, New York.

Enoch, Henry
Enoch owned a plantation in Hampshire County, Virginia northwest of Winchester at the forks of the Cacapon River. Braddock's Army camped on his land during their march to Fort Cumberland, May 1755. Enoch's Fort was later built on his land.

Evans, John
His farm was at present-day Martinsburg, West Virginia. Braddock's army encamped on his land during its march to Winchester in April, 1755. Evans' Fort was later built on his land.

Fairfax, George William (1725–1787)
The son of Colonel William Fairfax, George William was born in Providence, Bahama Islands and educated in England. He joined his father in Virginia in 1746 and soon became the best friend of George Washington. He served as a Burgess for Frederick County in 1748–1749 and 1752–1755 and then sat for Fairfax County from 1756–1758. He served as a member of the governor's council, 1767–1773 when he moved to England to manage his family's affairs. Although sympathetic to the colonial cause he remained in England during the American War of Independence and died at Bath in 1787.

Fairfax, Hannah (1742–1808)
The youngest daughter of William Fairfax. She later married George Washington's cousin Warner Washington.

Fairfax, Sarah Cary (c. 1730–1811)
Sarah, or Sally, Fairfax was the wife of George William Fairfax. She was a correspondent of George Washington, who was much infatuated with her.

Fairfax, Thomas, 6ᵗʰ Baron Cameron (1693–1781)
Lord Fairfax became proprietor of the northern neck of Virginia, the land between the Potomac and Rappahannock Rivers, at age sixteen. He moved to Virginia in 1747 and made his seat at Greenway Court, near Winchester, in 1752. He was colonel of the Frederick County militia.

Fairfax, William (1691–1757)
Fairfax was the cousin of Lord Fairfax and resident manager of his holdings in Virginia beginning in 1734. He was colonel of militia of Frederick County and a member of the governor's council.

Falconer (Faulkner), Thomas
A lieutenant in the 44th Regiment who fought at the Battle of the Monongahela. He was promoted to captain in November, 1755.

Fitzgerald, James
Fitzgerald was a private in the 48th Regiment who was court-martialed on May 14, 1755 for theft and sentenced to receive 800 lashes.

Floyer, Matthew (d. 1755)
A captain of the 40th Regiment garrisoned in Nova Scotia. He arrived in Virginia with dispatches for General Braddock in June, 1755. He joined Braddock just prior to the Battle of Monongahela where he was killed, July 9, 1755.

Force, Peter (1790–1868)
Force was a printer and archivist from Washington DC who gathered a massive collection of rare colonial manuscripts and pamphlets that he eventually sold to the Library of Congress for $100,000. "Braddock's Orderly Books" were part of the collection.

Franklin, Benjamin (1706–1790)
Printer, scientist, philosopher, and politician from Philadelphia. Franklin contracted with Braddock to supply wagons for the expedition.

Fraser (Frazier), John (d. 1773)
A fur trader, blacksmith, and gunsmith of Scottish origin who immigrated to Pennsylvania and settled in the Cumberland Valley, in the 1720s. He built a storehouse at Venango, 1741. He was forced to abandon his post when the French occupied his house the mouth of French Creek in 1753. He then moved to the mouth of Turtle Creek that Washington visited on his mission to the French forts in 1753. He next settled near Fort Cumberland where he served the fort as gunsmith. He served as a captain of guides and gunsmith under Forbes in 1758. Shortly thereafter he moved his family to Raystown where he resided until his death.

French, Ensign

An officer (possibly a naval officer) assigned by Braddock to oversee the crossing of supplies at the mouth of Rock Creek, in what is now Washington, DC.

Gage, Thomas (1719–1787)

The second son of an Irish peer, Gage entered the army as an ensign sometime between 1736 and 1740. He was commissioned a lieutenant in January, 1741, captain lieutenant in May, 1742, and captain in January, 1743. He was in Flanders in 1744 and served as an aide to the Duke of Albemarle from 1745–1748. He was promoted to major of the 44th Regiment in 1748 and was commissioned lieutenant colonel on March 2, 1751. Gage commanded the van of the British column at the Battle of Monongahela where he was wounded slightly in the belly. He served in New York in 1756 and on the aborted expedition against Louisbourg in 1757. In January, 1758, Gage became colonel of the 80th Light Infantry Regiment. He was serving as a brigadier general and second in command at the Battle of Ticonderoga, where he commanded a portion of the advance guard and was wounded. He commanded the rear guard of Amherst's army in 1760. Gage served as governor of Montreal 1760–1763 and was promoted to Major General, 1761. Gage served as commander-in-chief of British forces in North America from 1763–1775, and commanded the British forces in Boston in 1774–1775. He was recalled to Britain in October, 1775. Gage was promoted to full general in 1782 and died at the family estate of Portland Place, in Kent on April 2, 1787.

Gates, Horatio (1728–1806)

The godson of Horace Walpole, Gates served under Edward Cornwallis in Nova Scotia as a lieutenant, 1749–1754. He was commissioned captain of a New York Independent Company in September, 1754 and served in that capacity until 1759. His company was stationed at Fort Cumberland 1754–1755. He fought in the van and was wounded at Battle of Monongahela. Gates was commissioned major in the 60th Regiment in 1764. He rose to the rank of major general during the War of American Independence.

224

Gethins (Gethius), Richard (d. 1755)

A captain in the 44th Regiment. Gethins was killed at the Battle of Monongahela.

Gist, Christopher (1706-1759)

Gist was a fur trader living in North Carolina in 1750 when he was hired by the Ohio Company to survey their western land grant in 1750–1751. He visited western Pennsylvania on the company's behalf in 1751–1752 and attended a council at Logstown in May, 1752. In 1753, he began Gist's Settlement on the western side of Chestnut Ridge near present–day Brownsville, PA. Gist served as Washington's guide on his mission to the French forts on the Ohio in 1753. In 1754 he moved to Opechon, Maryland, across from the Wills Creek storehouse. Gist fought at the Battle of Great Meadows in 1754 and served as a scout on Braddock's expedition in 1755. He was appointed captain of the Virginia company of scouts in October, 1755. Gist was appointed deputy agent for Indian affairs in the southern department under Edmond Atkin in July, 1757. He died of small pox in July, 1759.

Gladwin, Henry (d. 1791)

Gladwin was serving as a lieutenant in the 48th Regiment in 1755 and was wounded at the Battle of Monongahela. He was appointed a captain in the 80th Light Infantry in December, 1757, and was appointed major in June, 1759. Gladwin was appointed commander at Fort Detroit in 1762 and commanded the fort during Pontiac's siege in 1763. He was promoted to lieutenant colonel in and deputy adjutant general in America in September, 1763. Promoted to colonel in 1777 and Major General in 1782.

Gordon, Harry (d. 1787)

Gordon joined the Royal Engineers in 1742 and served under the Duke of Cumberland in Flanders in 1745 and again in 1747–1748. Cumberland personally recommended him to serve as engineer under Braddock and was considered a road-building specialist. He was assigned to St. Clair's working party and was wounded in the arm at the Battle of Monongahela. Gordon was attached to the 60th Regiment in 1756, and was commissioned engineer in ordinary and captain in January, 1758. He served under Forbes in 1758 and helped lay out his road through Pennsylvania. He also designed Fort Ligonier in 1758 and Fort Pitt in 1759. Gordon traveled from Fort Pitt to Illinois in 1766 and from there down the Mississippi to Mobile. He was promoted to major in 1773, lieutenant colonel in 1777, and colonel in 1782.

Grey, John
Grey served as an ensign in the South Carolina Independent Company and fought at the Battle of the Great Meadows in July 1754. He was serving as a lieutenant in 1755 and was wounded at the Battle of the Monongahela.

Halkett, Francis
The son of Colonel Peter Halkett, Francis Halkett was commissioned a captain in the 44th Regiment on May 2, 1751. He served as brigade major under Braddock and was wounded at the Battle of the Monongahela. He later served as aide-de-camp and brigade major to General Forbes in 1758.

Halkett, James (d. 1755)
A lieutenant in the 44th Regiment and son of Colonel Peter Halkett. He was killed at the Battle of the Monongahela over the body of his dead father.

Halkett, Sir Peter, (1695–1755)
Halkett was a member of Parliament and a Scottish Baronet. He had served with distinction as lieutenant colonel of the 44th Regiment at the Battle of Prestonpans in September, 1745. He was commissioned colonel of the 44th Regiment on February 26, 1751. Halkett was killed at the Battle of Monongahela.

Hamilton, John (d. 1755)
Hamilton was commissioned a lieutenant in Captain William Poulson's company of Virginia Rangers in November, 1754. He was killed the Battle of Monongahela.

Hansard, Jonathan (d. 1755)
Lieutenant Jonathan Hansard was an officer in the 48th Regiment. He was killed at the Battle of Monongahela.

Harrison, Henry
Harrison was an ensign in the 48th Regiment. He fought at the Battle of Monongahela.

Hart, John (d. 1755)
A lieutenant in the 48th Regiment, Hart was killed at the Battle of Monongahela.

Hawthorn (Hathorn), John
Hawthorn was a lieutenant in the 48th Regiment. He served at the Battle of the Monongahela.

Haynes, Midshipman
Haynes has not been positively identified. He was a naval officer who served in the detachment of Lieutenant Charles Spendelowe. He fought at the Battle of the Monongahela.

Hobson, Samuel
Samuel Hobson was a captain in the 44th Regiment. He fought at the Battle of the Monongahela.

Hogg, Peter (1703-1782)
Hogg was a native of Scotland who settled in Augusta County, Virginia sometime in 1745. He was commissioned a captain in the Virginia Regiment on March 9, 1754 and fought at the Battle of Great Meadows on July 3. In June, 1755, Braddock assigned his company to provide sentry duty for workers on a supply road being built in Pennsylvania to link up with his march route. He was placed in command of the southwest frontier of Virginia in September, 1755, and in 1756 was given responsibility for overseeing the construction of a line of forts meant to protect that frontier. Washington dismissed him on July 24, 1757 for failing to fulfill this duty. Hog practiced law in Augusta County after the war and was heavily involved in land speculation in West Virginia and Kentucky.

Howarth, Probart (Robert)

A lieutenant in the South Carolina Independent Companies. Howarth had served as a lieutenant in Oglethorpe's Regiment in the 1740s. In 1749 he was named a lieutenant in one of the South Carolina Independent Companies. He fought at the Battle of Great Meadows on July 3, 1755. He was then wounded at the Battle of the Monongahela. Howarth was serving as adjutant of Fort Loudoun in the Cherokee Country in 1757, and was give a provincial commission as lieutenant colonel of the South Carolina Regiment in July, 1757. In 1760 he was promoted to captain in the British Army and placed in command of Fort Johnson near Charleston. He remained in that position until he was banished as a Loyalist in 1777.

Hughes, James

A private in the 48th Regiment who was court-martialed and sentenced to 800 lashes on May 14, 1755.

Hunter, John

A colonel of militia and justice of the peace for Elizabeth City County. He was named agent in North America for the London merchant firm of Thomlinson & Hanbury in December, 1754. This firm contracted with the army to transfer funds to the forces in North America. He sold out his interest in the firm and moved to England in 1766.

Igo, John

Igo was a convict servant who was court-martialed for theft on June 6, 1755 and sentenced to receive 500 lashes.

Innes, James (d. 1759)

Innes was born in Scotland and immigrated to North Carolina sometime after 1733. He had served as captain of the Cape Fear Company in the campaign against Cartagena in 1741. He served as colonel of the North Carolina Regiment in 1754 and was named overall commander of the Ohio Expedition of 1754. He then commanded at Fort Cumberland from 1754 until September, 1755 when he returned to North Carolina on personal business. He returned to Fort Cumberland for a short period in 1756.

Jackson, Robert (d. 1764)
Jackson was a merchant from Fredericksburg and a friend of the Washington family.

Johnston, William
Johnston was deputy paymaster general in North America and arrived in Virginia in March, 1755. He later served under Lord Loudoun in Albany.

Kennedy, Quentin
Kennedy was serving as a lieutenant in the 44th Regiment and was wounded at the Battle of Monongahela. He later commanded a party of Mohawk and Stockbridge scouts that fought in the Expedition of 1761 against the Cherokee.

Keyes, Gersham (d. 1766)
Keyes owned land on the west bank of the Shenandoah River near the present site of Charlestown, West Virginia.

La Péronie, William (d. 1755)
La Péronie was a Huguenot native of France who immigrated to Virginia around 1750. He was commissioned an ensign in the Virginia Regiment on April 20, 1754 and named adjutant in June. He fought at the Battle of Great Meadows, July 3, 1754, where he was wounded. La Péronie was promoted to captain on August 25, 1754. He commanded a company of Virginia rangers at the Battle of Monongahela where he was killed and scalped.

Le Roy, Abraham (d. circa 1765)
Le Roy was a Huguenot clock maker who had settled in Pennsylvania in 1754. He served as a steward for General Braddock.

Leake (Lake), Robert
Leake served as commissary general of stores and provisions in North America throughout the Seven Years' War.

Lee, Jonathan
Lee was the surgeon's mate of the 48th Regiment. He served at the Battle of Monongahela.

Legardeur de Saint-Pierre, Jacques (1701-1755)
Legardeur de Saint-Pierre had spent many years serving in the French posts in the west. He was commissioned and ensign in the *Troupes de la marine* in 1732 and had served as a lieutenant in the Chickasaw campaign of 1739. He was serving in Acadia in 1746. He was sent to Fort Rivière aux Boeufs in November, 1753, and took command of French forces in the Ohio on his arrival. He received George Washington on his mission to the French Forts in December, 1753. Legardeur de Saint-Pierre was recalled to Canada in early 1755. He was serving in command of Native American allies during the Battle of Lake George, where he was killed on September 8, 1755.

Leslie, Matthew
Leslie was a lieutenant in the 44th Regiment and assistant deputy quartermaster general serving under Sir John St. Clair. He was wounded at the Battle of Monongahela. Leslie was promoted to captain in 1760.

Lewis, Betty Washington (1733-1797)
The sister of George Washington and wife of Fielding Lewis.

Lewis, Fielding (1725-1782)
Fielding Lewis was the husband of Betty Washington and brother-in-law of George Washington. He was a member of the House of Burgesses.

Lewis, Warner (1755-1756)
Born on June 24, 1755, he was the son of Fielding Lewis and Betty Washington Lewis. He died in 1756.

Liénard de Beaujeu, Daniel-Hyacinthe-Marie (1711-1755)
Liénard de Beaujeu had served for years in the western posts and was commissioned a captain in the *Troupes de la marine* in 1748. He had served as commander at Fort Niagara, 1750–1751. He was serving as

commandant of Fort Michilimackinac in October 1754 when he was appointed to take command at Fort Duquesne. He arrived at Fort Duquesne in July, 1755 and commanded the French forces at the Battle of Monongahela. He was killed in the third volley of the battle.

Littler (Sittler), William
A lieutenant in the 44th Regiment. He fought and was wounded at the Battle of Monongahela.

Lock, Robert
A lieutenant in the 44th Regiment who fought and was wounded at the Battle of Monongahela. He served as a lieutenant in the 44th until 1764.

Lowdermilk, William H.
Lowdermilk was the first to publish Braddock's Orderly Books in his *History of Cumberland* in 1878.

Mackay, James (d. 1785)
Mackay had immigrated to Georgia with Oglethorpe and was appointed an ensign in the Georgia Independent Company, 1737. He was promoted to lieutenant in 1740 and captain lieutenant in 1742. In 1745 he was named a captain in Oglethorpe's Regiment and then became captain of a South Carolina Independent Company in 1749. Considered to be experienced in border warfare, he commanded the South Carolina Independent Company at the Battle of Great Meadows, July 3, 1754. Mackay retired from the army in September or October, 1755 and settled in Georgia where he became an extensive landowner and was active in politics. In 1768 he was appointed to oversee the survey of the Georgia-Lower Creek Boundary.

MacKellar, Patrick (1717–1778)
MacKellar had begun his career in the ordnance service as a clerk in 1735 and was warranted a practitioner engineer, in 1742. He worked for the ordnance board in Minorca throughout the 1740s until his recall in 1754. He came to North America in 1755 as the second ranking engineer in Braddock's Army and was considered an expert in fortifications.

He fought and was severely wounded at the Battle of Monongahela and later drew precise maps of the battlefield and order of march. MacKellar served at Fort Oswego in 1756 and was taken prisoner at its capitulation on August 14, 1756.

MacKellar was exchanged to England in 1757 and commissioned captain in the corps of engineers. In January, 1758 he was promoted to sub-director and major of engineers, and was appointed second engineer on the Louisbourg Expedition later in that year. He then served as chief engineer at the Siege of Quebec in 1759. He was severely wounded at the Battle of Montmorency Falls, July 31, 1759. MacKellar served in the garrison at Quebec during the winter of 1759–1760, and directed the artillery at the Battle of Ste. Foy on April 28, 1760, where he was again wounded. He was appointed chief engineer at Halifax in November, 1760. He served as chief engineer on the expedition against Martinique in 1761 and the Siege of Havana in 1762. He was appointed lieutenant colonel of engineers in 1775 and director of engineers and colonel in 1777.

Marin, Pierre-Paul de la Malgue (1692–1753)
Marin was a long-time veteran of the western forces, serving at Green Bay in 1729–1730. He was serving as an ensign in 1732. He served in Acadia and in the campaigns in upstate New York during the War of Austrian Succession and was promoted to captain in 1748. In 1749 he was given a license to trade in the upper Mississippi Valley and traveled to Sioux Territory in 1750. He was placed in command of the French Expedition to the Ohio River in 1753 and died at Fort Rivière aux Beoufs on October 29, 1753.

Martin, Thomas Bryan (1731–1798)
Martin was the nephew of Thomas, Lord Fairfax and arrived in Virginia from England in 1752 to serve as his land agent. He lived at Fairfax's estate of Greenway Court, near Winchester, Virginia. He was a colonel in the Hampshire County militia.

McCuller (McCulloch), Jonathan
A lieutenant in the Royal Artillery who fought and was wounded at the Battle of Monongahela.

McDonald, John
A soldier in the 44th Regiment who was court-martialed for theft on June 6, 1755 but acquitted.

McMullen, Alexander
An ensign in the 48th Regiment who fought at the Battle of Monongahela.

McNeill, Hector
Commissioned an ensign in the Virginia troops in December, 1754, McNeill fought in Captain William Poulson's Ranger Company at the Battle of the Monongahela and was the only officer in the company to survive the battle.

Memeskia (d. 1752)
Also known as Old Britain, la Desmoiselle, Twaatwaa, and Pianguisha. Memeskia was Piankashaw who had married into the Miami tribe. He became the principal chief of the pro-British faction of the Miami Confederacy. He founded the village of Pickawillany in present-day Piqua, Ohio in 1747. This village became a center for British traders in the Ohio. He was killed and eaten by Ottawa and Ojibwa warriors in an attack led by Charles-Michel Mouet de Langlade on June 21, 1752.

Menneville, Marquis Duquesne, Ange de (circa 1700–1778)
Governor of New France, 1752–1755. He ordered the French occupation of the Ohio that led to the outbreak of the French and Indian War.

Mercer, George (1733–1784)
Mercer was a member of the Ohio Company and had surveyed the forks of the Ohio in April, 1753. He enlisted as a lieutenant in the Virginia Regiment in February, 1754 and was promoted to Captain on June 4, 1752. He commanded a company of Virginia Carpenters at the Battle of Monongahela where he was wounded. He was named aide-de-camp to George Washington in September, 1755, and served at Fort Loudoun in Winchester, Virginia in 1756, and Charleston, South Carolina, and Savannah, Georgia in 1757. He was promoted to lieutenant colonel of the 2nd Virginia Regiment in March, 1758 and served on the Forbes Expedition, where he participated in the Battle at Loyalhannon on November 12.

Mercer remained with the Virginia forces as a volunteer after the 2nd Virginia is disbanded and General John Stanwix appointed him assistant deputy quartermaster general for Maryland and Virginia in August 1759. In 1763 Mercer moved to London as agent for the Ohio Company. He returned to Virginia for a brief period in 1766 as an agent under the Stamp Act but sailed back to England after being forced to resign his position in the face of rioters. He died in London in April, 1784.

Minor, Nicolas (d. 1782)

Minor operated an inn at the present-day site of Leesburg, VA. He was a captain in the Fairfax County militia and commanded a company of militia that operated in the area around Winchester, Virginia in the summers of 1756 and 1757.

Montresor, John (1736-1799)

John Montresor accompanied his father James Montresor to North America with Braddock in 1755. Montresor was commissioned an ensign in the 48th Regiment and appointed an engineer in June, 1755. He was promoted to lieutenant in July, 1755 and was wounded at the Battle of Monongahela. In 1756 he was employed on the works at Fort Edward and served on Lord Loudoun's aborted expedition to Louisbourg in 1757. He was commissioned a practitioner engineer in May, 1758 and lost his commission in the 48th Regiment. He served at Louisbourg in 1758 and Quebec in 1759. He remained in Canada after the war. In 1763 he delivered dispatches to Fort Detroit during the siege by Pontiac. In 1766 he was promoted to captain lieutenant and chief barrack-master of ordnance in North America. He served as an engineer in North America during the War of American Independence and was promoted to captain in January, 1776. Montresor retired from the army and returned to England in 1778.

Morris, Robert Hunter (circa 1700-1764)

Morris was born in Morrisiana, New Jersey about 1700. He had served under his father, Lewis Morris, as councilor and chief justice of New Jersey in the late 1730s. in 1739 he went to England where Thomas Penn chose him to be governor of Pennsylvania in 1754. He arrived in Philadelphia in October, 1754 and served as governor until August, 1756.

Morris, Roger (1727–1794)

Roger Morris was commissioned captain in the 17th Regiment in September, 1745. He was serving in the 48th Regiment in 1755 and was appointed an aide-de-camp to General Braddock. Morris was wounded in the nose at the Battle of Monongahela. He served as an aide-de-camp to General Daniel Webb, 1756–1758. Morris was appointed lieutenant colonel of the 47th Regiment in May, 1760. He resigned his commission in 1764 and settled on an estate along the Hudson River. He later served on the governor's council of New York. During the War of American Independence Morris was condemned as a loyalist and had his property was confiscated. He then returned to England.

Mouet de Langlade, Charles-Michel (1729–1801)

Born at Fort Michilimackinac, the son of a fur trader and Domitilde, the sister of the Ottawa chief Nissowaquet, Mouet de Langlade held significant influence among the Ottawa through his relationship with Nissowaquet. He was serving as a cadet in the *Troupes de la marine* in 1751 when he led an attack by Ottawa and Ojibway warriors against the pro-English Miami village of Pickawillany at present-day Piqua, Ohio. He was commissioned an ensign in March 1755 and commanded parties of his Indian allies throughout the French and Indian Wars, serving at the Battle of Monongahela in 1755 and again in the Ohio Valley in 1756. He served at Fort Carillon in 1757 where he fought against Rogers' Rangers in January, 1757, and participated in the Battle at Sabbath Day Point on Lake George on July 25, 1757. He served in the Siege of Quebec in 1759 and skirmished with a reconnaissance force led by General James Wolfe along the banks of the Montmorency River on July 26. Mouet de Langlade was promoted to lieutenant on half pay in 1760 and appointed commander of Fort Michilimackinac where he served until the arrival of the British in September, 1761. Langlade saved the lives of several of the men serving in the garrison at Fort Michilimackinac during Uprising of 1763. He went on to serve the British as an Indian agent and led parties of warriors on various expeditions throughout the American War of Independence. He died at his home in Baie-des-puant (Stinking Bay), present-day Green Bay, Wisconsin in the winter of 1800–1801.

Mullican, Charles
A soldier who fought at the Battle of Monongahela and was wounded in the foot. His mother, Priscilla Mullican, was an acquaintance of Mary Ball Washington.

Mullican, Priscilla
The mother of Charles Mullican.

Murdoch, Robert
The surgeon of the 48th Regiment. Murdoch had earned his medical degree from the University of Edinborough in 1754. He may be the same Dr. Murdoch who was serving in the garrison at Fort Pitt in the 1760s.

Napier, James
Dr. James Napier was serving as the director of the general hospital in North America under Braddock in 1755. The general hospital remained at Fort Cumberland when Braddock left for the Ohio.

Nicholas, Ann Cary (1735–1786)
The wife of Robert Carter Nicholas, they married in 1751. She was the sister of Sarah Cary Fairfax.

Nicholas, Robert Carter (1728–1780)
Nicholas served in the House of Burgesses from 1756–1776 and succeeded John Robinson, Jr. as treasurer of the colony of Virginia in 1766. He was appointed to the Court of Chancery in 1778. He had married Ann Cary Nicholas in 1751.

Nortlow, William (d. 1755)
Nortlow was an ensign in the 44th Regiment. He was killed at the Battle of Monongahela.

Nugent, John
A solider in the 44th Regiment, he was court-martialed for theft on May 26, 1755 and sentenced to receive 1000 lashes and was drummed out the regiment.

Ord, (Orde) Thomas

Ord was a captain in the Royal Regiment of Artillery and commanded the artillery detachment in Braddock's army. He fought at the Battle of Monongahela. Ord was promoted to lieutenant colonel in the Royal Artillery in 1760.

Orme, Robert (d. 1790)

Sir Robert Orme was serving as an ensign in the 34th Regiment when he was commissioned an ensign in the Coldstream Guards in September, 1745. He was promoted to lieutenant on April 24, 1751, with the rank of captain in the line. He served with Braddock as an aide-de-camp in 1755 and was severely wounded in the thigh at the Battle of Monongahela. Orme had the reputation of being imperious and insubordinate toward the field officers serving under Braddock. After the campaign, he wrote many letters and a journal vindicating Braddock's actions during the battle. He resigned his commission in October, 1756 and returned to England. He later left his wife and children and married Audrey Townshend. Orme died in Hertford, England in 1790.

Owens, Lawrence

Lawrence Owens operated an inn about fifteen miles west of Rock Creek and eight miles below the Falls of the Potomac in present-day Rockville, Maryland. Dunbar's Division encamped at his inn on their march to Fort Frederick.

Pelkington, Henry

Pelkington was a soldier in the 48th Regiment who was shot by Henry Dalton, May 1755. The shooting was ruled an accident and Dalton was acquitted on May 26.

Pennington, George

An ensign in the 44th Regiment who was promoted to lieutenant effective June 6, 1755. He fought at the Battle of Monongahela.

Polls (Potts), George

The homestead of George Polls was located on a hill just outside of present-day Gainesboro, Virginia.

237

Pottinger, James (d. 1758)

Pottinger had served as a volunteer in Flanders during the War of Austrian Succession and was commissioned an ensign in the 44th Regiment after serving in the siege of Bergen op Zoom. He purchased a lieutenant's commission in 1752. Pottinger served with the 44th Regiment at the Battle of Monongahela. He soon afterwards fell into dishonor due to debt, alcoholism, and indiscretions with a camp follower and was forced to leave the service. Lord Loudoun gave him a second chance and Pottinger became a cadet in Rogers' Rangers in September, 1757. He was commissioned a lieutenant on January 14, 1758. Pottinger was killed in the Battle at Rogers' Rock on March 13, 1758.

Poulson, William (d. 1755)

Poulson was a Scot who immigrated to Virginia around 1746. He was commissioned a lieutenant in the Virginia Regiment on February 18, 1754 and fought at the Battle of Great Meadows, July 3, 1754. He was promoted to captain on July 21, 1754. Poulson commanded a company of Virginia carpenters and artificers at the Battle of Monongahela. He was shot through the heart and killed by fire from the British regulars while leading his men in an attempt to take the main enemy position on the hill.

Preston, William

An ensign in the 44th Regiment who fought at the Battle of Monongahela.

Robinson, John, Jr. (1705–1766)

Robinson was speaker of the House of Burgesses and treasurer of the colony from 1738–1766, and was one of the most influential men in Virginia. He was a member of the committee authorizing expenditures for the Virginia forces, 1754–1755. After his death in 1766 it was revealed that he had maintained much of his influence by providing illegal loans from the treasury to many Virginia politicians.

Ross, Robert

Ross was a captain in the 48th Regiment and was wounded at the Battle of Monongahela. He served with the regiment as major at Louisbourg in 1758 and Quebec in 1759. Ross was promoted to lieutenant colonel of the 48th Regiment in 1762.

Rutherford, John (1712-1758)

Rutherford received a captain's commission in 1741 in exchange for his seat in Parliament. He was named the captain of a New York Independent Company and arrived in New York in 1742. He was given a seat in the New York Council in 1745. Rutherford's company served in Virginia, 1754–1755. He served in Dunbar's Division during Braddock's march. Rutherford was commissioned a major in the 60th Regiment in 1756 and was killed at the Battle of Ticonderoga, July 8, 1758.

Saint Clair, Sir John (d. 1767)

Saint Clair became the 3rd Baronet St. Clair in 1726. He was commissioned major in 22nd Regiment and served under Marshall von Browne in Italy during the War of the Austrian Succession. St. Clair was appointed deputy quartermaster general of the British Army in North America on October 15, 1754, where he served in that capacity until 1767. He arrived in Virginia in January, 1755 and began to prepare the way for Braddock's arrival. St. Clair commanded the working party at the Battle of Monongahela, where he was wounded in the early stages of the fight. He was commissioned lieutenant colonel in the 60th Regiment on March 20, 1756. In January, 1758, he was promoted to the rank of colonel in North America. St. Clair acted as quartermaster general under Forbes in 1758 and was commissioned a colonel on February 19, 1762.

Sary, Caleb

A soldier in the company of North Carolina Rangers who was court-martialed for desertion on June 6, 1755 and sentenced to receive 1,000 lashes.

Scarroyady (d. 1756)

An Oneida Chief who represented the Iroquois on the Ohio and was pro-British. He served as one of Washington's guides in 1753 and was present at battle of Jumonville Glen, May 28, 1754. Scarroyady was said to have a tattoo of a tomahawk on his chest and a bow and arrow on each cheek. He became leader of the Ohio Iroquois after the death of Tanaghrisson in October, 1754 and served as chief Indian scout on Braddock's expedition. He is said to have been present at the Battle of the Monongahela. Scarroyady died in Pennsylvania in 1756.

Scott, John
He served as wagon master on the Braddock Expedition.

Sharpe Horatio (1718-1790)
Sharpe was born in Yorkshire, England and had been a captain of marines and served in the 20th Regiment. He served as Lieutenant Governor of Maryland from 1753–1768. He was commissioned a lieutenant colonel and named acting commander in chief of the planned Ohio Expedition from October, 1754 until the arrival of General Braddock. Sharpe commanded at Fort Cumberland during the Forbes Expedition of 1758.

Shelton, Michael
A soldier in the company of North Carolina Rangers who was court-martialed for desertion on June 6, 1755 and sentenced to receive 1,000 lashes.

Shirley, William (1694-1771)
Shirley was born in London where he practiced law from 1720–1731 when he immigrated to Boston. Shirley became advocate general of Massachusetts in 1733 and served as Lieutenant Governor from 1741–1756. Shirley actively organized colonial forces throughout King George's War including the expedition against Louisbourg in 1745. After the war he served on the commission appointed to negotiate the borders with France from 1750–1753. He was appointed colonel of the 50th Regiment in 1755 and commanded the expedition against Niagara of that year. He served as commander-in-chief of British forces in North America from the death of Edward Braddock until June, 1756, when he was recalled to Britain.

Shirley, William, Jr. (1721-1755)
The eldest son of Governor William Shirley. He served as a naval officer in Boston, 1741. He later went to England to attend to family affairs and was appointed secretary to General Braddock without rank, in the fall of 1754. He was shot in the head and killed at the Battle of Monongahela.

Simpson, Andrew

A lieutenant in the 44th Regiment who was wounded at the Battle of Monongahela.

Simpson

A servant of George William Fairfax who was serving in Braddock's Army at Fort Cumberland, June, 1755.

Smith, Robert (d. 1755)

A captain lieutenant in the Royal Regiment of Artillery. Smith died from wounds received at the Battle of Monongahela.

Soumain, Simon (d. 1755)

Soumain was a lieutenant in the New York Independent Company. He was killed at the Battle of Monongahela.

Sparke, William (circa 1698–1777)

Sparke was commissioned an ensign in the 48th Regiment in 1734 and was serving as a captain in 1740. He was commissioned major on June 3, 1752. Sparke was wounded at the Battle of Monongahela and served in North America until 1758, when he sold his commission and returned to England.

Spearing, Ann

Ann Spearing was the wife of Lieutenant Thomas Spearing of Captain Horatio Gates' New York Independent Company. She lived at Belvoir in 1754–1755 while Lieutenant Spearing was stationed in the garrison at Fort Cumberland and during his service under Braddock.

Spendelowe, Charles (d. 1755)

Spendelowe was commissioned a lieutenant in the Royal Navy on May 1, 1752. He commanded the detachment of sailors from the *HMS Norwich* who served under Braddock in 1755. He is best known for discovering the route around Wills Mountain known as Spendelowe's Road. He was killed at the Battle of Monongahela.

Splitdorph, Carolus Gustavus (d. 1755)

Splitdorph was an immigrant from Sweden who had served as a volunteer on Washington's expedition to the Ohio in 1754. He was commissioned an ensign in the Virginia Regiment on July 21, 1754 and was promoted to lieutenant, October 29, 1754. Splitdorph was killed at the Battle of Monongahela.

Stephen, Adam (c. 1718–1791)

Stephen was a native of Scotland who had earned a degree as a surgeon from the University of Edinburgh and briefly pursued a career in the British Navy before immigrating to Fredrick, Maryland in 1745. He served as lieutenant colonel of the Virginia Regiment in 1754 and fought at the Battle of Great Meadows, July 3, 1754. When the regiment was disbanded in October of that year Stephen became captain of one of the independent companies formed in its place. Stephen fought at the Battle of the Monongahela where he was wounded. He again served as lieutenant colonel when the Virginia Regiment was reconstituted later in 1755. He then commanded the Virginia troops garrisoned at Fort Cumberland until June, 1757, when he was placed in command of the Virginian contingent sent to Charleston, South Carolina. He served in Forbes' expedition to the Ohio in 1758. Stephen served as colonel of the Virginia Regiment in 1761 and also commanded regiments raised to participate in Pontiac's Rebellion in 1764. He was appointed colonel of the 4th Virginia Regiment in 1776 and was promoted to brigadier general in September, 1777. Stephen fought at Battle of Brandywine but was later dismissed by Washington and court-martialed in November, 1777 for being drunk and incapacitated at the Battle of Germantown. Stephen later settled in Berkeley County (now West Virginia), became a member of the House of Burgesses, and a member of the Virginia Convention to ratify the U.S. Constitution in 1788.

Steuart (Stewart), Walter (c. 1732–1782)

Steuart was a Scot from the Orkney Islands. He was Commissioned 4th Ensign of the Virginia Regiment in July, 1754 and promoted to lieutenant later that month. He served in Thomas Waggoner's Company of rangers in 1755. Steuart served with Waggoner's Company on the South Branch of the Potomac in 1755–1756 and served in South Carolina and Georgia in 1757. Commissioned a captain in June, 1758, Steuart served on the Forbes Expedition as brigade major for the Virginia troops and was wounded in Grant's Raid on Fort Duquesne on September 14. He resigned his commission in October, 1758 and traveled to New York seeking a royal commission. In 1759, Steuart served with the 17th Regiment as a volunteer. He was then commissioned an ensign and later a lieutenant in the 17th Regiment in 1760. Steuart retired from the 94th Foot in 1763 on half pay.

Stewart, Robert

Stewart was a native of Scotland who fought and was wounded at the Battle of Great Meadows in July, 1754. He was promoted to captain in the Virginia forces on November 1, 1754. Stewart commanded the troop of Virginia light horse on Braddock's expedition. His unit served as escort for General Braddock and fought at the Monongahela. Stewart remained close to Washington throughout the war, accompanying him to Boston to meet with General William Shirley in 1756, and to Philadelphia to meet Lord Loudoun in 1757. Stewart again commanded the Virginia cavalry in the Forbes Expedition of 1758. He was appointed a lieutenant in the 60th Regiment in January, 1759 but continued to serve in the Virginia Regiment being promoted to major later that year. Stewart spent much of the 1760 campaign in command at Fort Venango. He served with the Regiment on the southwest frontier in 1761 and served as lieutenant colonel of the Virginia Regiment in 1762. Stewart returned to England in 1763 and was sent to Kingston, Jamaica as comptroller of Customs in 1768 where he remained for most of the next decade. Stewart maintained a regular correspondence with Washington for several years after the war.

Stirling, Robert

An ensign in the 48th Regiment who was wounded at the Battle of Monongahela.

Stone, Captain (d. 1755)

Stone was an officer in the 47th Regiment of Foot who had arrived in Virginia in June, 1755 with dispatches for General Braddock. He fought as a volunteer at the Battle of Monongahela where he was killed.

Strother, Anthony, Sr.
Strother was a merchant from Fredericksburg, Virginia and an old friend of the Washington family. Washington aided his son in getting a commission in the 48th Regiment.

Strother, Anthony, Jr. (1736–1790)
Washington aided Strother in obtaining a commission as ensign in the 48th Regiment, June 1755.

Swearingen, Thomas
Swearingen was a captain in the militia of Frederick County, Virginia. He had settled in the Shenandoah Valley and acted as a justice of the peace in the 1740s. Swearingen began operating a ferry on the Potomac in 1754–1755 on his land near present-day Shepherdstown, Virginia. He served in the House of Burgesses from 1755–1758. He was commissioned a lieutenant in Captain Robert Rutherford's Company of Virginia Rangers in November, 1757.

Talbot, Midshipman (d. 1755)
Talbot was a naval officer who served in Lieutenant Charles Spendelowe's detachment and was killed at the Battle of Monongahela.

Tatton, Charles (d. 1755)
A captain in the 48th Regiment who was killed at the Battle of Monongahela. It is said he was shot by British grenadiers.

Thompson, Edward
Thompson owned an inn in present-day Hillsboro, Virginia. Braddock's Army encamped there on the way to Fort Cumberland.

Townshend, Robert (d. 1755)
A lieutenant in the 44th Regiment who was killed at the Battle of Monongahela.

Treby, John
Treby was a lieutenant in the 44th Regiment who fought and was wounded at the Battle of Monongahela.

244

Vestal, John
Vestal operated a ferry over the Shenandoah River about six miles east of present-day Charlestown, West Virginia.

Waggener, Edmund (d. 1755)
Waggoner was the brother of Captain Thomas Waggener and was commissioned ensign in his ranger company in January 1755. He was killed at the Battle of Monongahela, 1755.

Waggener, Thomas (d. 1760)
Waggener had served as an officer in the aborted expedition against Canada in 1746. He was commissioned a lieutenant in the Virginia Regiment on February 2, 1754. He was wounded in the skirmish at Jumonville Glen on May 28, 1754 and fought at the Battle of Great Meadows on July 3, 1754. Waggener was promoted to captain on July 20, 1754 and commanded a company of Virginia rangers at the Battle of Monongahela, 1755. Waggener commanded Virginia forces on the South Branch of the Potomac from 1755–1758. He served on the Forbes Expedition in 1758 and served in the garrison at Fort Pitt from December, 1758 until his death sometime in early 1760.

Walsam (Walsham), John
A lieutenant in the 48th Regiment who fought at the Battle of Monongahela.

Wardrop, Leticia Lee (d. 1776)
The wife of James Wardrop of Upper Marlboro, Maryland. General Braddock is said to have been fond of her cooking.

Washington, Ann Aylett (1721–1773)
The wife of Augustine Washington and sister-in-law of George Washington.

Washington, Ann Fairfax (d. 1761)
The daughter of William Fairfax and wife of George Washington's brother Lawrence Washington. After Lawrence's death she married George Lee (1714–1761). Washington leased Mount Vernon from her in December, 1754, and inherited the estate after her death in 1761.

Washington, Augustine (1720–1762)
George Washington's older half brother. He was serving as a Burgess for Westmoreland County in 1755.

Washington, George (1732–1799)
Washington had begun his military career in 1752 as adjutant of Virginia militia for the Southern District with the rank of major. In 1753 he volunteered to deliver a message to the French on the Ohio River ordering them to withdraw immediately. He was then commissioned lieutenant colonel of the Virginia Regiment on January 25, 1754, and was promoted to colonel in May 1754. He commanded the Virginia forces in the skirmish at Jumonville Glen on May 28, 1754, which triggered the French retaliation that resulted his defeat at the Battle of Great Meadows, July 3, 1754.

When the Virginia Regiment was disbanded in October, 1754 he resigned his commission rather than be demoted to captain of an independent company. Washington served as a volunteer aide-de-camp to General Braddock in 1755. He accepted a commission as colonel of the newly reorganized Virginia Regiment on August 31, 1755 and served in command of the frontier defenses of Virginia until December 1758, when he resigned his commission after that capture of Fort Duquesne.

Washington, John (Jack) Augustine (1736–1787)
The younger brother of George Washington, John Augustine managed Washington's estate at Mount Vernon throughout the French and Indian War while Washington was away.

Washington, Mary Ball (1706–1789)
The mother of George Washington, she married Augustine Washington on March 6, 1730. She lived on her estate at Ferry Farm near Fredericksburg.

Washington, Townshend, Jr. (1736–1761)
A distant cousin of George Washington. Washington procured him a position as an assistant to commissary Robert Leake.

Webster, Robert
A captain in 44th Regiment, Webster served as provost marshal in Braddock's army. He served with Dunbar's Division and did not participate in the Battle of Monongahela.

Widman, William (d. 1755)
A lieutenant in the 48th Regiment, Widman was killed at the Battle of Monongahela.

Williamson, Adam
A captain lieutenant of Engineers who was wounded at the Battle of Monongahela. He served at Fort William Henry during the siege in August 1757. In 1758, he served at the Siege of Louisbourg.

Woodward, Henry
Woodward was a former naval officer who was commissioned a lieutenant in the Virginia Regiment on December 13, 1754. He served in Captain Thomas Waggoner's company of Virginia rangers at the Battle of Monongahela. Woodward was promoted to captain on August 25, 1755 and served in garrison at Winchester, Fort Cumberland, and Vass' Fort from 1755–1758. He served on the Forbes Expedition in 1758. Woodward was stationed at Fort Ligonier in May 1759. He served at Fort Chiswell on the southwest frontier in July 1761. Woodward returned to England in late 1761 seeking an appointment to command a vessel on the Great Lakes.

Woodward, Luke
A soldier in the 48th Regiment who was court-martialed for desertion and sentenced to death on May 14, 1755.

Wright, John (d. 1755)
Wright was a lieutenant in William la Péronie's Company of Virginia Rangers. He was killed at the Battle of Monongahela.

Bibliography

Primary Sources: Archives

Library of Congress: George Washington Papers. Series 2: Letterbooks, Series 4: General Correspondence, Series 6: Military Papers. Accessed through the Library of Congress internet site.

Primary Sources

Abbott, W. W., Dorothy Twohig, et. al., eds. *The Papers of George Washington: Colonial Series.* 10 Vols. Charlottesville, VA: University Press of Virginia, 1983–1995.

Brock, R. A., ed. *The Official Records of Robert Dinwiddie Lieutenant-Governor of the Colony of Virginia, 1751–1758.* 2 vols. Richmond, VA: Virginia Historical Society, 1883.

Fitzpatrick, John C., ed. *The Writing of George Washington from the Original Manuscript Sources.* 38 volumes. Washington, DC: Government Printing Office, 1931–1944.

Franklin, Benjamin. *The Autobiography and other Writings.* Edited by L. Jessie Lemisch. New York: Signet Classics, second printing; 1963.

Grenier, Fernand, ed. *Papiers Contrecoeur et autres documents concernant le conflit anglo-français sur l'Ohio de 1745 à 1756.* Quebec: Les Presses Universités Laval, 1952.

Hamilton, Charles, ed. *Braddock's Defeat.* Norman, OK: Oklahoma University Press, 1959.

Pease, Theodore Calvin, and Ernestine Jenison, eds. *Illinois on the Eve of the Seven Years' War, 1747–1755.* Collections of the Illinois State Historical Library, Vol. XXX. Springfield, IL: Trustees of the State Historical Library, 1940.

Pargellis, Stanley M., ed. *Military Affairs in North America, 1748–1765.* New York: D. Appleton-Century Company, 1936.

Sargent, Winthrop, ed. *A History of an Expedition Against Fort Duquesne in 1755; Under Major General Edward Braddock.* Philadelphia: Lippincott, Grambo & Co., 1855; repr. New York: Arno Press, 1971.

Sullivan, James, et. al., eds. *The Papers of Sir William Johnson.* 10 Vols. Albany: University of the State of New York, 1921–1939.

Washington, George. *The Diaries of George Washington.* 6 Vols. Edited by Donald Jackson and Dorothy Twohig. Charlottesville, VA: University Press of Virginia, 1976–1979.

Secondary Sources

Albert, George Dallas. *Report of the Commission to Locate the Site of the Frontier Forts of Pennsylvania, Volume Two: The Frontier Forts of Western Pennsylvania.* Second ed., edited by Thomas Lynch Montgomery. Harrisburg, PA: Wm. Stanley Ray, State Printer, 1916.

Anderson, Fred. *The Crucible of War: The Seven Years' War and the Fate of Empire in British North America, 1754–1766.* New York: Alfred A. Knopf, 2000.

Brady, Cyrus Townsend. *Colonial Fights and Fighters: Stories of Exploration, Adventure & Battle on the American Continent Prior to the War of the Revolution.* New York: McClure, Phillips & Co., 1901.

Loescher, Burt Garfield. *The History of Rogers Rangers, Volume III: Officers and Non-Commissioned Officers.* Bowie, MD: Heritage Books, 2001.

Malone, Dumas, ed. *Dictionary of American Biography.* 21 vols. New York: Scribner's, 1943.

Netherton, Ross. *Braddock's Campaign and the Potomac Route to the West.* Falls Church, VA: Higher Education Publications, Inc., 1989.

Nixon, Lily Lee. "Colonel James Burd in the Braddock Campaign," *The Western Pennsylvania Historical Magazine.* Vol. 17, No. 4, December 1934, pp. 235–46.

Freeman, Douglas Southall. *George Washington: A Biography.* 7 vols. New York: Charles Scribner's Sons, 1948.

Gipson, Lawrence Henry. *The British Empire Before the American Revolution, Volume VI. The Great War for Empire: The Years of Defeat, 1754–1757.* New York: Alfred A. Knopf, 1946.

Hough, Walter S. *Braddock's Road Through the Virginia Colony.* Winchester, VA: Frederick County Historical Society, 1970.

James, Alfred Procter. *George Mercer of the Ohio Company: A Study in Frustration.* Pittsburgh: University of Pittsburgh Press, 1963.

Jones, Charles H. *History of the Campaign for the Conquest of Canada in 1776: From the Death of Montgomery to the Retreat of the British Army under Sir Guy Carleton.* Philadelphia: Porter & Coates, 1882.

Kopperman, Paul E. *Braddock at the Monongahela.* 2d printing. Pittsburgh: University of Pittsburgh Press, 1992.

Lowdermilk, William H. *History of Cumberland, (Maryland) from the Time of the Indian Town, Caiuctucuc, in 1728, up to the Present Day, Embracing an Account of Washington's First Campaign, and Battle of Fort Necessity, Together with a History of Braddock's Expedition.* Washington, DC, 1878.

McCardell, Lee. *Ill-Starred General: Braddock of the Coldstream Guards.* Pittsburgh: University of Pittsburgh Press, 1958; reprint, 1986.

Pargellis, Stanley M. *Lord Loudoun in North America.* Yale University Press, 1933; repr. New York: Archon Books, 1968.

Scharf, J. T. *History of Maryland from the Earliest Period to the Present Day.* 3 vols. Baltimore, MD: Turnbull Brothers, 1874.

Index

failure with southern tribes 20
formation of Provincial Companies 36
identification 212
illustration 36
impatience of 170, 184
instructions to Washington 160
invitation to Washington 135
Lachlan Shaw recommended to
184
loss of papers 25
march through Maryland
105, 150
meeting with Benjamin Franklin
20
Mrs. Wardrop's cake 159
on casualty list 205
orderly books
location of 25
origins of 25, 33
orders concerning alcohol
72, 78, 81, 82, 85
orders concerning court-martials
84, 85
orders concerning fire from
Native Americans 42
orders concerning firearms 48
orders concerning gambling 84
orders concerning Rangers 52
orders concerning uniforms
52, 55
orders concerning women
93, 97
orders retreat 25
orders to Ensign French 69
orders to Gates 67
orders Washington to remain at
Little Meadows 178, 179
pay for road work 88
present from Robert Hunter
Morris 190

recruitment of additional men 20
report to 64
review of returns 55
reviews troops 44
to Little Meadows 169, 173
Washington's sympathy for 200
wound of 193
wounds of 190
Braddock, Pennsylvania 15
Braddock's Road
Pennsylvanian road to intersect
170
Brest, France
rumors of French squadron 184
Brierton, Percival, Lieutenant
assigned to Halkett's Division
122
dispatch to 69
identification 109, 128, 212
on casualty list 206
Bromley, Captain
death of 176
identification 213
Buchanan, Francis James,
Lieutenant
assigned to advance guard 122
identification 128, 213
on casualty list 207
Buffalo River 180
Bulkeley, Charles, Captain
company of rangers 127
Bullskin Plantation, West Virginia
location of 148
Washington at 148
Washington plans to visit 195
Washington's horse to 152
Burd, James, Colonel
builds road through Pennsylvania
169

Burton, Ralph, Lieutenant Colonel
  assigned to Halkett's Division
    118, 180
  at Battle of Monongahela 24
  compliments to 200
  identification 102, 213
  march from Fort Cumberland
    94, 169
  officer of the day
    45, 47, 49, 50, 51, 72, 74, 75,
    78, 81, 83, 89, 90, 91, 92, 118
  on casualty list 206
  wound of 190, 194
Burwell, Carter
  identification 143, 213
  letter to 143
Byrd, III, William
  identification 142, 213
  letter from Washington 141

C

Camp at the Grove
  location of 112
  orders from 96, 115
  renaming of 169
Campbell, John, 4th Earl of
    Loudoun, General
  Byrd as volunteer under 142
Canada 184
Canadian Militia
  at Battle of Monongahela 22
Carlyle, John, Major 37
  identification 100, 214
  letter to 155, 174
  seeks vessel for Robert Orme
    200
  Washington's boots to 155
Carlyle, Sarah Carlyle
  letter to 157, 175
Carlyle, Sarah Fairfax
  compliments to 155, 173, 174

  identification 157, 214
Carpenters, Virginia Companies
  brigading of companies
    49, 73, 74
  detachment to Little Meadows
    86
  formation of 36
  march from Fort Cumberland 92
  march of 116
  marching orders to 47
  monthly returns 55
  orders to 35, 70
  return 110
Cartagena, Siege of (1741) 112
Catawba, Native American Nation
  Braddock's failure with 20
  Byrd as agent to 142
Caton, Thomas, Captain
  at Fort Cumberland 187
  identification 187, 214
Chapman, Russell, Major 101
  advanced guard 21
  assigned to 2nd Division 180
  detachment to Little Meadows
    86, 169, 173
  identification 102, 214
  naming of Chapman's Camp
    108
  officer of the day
    48, 50, 81, 82, 118
  wagons from detachment 96
Chapman's Ordinary 108
Charles City, Virginia 142
Charlestown, West Virginia 106
Cherokee, Native American Nation
  Braddock's failure with 20
  Byrd as agent to 142
Chissels Ordinary. See Chiswell's
  Ordinary
Chiswell's Ordinary
  location of 162

256

259

transport supplies to 20
Washington at
154, 155, 173, 194
Fort des Miamis 15
Fort Detroit 27
Fort Duquesne 15, 27, 174, 179
attack plans 19
attack plans by "flying column"
22
British approach 22, 193
French reinforcements to
171, 176
proposed road to 170
Fort Frederick 37
bat men at 62
camp at 61, 62, 64, 67
delivering hospital stores 50
description of town 152
march route from 64, 65
march to 20, 57, 69
regarding bat-horses 58
subaltern to 55
wagons to 62
Washington arrives 150
Washington at 20, 154
Fort Machault
location of 183
Fort Michilimackinac 27
Fort Necessity
capitulation of 18
Fort Niagara 19, 27
Fort Oswego
French reinforcements seen
171, 174, 176
Fort Presqu'Isle
construction of 16
location of 27
Fort Rivière aux Boeufs
construction of 16
location of 27

Washington's visit 17
Fort Wayne, Indiana 27
Fort William Henry 28
Franklin, Benjamin
identification 223
meeting with Braddock 20
Franklin, Pennsylvania 183
Fraser, John. See Frazier, John
Frazier, John
cabin of near battlefield 193
grass guard at 70
identification 109, 194, 223
Frederick County, Virginia
militia 169
Fredericksburg, Virginia
37, 38, 153, 173
French
at Battle of Monongahela
22, 191
forced from the Ohio Country
184
Native American alliances
15, 21
possible withdrawal from Ohio
155
French Creek 183
French, Ensign
at Rock Creek 64, 108
identification 224
orders from Braddock 69
Frostburg, Maryland 111, 126

G

Gage, Thomas, Lieutenant Colonel
101
assigned to Halkett's Division
180
at Battle of Monongahela
22, 24
command of artillery 20

Lee, Jonathan, surgeon's mate
  identification 128, 230
Leesburg, Virginia 106
Legardeur de Saint-Pierre,
  Jacques, Captain 17
  identification 27, 230
Leslie, Mathew, Lieutenant
  applications for guide 54
  identification 105, 230
  on casualty list 205
  review of stores 52
  supplying 44th Regiment 60
  supplying artillery 61
Lewis, Betty Washington
  compliments to 189
  identification 230
Lewis, Fielding
  compliments to 189
  identification 189, 230
Lewis, Warner
  identification 189, 230
Library of Congress 25, 26, 33
Liénard de Beaujeu, Daniel-
    Hyacinthe-Marie, Capt.
  at Battle of Monongahela 22
  commander French forces 15
  death of 22, 25
  identification 27, 230
  illustration 17
Light Horse, Virginia Troop of
  encampment of 74
  expected at Winchester
    162, 167
  formation of 36
  march from Little Meadows 122
  monthly returns 55
Little Cacapon River
  camp at mouth of 65, 108
Little Meadows
  arrival at 126
  camp at 121, 179

council at 22, 169, 180
detachment to
  86, 112, 169, 173
march to 21
wounded officers at 190
Littler, William, Lieutenant
  assigned to advance guard 122
  identification 127, 231
  on casualty list 205
Lock, Robert, Lieutenant
  assigned to Halkett's Division
    122
  compliments to 184
  identification 128, 231
  on casualty list 206
London, England 19
Loramie Creek, Ohio 27
Lottery Bill
  debates in House of Burgesses
    184
Lowdermilk, William H. 25, 26
  identification 231

M

Mackay, James, Captain 17
  identification 28, 231
MacKellar, Patrick, Captain
  builds bridge 106
  identification 231
  on casualty list 207
Maidstone, Virginia 187
Marin de la Malgue, Paul, Captain
  death of 16
  identification 27, 232
Martin, Thomas Bryan, Colonel
  identification 151, 232
Martin's Plantation
  camp at 118
  grass guard at 76, 78
  location of 111, 126

Morris, Roger, Captain *(cont.)*
  assigned to advance guard
    122, 126
  compliments to 165, 200
  identification 101, 235
  letter to Washington 178, 202
  on casualty list 205
  orders for pack horse guard 120
  wound of 190
Mouet de Langlade, Charles-
  Michel 15
  identification 27, 235
Mount Vernon
  identification of 139
  John Augustine Washington at
    158, 176, 177, 195
  Mary Ball Washington at 173
  Washington at
    137, 141, 143, 144, 146, 200
  Washington leaves 109
Mullican, Charles
  identification 192, 236
Mullican, Priscilla 192, 236
Murdoch, Robert, Doctor
  identification 178, 236
  treats Washington 178

N

Napier, James, Doctor 99
  identification 111, 236
  orderlies for General Hospital
    80, 99
Napper, James, Doctor *See*
  Napier, James, Doctor
Native Americans
  at Battle of Monongahela 22
  at Fort Cumberland 109
  council with Braddock
    21, 78, 109
  failure to attend council 20

  French alliances 15, 21
  orders concerning fire from 42
  prohibition of liquor
    21, 72, 78, 81
  reinforce French in Ohio 154
  relations with Braddock 21
Nemacolin, Delaware chief
  106, 108
New England 15
New York 15
Nicholas, Ann Cary
  identification 147, 236
Nicholas, Robert Carter 146
  identification 147, 236
Nortlow, William, Ensign
  assigned to Halkett's Division
    122
  identification 127, 236
  on casualty list 206
Nugent, John
  court-martial of 85
  identification 236

O

Occoquan, Virginia 99
  ferry at 37
Ohio
  Country 15
    British army marches to
      21, 177, 184
    British army sent 17
    British incursions 16
    French occupation
      16, 18, 173
    hoped for French withdrawal
      155
    intelligence from 154
    lack of intelligence from 176
Ohio Expedition
  failure of 25

Rutherford, John, Captain
brigading of company 73
detachment to Little Meadows
86
Rutherford, John, Captain
brigading of company 73
detachment to Little Meadows
86
identification 109, 239
orders regarding arms 96
return of company 110

S

Saint Clair, John, Lieutenant
Colonel 24
advance to Little Meadows
21, 106, 169, 175, 176
advanced guard 21
builds bridge 106
detachment of 181
identification 101, 239
on casualty list 205
orders regarding
42, 45, 80, 81, 84
recommendation for camps
99, 100
regarding wagons 57
wound of 194
Saint-Pierre, Jacques Legardeur
de, Captain 17
identification 27
Sainte Foy, Battle of (April 28,
1760) 29
Sary, Caleb
court-martial of 93
identification 239
Savage River
location of 126
troops arrive at 120

Scarroyady, Iroquois Chief
at Fort Cumberland 20
identification 239
Scotland
rebellion of (1745) 73, 101
Scott, John, wagonmaster
appraises value of horses 169
identification 126, 240
orders regarding 84, 120
Seamen, Naval Detachment 57
brigading of 74
Camp at the Grove 116
march from Fort Frederick 67
march from Little Meadows 124
Sharpe, Horatio, Governor
at Fort Frederick 62
conference with Braddock 146
identification 107, 240
illustration 63
Shaw, Lachlan, Captain
delivers message from England
184
identification 184
recommended to Braddock 184
Shawnee Old Town, Maryland 108
Shelton, Michael
court-martial of 93
identification 240
Shenandoah River
ferry at 54, 106
Shippensburg, Pennsylvania 171
Shirley, William, Governor
and return of regiments to
Philadelphia 202
campaign against Niagara 155
conference with Braddock 146
council at Annapolis 138
identification 240
letter from William Fairfax 138
Washington meets 146

Y

Youghangany River. *See*
    Youghiogheny River
Youghiogheny River. *See also:*
    Great Crossing
    camp at 178, 182
    great crossing of 182
    Pennsylvania road to 171

www.ingramcontent.com/pod-product-compliance
Lightning Source LLC
Chambersburg PA
CBHW020518100426
42813CB00030B/3293/J

* 9 7 8 0 9 7 4 8 6 9 0 1 8 *